Agamben and Politics

THINKING POLITICS

Series Editors: Matthew Sharpe and Geoff Boucher

Politics in the twenty-first century is immensely complex and multi-faceted, and alternative theorisations of debates that radically renew older ideas have grown from a trickle to a flood in the past twenty years. The most interesting and relevant contemporary thinkers have responded to new political challenges – such as liberal multiculturalism, new directions in feminist thinking, theories of global empire and biopolitical power, and challenges to secularism – by widening the scope of their intellectual engagements and responding to the new politics. The thinkers selected for inclusion in the series have all responded to the urgency and complexity of thinking about politics today in fresh ways.

Books in the series will provide clear and accessible introductions to the major ideas in contemporary thinking about politics, through a focus in each volume on a key political thinker. Rather than a roll-call of the 'usual suspects', it will focus on new thinkers who offer provocative new directions and some neglected older thinkers whose relevance is becoming clear as a result of the changing situation.

www.euppublishing.com/series/thpo

AGAMBEN AND POLITICS
A CRITICAL INTRODUCTION

Sergei Prozorov

EDINBURGH
University Press

To my family

© Sergei Prozorov, 2014

Edinburgh University Press Ltd
The Tun – Holyrood Road
12 (2f) Jackson's Entry
Edinburgh EH8 8PJ
www.euppublishing.com

Typeset in Sabon by
Servis Filmsetting Ltd, Stockport, Cheshire,
and printed and bound in Great Britain by
CPI Group (UK) Ltd, Croydon CR0 4YY

A CIP record for this book is available from the British Library

ISBN 978 0 7486 7620 0 (hardback)
ISBN 978 0 7486 7621 7 (paperback)
ISBN 978 0 7486 7622 4 (webready PDF)
ISBN 978 0 7486 7624 8 (epub)

Contents

Expanded Contents List

Introduction

The best introduction to Agamben's political thought is a stack of Agamben's volumes. This book can therefore only aim to be second-best and would be able to attain this goal if it succeeded in getting students of political science, international relations, philosophy, sociology, history and other disciplines to read this Italian philosopher, if it managed to assure them of the relevance of his erudite, elliptical and admittedly arcane writings to the key concerns of contemporary world politics, if they finished this book with the dissatisfaction of not having learned enough about Agamben's politics and the desire to find out more. For this reason, this book is not intended as a summary of all Agamben's writings and statements on politics, an exhaustive treatment of his philosophy in the context of the wider history of political thought or an illustrative application of his political thought to historical or contemporary situations. It is rather an invitation to read Agamben that ventures to demonstrate the originality of his political thought in the contemporary theoretical and sociopolitical context, its capacity to disturb our familiar assumptions about politics, provoke unease about the political positions we uphold and offer new perspectives on the key political issues of our time. To be successful in this task the book should demonstrate why Agamben's works are important for anyone interested in politics.

Yet it is here that things become somewhat complicated, since Agamben is neither a political scientist nor a political theorist in the usual sense of the term and we would look in vain for a fully articulated theory of politics in his work. While the scope of his interests is remarkably broad and certainly includes politics, his approach to it is quite distinctive. The readers interested in what Agamben has to say about various issues in contemporary politics, from the financial crisis to the war on terror, from the Arab Spring to anti-Putin protests, from gay marriage to gun control, are bound to be disappointed. With a few exceptions Agamben's works rarely address concrete contemporary or historical events and when they do, it is usually in an abstruse historico-philosophical context that is apparently devoid of immediate political significance. Moreover, Agamben's own repeated references to the 'eclipse' of politics in our day and age (2000: ix; 1998: 4) may create an impression of an apolitical philosopher who loftily dismisses all present-day concerns and has little to say to us about contemporary politics.

And yet almost all of Agamben's books make explicit or implicit references or allusions to politics and the most esoteric philosophical formulations are presented as responses to an immediate political exigency. Moreover, these references never fail to highlight that this politics is not yet practised, let alone encapsulated in a fixed form of regime or system, but rather remains entirely to be invented (Agamben 1998: 11) Politics is thus central to Agamben's philosophy but it is a *different kind* of politics. To talk about Agamben and politics, as this book does, is thus not to interpret Agamben's views *on* politics as we know it but to probe into Agamben's own redefinition and reinvention *of* politics, a task that will take us to the places that the more conventional political theory tends to ignore and avoid. It therefore should not be surprising that many of the pages of this book are devoted to things that are ostensibly far away from politics: personal pronouns, the axolotl, Kafka, St Paul, boredom, etc. Yet, as we shall demonstrate, it is precisely through the reinterpretation of these ostensibly non-political phenomena that Agamben is able both to problematise the entire political tradition which we continue to inhabit and advance a thoroughgoing alternative that seeks to deactivate this tradition, or, in Agamben's terminology, render it inoperative. The central focus of this book is thus on Agamben's politics as a philosophical *invention*, produced both through a critical engagement with the existing traditions of political thought and practice and through a reconsideration of what these traditions exclude as non-political. Overturning the distinction between the political and the non-political, Agamben finds in the former little more than traces of a profound depoliticisation and instead surveys the latter for the signs of a coming new politics. Any assessment of Agamben's critical studies of historical or contemporary politics would therefore be incomplete without the consideration of his engagement with the ostensibly non-political subject matter as the source for a new political affirmation.

This reading of Agamben is distinct from the dominant mode of reception of his thought in the English-speaking academia that emphasises his critique of the Western political tradition at the expense of his affirmation of a radically new politics, which tends

2

to be dismissed as utopian, naive and incoherent or simply ignored. Agamben is thereby read as a strident if not outright shrill critic of the occidental tradition of politics, particularly in its modern versions which, notwithstanding ideological differences between, for example, liberal democracy and Nazi or Stalinist totalitarianism, all appear to lead inescapably to the concentration camp that is posited as the paradigmatic site of modern politics (see Mesnard 2004; Bernstein 2004; Laclau 2007; Connolly 2007; Patton 2007). While this reading is not, strictly speaking, incorrect, it obscures the affirmative attunement that grants this critique both its meaning and its power. In contrast, we shall begin with this affirmative attunement as the context necessary for grasping Agamben's critical project and evaluating its strengths and weaknesses. Prior to addressing Agamben's most controversial theses about, for example, the indistinction of democracy and totalitarianism or the camp as the paradigmatic political space of modernity we shall illuminate the overall disposition that makes these theses more intelligible and rather less extreme than when they appear out of context.

This approach to Agamben's politics determines the structure of the book. In Chapter 1 we shall reconstitute what we shall term the 'comic mood' of Agamben's philosophy. Drawing on Agamben's own rejection of the 'tragic paradigm' in politics and ethics, we shall present the break with the tragic vision of politics and the embrace of comic affirmation as the fundamental *attunement* or mood of Agamben's philosophy. While this argument may be counterintuitive, given the morbid subject matter of many of Agamben's key works, we shall argue that this 'negative' image is secondary and subordinate to the affirmative aspect of Agamben's thought that accords with the understanding of comedy in classical aesthetics as the passage from a 'foul' beginning full of misfortunes to a happy end. Agamben's detailed analyses of the lethal contradictions of established forms of politics are not intended as tragic ruminations on the inaccessibility of redemption but rather as the proper pathway towards it. It is only by engaging with the existing forms of power at their most extreme points that it is possible to bring their operation to a 'happy ending'. Thus, Agamben's genealogical studies of the most tragic moments of the Western political tradition function as *diagnostic tools* in the service of its comic overcoming.

Chapter 2 elucidates the logic of the comic affirmation that defines Agamben's politics. While numerous passages on the 'coming politics' and 'happy life' in Agamben's texts are often dismissed as naive utopianism at odds with the clinical detachment of his critical analyses, this dismissal is due to the misunderstanding of the logic of comedy: happiness is possible but only at the *end*. The key to understanding Agamben's politics is his rethinking of the very idea of ending, of coming or bringing something to an end. The 'happy end' that his politics affirms is neither the teleological fulfilment of a process nor a merely negative disappearance of something but rather the process of becoming or rendering something *inoperative*, neutralising its ordering force and making it available for free use. The chapter introduces inoperativity as the fundamental concept of Agamben's thought, marking the continuity of his philosophical project from the earliest work onwards. Drawing in particular on Agamben's reading of Aristotle, we shall reconstitute the original for-mulation of this problematic and its linkage with another key concept of Agamben's thought, i.e. potentiality. We shall then elucidate the functioning of the logic of inoperativity in Agamben's conceptual apparatus by considering a series of paradigmatic examples from the most diverse spheres: the glorious body in Christianity, the Sabbath in Judaism, the religious hymn, the empty throne, etc. Since the most famous and extreme example of inoperativity in Agamben's work is the protagonist of Melville's novella *Bartleby the Scrivener*, we shall devote particular attention to the critical analysis of Agamben's reading of Bartleby.

The four remaining chapters elaborate the logic of inoperative politics in four key domains of Agamben's political thought: lan-guage, statehood, history and humanity. Justin Clemens has argued that 'Agamben's net is wide but he catches the same fish time after time' (2008: 55). In our view, this statement ought not to be taken as criticism but rather as an indication of both the fundamental consistency of Agamben's political philosophy and his fidelity to its key principles. As we shall see, the affirmative logic of Agamben's politics remains the same across the dazzling variety of thematic concerns and spatiotemporal contexts, persistently tracing the pos-sibility of rendering inoperative the structures of power that capture and confine human existence.

Since Agamben's thought is remarkably diverse in its thematic foci, intellectual influences and methodological strategies, any choice of domains to be covered is bound to exclude something of interest and this book is no exception. It is with some regret that we have to bracket off the discussion of Agamben's fascinating interventions into the field of aesthetics, particularly poetry and literature, or his rethinking of commodity fetishism and the capitalist 'society of the spectacle'. Nonetheless, there is one aspect of Agamben's thought that has become so prominent in recent works that its apparent exclusion requires justification. This is theology, which plays an ever more important role starting from *The Kingdom and the Glory* (2011, see also Agamben 2013). In our reading, theology does not constitute a separate domain of Agamben's work but is rather a fundamental aspect of his reinvention of politics as such that has arguably been present all along (cf. Dickinson 2011; De la Durantaye 2009: 367–82; cf. Toscano 2011, Sharpe 2009). Suffice it to recall that Agamben's discussion of post-statist community (1993a) makes numerous references to the limbo, halos, Kabbalah, Shekinah, etc, while his theorisation of politics beyond the law and the logic of sovereignty is phrased in unequivocally messianic terms (2005a). As Agamben has argued, 'it is only through metaphysical, religious and theological paradigms that one can truly approach the contemporary – and political – situation' (Agamben cited in De la Durantaye 2009: 369) At the same time, Agamben's works are clearly 'confrontations with theology' (ibid.): his use of theological genealogies of the most familiar aspects of our political tradition is a part of his effort to render this tradition inoperative and open it to free use that he calls profane. We shall therefore encounter theological themes in each of the four domains that we shall cover in this book, which makes any separate consideration of the theological realm superfluous for our purposes.

The choice of the domains of language, statehood, history and humanity is determined by their significance for understanding the logic of Agamben's inoperative politics in its historical development. While at first glance it would be more logical to begin the account of Agamben's politics with his work in the sphere of statehood and law, the foundations for his arguments in this sphere are laid by his earlier critique of the negative foundations of language. Indeed, the main thesis of *Homo Sacer* is already contained in the conclusion to the 1982 book *Language and Death* (Agamben 1991). Similarly, Agamben's affirmative rethinking of the experience of language prior to and beyond all signification paves the way for his theorisation of political community beyond every particular identity, which is a precondition for any post-statist politics. This post-statist politics is in turn explicitly posited as post-historical, not in the more familiar Kojèvian or Fukuyaman sense of the final fulfilment of the historical process but in the sense of a deactivation of this very process, the suspension of the dialectical negating action that subjected human existence in the present in the name of its future emancipation. Finally, insofar as historicity has been traditionally posited as constitutive of human existence as such, this reconsideration of the end of history brings up the question of the effect of inoperative politics on the very distinction between humanity and animality.

The order of our presentation of these four domains roughly corresponds to the historical development of Agamben's political thought: the work on language and community of the late 1970s to early 1980s, on law and the state in the late 1980s to 1990s, on history and messianism in the late 1990s to early 2000s and on humanity/animality during the 2000s. Yet, more importantly, this order corresponds to the radicalisation of the ambitions and claims of Agamben's philosophy of inoperativity, which begins with the more restricted technical and philosophical problem of the negative foundations of language and progressively expands its focus to law, history and ultimately humanity as such. The variations on the theme of inoperativity that we shall analyse in Chapters 3–6 thus produce a crescendo effect as Agamben's affirmation of a path out of the tragedy of modern politics becomes ever more exigent.

Chapter 3 addresses the operation of the logic of inoperativity in the domain of language, central to Agamben's work of the 1970s and the 1980s. In a series of works from this period Agamben demonstrates that the Western philosophy of language has been guided by the logic of negative foundation, whereby the positivity of human language as signifying discourse is conditioned by the negation of natural or animal sound. It is this moment of negation, which Agamben terms Voice, that remains inaccessible to speech as such, making the foundation of language ineffable and ultimately mystical. Agamben then seeks to render this negativity of Voice inoperative in a pure experience of language (*experimentum linguae*) that brings the unspeakable to speech in the suspension of signification. This logic is then transferred to the domain of political community, which is rethought in the absence of any predicates of identity and conditions of belonging, as the precise correlate of the pure experience of language. It is this community of 'whatever being', founded solely on the basic fact of human multiplicity, that becomes the subject of a new, singularly universalist politics that seeks to deactivate all particular communities and political orders.

The analysis of Agamben's rethinking of language and community prepares the ground for our interpretation of his best-known political texts in the *Homo Sacer* series from the perspective of inoperativity in Chapter 4. Starting with the discussion of Agamben's reinterpretation of Foucault's theory of biopolitics and Schmitt's theory of sovereignty, we shall demonstrate how the notion of bare life as the object of biopolitical sovereignty corresponds to the idea of the ineffable Voice in the philosophy of language. We shall then address Agamben's account of the confinement of bare life in the state of exception, including the familiar figures of *homo sacer* and the *Muselmann*, and probe into his resolution of the problem of sovereignty. In accordance with the general logic of inoperativity, this resolution does not take the form of either the revolutionary takeover or the anarchist destruction of the state and the legal apparatus but rather consists in the *deactivation* of their ordering power in what Agamben, following Walter Benjamin, terms the 'real state of exception', in which human praxis is severed from all relation to the law. We shall conclude with the analysis of Agamben's notion of 'form-of-life' as the effect of the reappropriation of bare life from its capture in the logic of sovereignty.

Chapter 5 traces the operation of the logic of inoperativity in the domain of history. While in the early 1990s Agamben joined other continental thinkers in the criticism of the recycling of the Hegelo-Kojèvian thesis on the end of history by Francis Fukuyama, he went beyond the derisive dismissal of this argument and developed an alternative account of historicity and its deactivation. Tracing Agamben's critical engagement with Hegel's and Kojève's thought, we shall reconstitute Agamben's 'happy ending' of history as the suspension of the Hegelian Master–Slave dialectic by the figure of the Slave that ceases to work without striving to attain mastery. As we shall argue, for Agamben history does not end by fulfilling its immanent logic but is rather *brought to an end* in emancipatory social practices that suspend its progress and thus render inoperative the positions of both Master and Slave. We shall then elaborate this logic of suspension by addressing Agamben's reinterpretation of Pauline messianism, focusing in particular on the notion of messianic time as the eruption of the *kairos*, a critical moment of emancipatory possibility, within the chronological time of history. We shall elaborate this 'profane messianism' by contrasting it with the 'katechontic' logic that restrains and delays the messianic *parousia*, perpetuating the reign of sovereign power.

Chapter 6 probes Agamben's affirmation of inoperativity at the very site where the subject of politics emerges, i.e. humanity. If human existence has been understood as constitutively historical, then what are the implications of the end of history for our very notion of humanity? In his recent work Agamben has explicitly engaged with the problem of anthropocentrism in the Western political tradition, overcoming its vestiges in his own earlier texts. In this chapter we shall analyse Agamben's figure of the anthropological machine as the historical apparatus of distinguishing humanity from animality and address his attempts to bring this machine to a halt. In particular, we shall focus on Agamben's critical reinterpretation of Heidegger's attempt to distinguish humanity from animality on the basis of the exclusively human faculty of the disclosure of the world. In an intricate reversal of Heidegger's argument Agamben demonstrates that rather than authorise any distinction this faculty rather points to an extreme affinity between humanity and animality, rendering any opposition between them inoperative in the figure of 'saved life' beyond all separations and divisions. We shall address this figure of post-anthropocentric 'saved life' as the most radical version of the affirmation of inoperativity in Agamben's work, whereby his attempts to break outside the confines of signification, law and history lead his form-of-life 'outside of being' as such.

In conclusion we shall address the immanent critique of Agamben's work, focusing in particular on the paradoxical and somewhat counter-intuitive optimism that Agamben has repeatedly professed with regard to his vision of the coming politics. We shall argue that the central problem of Agamben's affirmative politics is his principled opposition to any form of a voluntarist project, which leaves him incapable of accounting for the process of the constitution of the political subject, including the inoperative community of whatever being. Having demonstrated the violent and vacuous character of particularistic political communities governed by biopolitical sovereignty and pointed the pathway for escaping their subjection and reclaiming the potentialities of existence confined in them, Agamben cannot demonstrate why this step outside would be taken by the subjects of contemporary societies. The principled affirmation of inoperativity as both the telos and the method of the coming politics makes it logically impossible to discuss this politics in the traditional terms of the composition of a social movement or a coalition of parties, of raising awareness and mobilising the civil society, of articulating and aggregating particular interests, etc. All that the definition of politics in terms of inoperativity permits is the affirmation of the sheer potentiality of the subtraction from the apparatuses that govern us and the coming together of singularities into an open and non-exclusive community of whatever being. Thus, Agamben's politics lacks not only teleological assurances but also the hope that could be invested in voluntarist action and is left with nothing to fall back on but its affirmation of its possibility, which is by definition also a possibility for it *not* to be actualised. While it is ultimately up to the reader to decide whether this problem is a weakness of Agamben's thought or the proof of its consistency, it is important to understand the reasoning behind it.

This book is explicitly pitched at two audiences. It is intended as both an introduction to Agamben's political thought for first-time readers and a critical interpretation of his work that will be of interest to the readers already acquainted with his thought. The focus on inoperativity as the logic of Agamben's affirmative politics serves both purposes. For newcomers to Agamben it provides an overarching frame for a dazzling and somewhat intimidating array of diverse themes that Agamben's political thought addresses, from angels to porn stars, from camps to pronouns, etc. For the more familiar readers, it offers a specific interpretive perspective that highlights the originality of Agamben's insights in the contemporary intellectual context, accentuating the stakes, achievements and problems of his vision of the coming politics. With respect to both audiences, this book will fulfil its purpose if it succeeds in its invitation to read Agamben, either for the first time or repeatedly.

Chapter 1

All's Well That Ends Well:
Agamben's Comic Politics

In this chapter we shall introduce the idea of mood as a methodological key to the interpretation of Agamben's political thought.
Approaching the idea of the *mood* as the fundamental attunement
characterising a philosophical standpoint, we shall argue that the
mood of Agamben's philosophy is *comic* in the sense used in aesthetic theory. While tragedy is understood in terms of a passage
from a pacific beginning to a terrible end, comedy is defined by the
reverse movement from a misfortune or predicament to a happy
resolution. In contrast to many orientations in continental philosophy, whose approach to politics is marked by the tragic awareness
of the limits of political possibility, Agamben's politics is radically
affirmative, emphasising the *contingency* of the *apparatuses* that
govern our existence and hence the possibility of their overcoming.
In the remainder of the chapter we shall elaborate the comic mood
of Agamben's philosophy by addressing his readings of Dante, Kafka
and other authors.

What is a Mood?

The primary task of this book is to elucidate the overall orientation
and development of Agamben's political thought from his earliest
works of the 1970s to the most recent writings. In our view, the best
way to do this is by grasping the fundamental attunement to politics
that characterises Agamben's writings. The concept of 'fundamental
attunement' or mood (*Stimmung*) was developed in the philosophy of
Martin Heidegger, the key influence on Agamben's intellectual development. In *Being and Time* (1962), Heidegger famously described
anxiety as a fundamental mood, in which the mode of human being-
there (*Dasein*) is disclosed. In this mood, distinguished from fear
by the lack of any determinate object, *Dasein* is separated from its
everyday immersion in the world and is able to gain access to its

being-in-the-world as a whole. In this experience the familiar world appears to us as uncanny and strange, which for Heidegger is the pre-condition for any authentic and free engagement with it. Similarly, in a later course of lectures, entitled *The Fundamental Concepts of Metaphysics* (1995), Heidegger posited 'profound boredom' as the mood of world disclosure, in which the world is rendered manifest as an opening, in which individual beings come to appearance. It is only when we are 'left empty' by beings that become indifferent for us and are 'held in limbo', all possibilities of our action suspended, that we experience the clearing of being as such. Such moods as anxiety and boredom are thus fundamental in the sense of giving us nothing less than an experience of being itself, making possible the phenomenal appearance of the ontological dimension.

The notion of a fundamental attunement may also be applied to the work of individual philosophers, for example Heidegger himself, whose own mood Agamben discussed in terms of a paradoxical 'openness to a closedness', being delivered over to something that refuses oneself (Agamben 2004b: 68). In this sense the notion of a mood indicates something like an ontological tenor of an author's philosophy, which permits one to grasp its fundamental orientation. By illuminating the mood of Agamben's politics and its unfolding in the key domains of his writings we may expect to gain an interpretive key to his often controversial, counter-intuitive or outright enigmatic claims about politics.

In his 1985 collection *Idea of Prose* Agamben devoted a separate vignette 'The Idea of Music' to the notion of mood, arguing both for the centrality of this notion to any philosophy and for its gradual descent into obscurity in contemporary thought:

> Our sensibility, our sentiments, no longer make us promises. They survive off to the side, splendid and useless, like household pets. And courage, before which the imperfect nihilism of our time is in constant retreat, would indeed consist in recognising that we no longer have moods, that we are the first men not to be in tune with a *Stimmung*. [And] if moods are the same thing in the history of the individual as are epochs in the history of humanity, then what presents itself in the leaden light of our apathy is the never yet seen sky of an absolute non-epochal situation in human history. The unveiling of being and language, which remains unsaid in each historical epoch and in each destiny, perhaps is truly coming to an end. Deprived of an epoch, worn out and without destiny, we reach the blissful threshold of our unmusical dwelling in time. Our word has truly reached the beginning. (Agamben 1995: 91)

This fragment is a good illustration of the tenor of Agamben's approach, presenting in a condensed, if also somewhat cryptic, manner a number of theses that, as we shall show in this book, are emblematic for Agamben's political thought: the assertion of a radical discontinuity in our contemporary condition, the mercilessly negative view of our current predicament, the argument for the exhaustion and vacuity of our traditions, the sense of a looming end that is then converted into the expectation of a new beginning. Despite Agamben's claim for the increasing oblivion of the idea of mood in our contemporary experience, this statement actually provides us with a glimpse into the fundamental mood of his own philosophy.

Taking Leave of Tragedy

This book argues that the basic mood of Agamben's political thought is *comic*. Those familiar at least with the subject matter of Agamben's books will certainly protest in disbelief. Comic? Isn't this the author who writes about concentration and refugee camps, about states of exception and state terror, and whose best-known conceptual personae are *homo sacer*, the being that can be killed with impunity, and the *Muselmann*, the emaciated and apathetic inmate of Nazi concentration camps? There certainly does not appear to be anything comic about that. On the contrary, what defines the reception of Agamben in many quarters of political and international relations theory is precisely the interpretation of his reading of the Western political tradition as tragic and, perhaps, *far too tragic*. Agamben's provocative theses about the concentration camp as the paradigmatic site of modern politics, the indistinction between democracy and totalitarianism with respect to the logic of sovereignty, the state of exception becoming the rule in modern politics have been frequently criticised as excessively totalising and ahistorical.

In fact, this 'tragic' reading has so far been the dominant mode of the reception of Agamben's work in Anglo-American political theory. Although Agamben's early works were translated into English starting from the early 1990s, the book that made him famous was the first volume of *Homo Sacer* (1998) and the context of its reception was dominated by the US-led War on Terror after the 9/11 attacks of 2001. Agamben's analyses of sovereignty, biopolitics, bare life and the camp were particularly topical in the context of American exceptionalism, preventive war without legal sanction, the Guantanamo camp, the Patriot Act, and so on. In this context, Agamben was read as an excessively pessimistic theorist who finds in the current events the manifestation of the underlying logic of the entire Western political tradition, making today's policies appear tragically predetermined by the millennia of history as the unfolding of the lethal paradox of sovereignty that was there already in Ancient Rome.

In line with this mode of reception, Ernesto Laclau accuses Agamben of positing an 'unavoidable advance towards a totalitarian society' (Laclau 2007: 17), '[dismissing] all political options in our societies and unifying them in the concentration camp as their secret destiny' (ibid.: 22). Similarly, William Connolly argues that '[Agamben] carries us through the conjunction of sovereignty, the sacred and biopolitics to a historical impasse. Agamben's analysis exacerbates a paradox that he cannot imagine how to transcend' (Connolly 2007: 27). The criticism of Agamben's tragic teleology is fortified even further by Andreas Kalyvas, for whom 'Agamben proposes a theory of history that does not seem to bring forth anything new' other than the 'survival of sovereignty over a period of 25 centuries', so that the history of Western politics ends up nothing but a 'history of repeated failures' (Kalyvas 2005: 111–12). Moreover, these failures are allegedly 'guided by the iron hand of historical necessity all the way to the camps' (ibid.: 112). William Rasch succinctly sums up the logic underlying this reading of Agamben: 'What reveals itself in the sovereign ban is the long, slow, but inevitable telos of the West, an ingrained imperfection that inheres as much in the democratic tradition as it does in absolutism or twentieth-century totalitarianism' (Rasch 2007: 100). Agamben's politics is thus not merely tragic as a matter of contingency, but rather as a matter of teleological necessity, from whose grip one apparently cannot twist loose, since every concrete instance of political praxis ultimately bears the full metaphysical weight of the millennia of tragedy: 'At the basis of Agamben's analyses of the law, the state and the citizen lies this fundamental premise that Western metaphysics is a metaphysics of death, a deadly metaphysics' (Deranty 2008: 175). Thus, the consensus among the critics is that Agamben's work is an exemplar of a 'radically pessimistic philosophy of history' (Marchart 2007: 13).

So far, so very non-comic. And yet, these readings of Agamben ignore (or scornfully, and a little too hurriedly, dismiss) the persistent references throughout his work to 'happiness' and 'redemption' that come at the end of the tradition whose reign has indeed been tragic and, moreover, going from bad to worse. To recall Agamben's fragment on moods, the experience of being 'deprived', 'worn out' and 'apathetic' simultaneously marks the 'true beginning' of our 'word'. The reversal of the tragic predicament into the possibility of a 'happy life' that we find in the final pages of almost all Agamben's books permits us to rigorously distinguish his thought from what we may term the tragic logic dominant in contemporary continental thought. The tragic reading of politics, which ranges from a Schmittian political realism to a Lacanian or Heideggerian poststructuralism, posits the ultimate goals of politics as radically unattainable, resigning us to, at best, temporary and unfinalisable outcomes that necessarily compromise our ideals and, at worst, a perpetual possibility of a relapse into violent antagonism. Particularly in the post-Cold War period, this tragic understanding of politics has been accompanied and reinforced by a melancholic interpretation of 'radical' or 'progressive' politics as necessarily harbouring its own failure, its own reversal into reaction or terror and usually both (see Žižek 2008: 1–8; Badiou 2009: 1–9; Bosteels 2011: 269–87). Thus, the 'tragic' approach in contemporary continental thought affirms the inescapable limits of political possibility and warns about the catastrophic results of every attempt at transgressing them.

In contrast to this tragic pathos, whose central motif is our best intentions going terribly wrong, Agamben's politics may be understood as comic, evidently not in the sense of being funny or humorous, but rather in the sense espoused by classical aesthetics. Whereas tragedy is marked by a pacific beginning after which things go wrong and end badly, comedy begins with various misfortunes only to lead at the end to what Agamben refers to as 'happy life' (Agamben 2000: 114). In aesthetic theory, comedy does not designate a genre that would be 'feelgood', hilarious or humorous throughout. After all, even Dante's famous book, in which all sorts of terrible things happen, is called *Divine Comedy*. It is specifically the movement *from* the misfortunes or mishaps at the beginning *to* happiness at the end that defines comedy. Indeed, it is precisely in his reading of Dante in *End of the Poem* (1999a) that Agamben elaborates his theory of comedy that has not been applied in the study of his politics, but in our view provides the best interpretive key for it. A brief analysis of this text will help us illuminate the fundamental mood of Agamben's political philosophy as thoroughly heterogeneous to the image of the prophet of doom constructed by his critics.

Why did Dante decide to entitle his masterpiece *Divine Comedy*? In his attempt to answer this question Agamben goes beyond the strictly stylistic opposition between the elevated style of tragedy and a more 'humble' or 'lowly' style proper to comedy and articulates the tragic/comic opposition on the level of content 'as an opposition of beginning and end: tragedy is marked by an "admirable" and "peaceful" beginning and a "foul" and "horrible" end; comedy by "horrible" and "foul" beginning and a "prosperous" and "pleasant" end' (Agamben 1999a: 6). In the context of the subject matter of Dante's poem, which deals with the question of humankind's salvation or damnation after the divine judgment, this opposition is concretised in the following manner:

> That Dante's poem is a comedy and not a tragedy means [that] man appears at the beginning as guilty but at the end as innocent. Insofar as it is a 'comedy', the poem is an itinerary from guilt to innocence and not from innocence to guilt. Tragedy appears as the guilt of the just and comedy as the justification of the guilty. (Ibid.: 8)

Thus, the tragic situation consists in the conflict between the subjective innocence of the hero and his objectively attributed guilt, whereby the just end up guilty despite themselves, while the logic of comedy consists in the overcoming of the subjective guilt that ensures a 'prosperous and pleasant' ending.[1] While the tragic logic is conventionally held to characterise the Ancient Greek world and the comic logic is made possible by the historical event of Christianity, this division is made more complex by Agamben through the introduction of another opposition, that of *nature* and *person*. The 'tragic guilt' that characterised the antiquity certainly persists in the Christian universe in the form of the doctrine of the original sin, in which it was, as it were, nature itself that sinned: '[as] natural and not personal guilt, as guilt that falls to every man through his own origin, original sin is a perfect equivalent of tragic *hamartia*, an objective stain independent of will' (ibid.: 11). It is Christ's passion that radically alters this situation, 'transforming natural guilt into personal expiation and an irreconcilable objective conflict into a personal matter' (ibid.: 12). The salvation that Christianity promises is not of a 'natural' or objective nature but is rather a matter of personal achievement that cannot be passed on to others. Rather than simply cancel out the original sin and restore the Edenic condition of humanity, Christianity transforms guilt from an objective condition to a question of personal practice: 'Transforming the conflict between natural guilt and personal innocence into the division between natural innocence and personal guilt, Christ's death thus liberates man from tragedy and makes comedy possible' (ibid.: 13).

From that point on, the only tragic experience that remains possible is that of love, insofar as the body with its desires remains in the state of original sin, resigning one to natural guilt despite one's personal innocence. It is precisely in this sphere that Dante ventures a comic reversal, whereby the erotic experience ceases to be a 'tragic' conflict between personal innocence and natural guilt and becomes a comic reconciliation of natural innocence and personal guilt. In the *Divine Comedy* this reconciliation takes the form of Dante's character's full assumption of shame: while tragic heroes, of which Oedipus is the best example, could not assume their shame due to their subjective innocence, the comic character renounces every claim to personal innocence as well as every attempt to return to the Edenic state and instead fully assumes the fracture between the natural and the personal within one's existence. Yet it is precisely this fracture that founds comedy by making it possible to assume one's (guilty) person without fully identifying with it. Relying on the originary etymological sense of 'person' as a mask, which he will invoke in many of his other works (2010: 46–54; 2007b: 55–60), Agamben emphasises the possibility to combine the assumption of personal guilt with a claim to natural innocence: 'the one who accomplishes the voyage of the Comedy is not a subject or an I in the modern sense of the word, but, rather, simultaneously a person (the sinner called Dante) and human nature' (Agamben 1999a: 20). Moreover, the one to be redeemed at the end of this journey is the 'creature' in its natural innocence and not the person, which ultimately remains nothing but a 'mask', a 'foreign person', a product of the external forces that may well be consigned to its guilt. What would be properly tragic is rather one's identification with this 'foreign person' (Agamben 1999a: 18–20), whereby it begins to define one's identity without any remainder, completely crowding out the innocent creature (Agamben 2007b: 59–60; 2010: 50–4). In contrast, the comic character resists this identification, reclaiming its natural innocence while leaving its guilty person to the external forces of the law.

Kafka and the Apparatuses of Tragedy

This logic of the overcoming of tragedy is elaborated in Agamben's reading of a more contemporary literary figure whose works have been routinely misinterpreted as tragic, Franz Kafka, who is the most important literary reference in Agamben's entire oeuvre (see Snoek 2012; Murray 2010: 99–107).

It is a very poor reading of Kafka's works that sees in them only a summation of the anguish of a guilty man before the inscrutable power of a God become estranged and remote. On the contrary, here it is God himself who would need to be saved and the only happy ending we can imagine for his novels is the redemption of Klamm, of the Count, of the anonymous, theological crowd of judges, lawyers and guardians indiscriminately packed together in dusty corridors or stooped beneath oppressive ceilings. (Agamben 1995: 85)

Contrary to the interpretations of Kafka as the founding figure of a specifically modern form of tragedy, in which the sheer fact of objective guilt remains despite the disappearance of its sense, Agamben approaches Kafka's literary gesture as a modern repetition of Dante's renunciation of tragedy. Kafka's novels seek less the redemption of the guilty than the redemption from the very idea of guilt, the redemption which can only be universal and pertain as much to those accused as to those who accuse, judge and punish. Rather than attempt to justify those considered guilty by reassigning guilt to others, Kafka seeks to dispense with guilt as such, understanding it as ultimately a product of our 'self-slander' before the law:

[Kafka's] universe cannot be tragic but only comic: guilt does not exist, or, rather guilt is nothing other than self-slander, which consists in accusing oneself of a nonexistent guilt (that is, of one's very innocence, which is the comic gesture par excellence). (Agamben 2010: 21)

In Agamben's interpretation of Kafka's novel *The Trial*, Joseph K *allows* himself to be captured in the trial and persists in this capture until his death due to his own fascination with law that he cannot escape and which eventually gets the best of him. The problem of guilt is ultimately the problem of the capture and confinement of human existence within what Agamben terms an 'apparatus' (2009c): a structure of ordering beings by endowing them with positive identities and roles.

The concept of the apparatus (*dispositif*) was originally developed by Michel Foucault in his *History of Sexuality* (1990a). In a methodological move typical of his later work, Agamben takes up Foucault's concept, traces its genealogy further back in the history of philosophy and generalises it far beyond its original articulation. While Foucault's *dispositif* referred to a heterogeneous set of discursive and nondiscursive practices that organises the relations of power and forms of knowledge in specific domains such as sexuality, punishment, law, and so on (see Deleuze 1992, 1988: 30–7),

Agamben relies on his theological genealogy of the notion of the economy (2011) to isolate the idea of *dispositio* as the generic activity of governing. The apparatus is thus generalised to designate 'a set of practices, bodies of knowledge, measures and institutions that aim to manage, govern, control and orient – in a way that purports to be useful – the behaviours, gestures and thoughts of human beings' (Agamben 2009c: 13). Thus, Agamben replaces Foucault's largely methodological notion of the apparatus with what amounts to a general theory of order:

> I wish to propose to you nothing less than a general and massive partitioning of beings into two large groups or classes: on the one hand, living beings (or substances), and on the other hand, apparatuses in which living beings are incessantly captured. On the one hand, then, to return to the terminology of the theologians, lies the ontology of creatures, and on the other hand, the *oikonomia* of apparatuses that seek to govern and guide them toward the good. (Agamben 2009c: 13)

This division ultimately corresponds to the Heideggerian difference between the ontological and the ontic. Only living beings (or what Agamben calls 'substances') have an ontological status, while the apparatuses are purely ontic figures of order that have no foundation in being (Agamben 2009c: 10; see also Agamben 2011: 53–66). While both categories refer to *beings*, only the beings of the former category are endowed with *being*. On the basis of this distinction Agamben defines the apparatus as

> [literally] anything that has in some way the capacity to capture, orient, determine, intercept, model, control or secure the gestures, behaviours, opinions, or discourses of living beings. Not only, therefore, prisons, madhouses, the panopticon, schools, confession, factories, but also the pen, writing, literature, philosophy, agriculture, cigarettes, navigation, computers, cellular telephones and – why not – language itself, which is perhaps the most ancient of the apparatuses. (Agamben 2009c: 14)

While many of these apparatuses are certainly themselves substantial, what constitutes them *as* apparatuses is not their materiality but their capacity to capture and order the existence of living beings. It is in the gap between the apparatuses and the beings they capture that Agamben locates a third class, that of *subjects* defined as products of the relation between the two, be it harmonious or antagonistic. From this perspective, the subject of tragedy is ultimately the product of the apparatuses of law, which alone are capable of adjudicating on one's guilt or innocence.

It is only when one enters, by force or willingly, into the domain of law that one can be found, or find oneself, guilty, paving the way for tragedy: '[When] Being is indicted, or "accused", within the sphere of law, it loses its innocence; it becomes a *cosa* (a thing), that is a *causa* (a case): an object of litigation' (Agamben 2010: 23). And yet Agamben's Kafka does not simply dismiss the idea of guilt in a nostalgic affirmation of the innocence of Being before any indictment. Indeed, in Agamben's often repeated methodological principle, 'history never returns to a lost state' (ibid.: 54. See also Agamben 2009b: 82–104; 2005a: 88) and whatever has been captured in an apparatus cannot simply return to innocence. In both Dante and Kafka, the liberation from tragic guilt takes the form of the full assumption or 'liberation' of shame: '[Kafka's] greatness is that he decided at a certain point to renounce theodicy and forego the old problem of guilt and innocence, of freedom and destiny, in order to concentrate solely on shame' (Agamben 1995: 65). When objective guilt is dissolved, our confinement within the apparatuses of law and politics appears to be nothing but a series of historical accidents, of which one cannot be guilty but can certainly be ashamed: 'One cannot be guilty or innocent of an accident, one can only feel embarrassed or ashamed as when we slip in the street on a banana skin' (ibid.: 84). From this perspective, the criticism that accuses Agamben of positing a teleological necessity to the Western political tradition appears misdirected. Not only is there no teleological argument or other claim to necessity in Agamben's works, but his critical exercise demonstrates precisely the radical *contingency* of the apparatuses of sovereign power, which in turn makes possible the liberation from one's tragic confinement within them.

Agamben's most explicit break with the logic of tragedy takes place in the context of his discussion of what is undoubtedly the most tragic event of the past century – the Shoah. In his book *Remnants of Auschwitz* (1999c), Agamben takes up the challenge of resuming ethical discourse after this horrendous event. Recognising how the experience of the camps makes meaningless, if not outright obscene, many of the ethical perspectives of the two preceding centuries, from Nietzsche's *amor fati* to Apel's discourse ethics, Agamben argues that the pathway to a post-Auschwitz ethics must begin with the abandonment of the tragic paradigm. Addressing the testimony of camp survivors, Agamben notes the inapplicability of the tragic logic, where the hero must assume its objective guilt despite his subjective innocence of the crime, to the experience of Auschwitz:

The deportee sees such a widening of the abyss between subjective innocence and objective guilt, between what he did do and what he could
feel responsible for, that he cannot assume responsibility for any of his
actions. With an inversion that borders on parody, he feels innocent precisely for that which the tragic hero feels guilty and guilty exactly where
the tragic hero feels innocent. (Agamben 1999c: 97)

Moreover, the model of tragic ethics is rendered suspect by the way
it was readily resorted to not by the victims but by the executioners,
who sought justification by pointing to the tragic conflict between
their objective guilt (as a result of following orders) and their subjective innocence of the acts they committed: 'The Greek hero has left
us forever; he can no longer bear witness for us in any way. After
Auschwitz, it is not possible to use a tragic paradigm in ethics' (ibid.:
99). In his Nobel lecture Joseph Brodsky famously argued, with reference to twentieth-century totalitarianism, that 'in a real tragedy, it
is not the hero who perishes; it is the chorus' (Brodsky 1987). Both
the scale and the senselessness of totalitarian violence destroy the
very possibility of adjudicating between the objective and the subjective, guilt and innocence that the chorus in Greek tragedy made possible, rendering the death of the hero insignificant in the literal sense
of being devoid of all meaning.

Bucephalus

Agamben's reversal of the tragic logic of politics may be elaborated
with the help of his reading of one of Kafka's explicitly comic texts,
'The New Advocate'. This short parable describes the entry of
Alexander the Great's renowned horse, Bucephalus, into the legal
profession, 'mounting the marble steps with a high action that made
them ring beneath his feet' (Kafka 2002: 58). The other lawyers 'in
general' accept Bucephalus into their field, understanding the 'dif-
ficulty' of his condition, which is that of a war horse without his
master in the times that no longer call for heroism:

[Nowadays] – it cannot be denied – there is no Alexander the Great.
There are plenty of men who know how to murder people; the skill
needed to reach over a banqueting table and pink a friend with a lance is
not lacking; but no one, no one at all, can blaze a trail to India. Today the
gates [to India] have receded to remoter and loftier places; no one points
the way; many carry swords, but only to brandish them, and the eye that
tries to follow them is confused.

So perhaps it is really best to do as Bucephalus has done and absorb oneself in law books. In the quiet lamplight, his flanks unhampered by the thighs of a rider, free and far from the clamour of battle, he reads and turns the pages of our ancient tomes. (Kafka 2002: 59)

In his reading of the story Walter Benjamin emphasised the fact that while Bucephalus *studies* the law, presumably diligently, he does not *practise* it. Absorbed in study, he remains 'free' and 'unhampered', which is what brings Benjamin to his famous claim that Agamben takes up on many occasions in his writings:

The law which is studied and not practiced any longer is the gate to justice. The gate to justice is learning. And yet Kafka does not attach to this learning the promises which tradition has attached to the study of the Torah. His assistants are sextons who have lost their house of prayer, his students are pupils who have lost the Holy Writ. Now there is nothing to support them on their 'untrammelled, happy journey'. (Benjamin 1968: 139; cf. Agamben 2005a: 59–64)

Indeed, we do not even know if Bucephalus's absorption in the pages of the ancient tomes produces any effects of knowledge – probably not, since it is, after all, a horse. But how can something be studied in the absence of any support and what could possibly be the purpose of such study? Benjamin concludes his essay on Kafka by bringing together the 'new advocate' Bucephalus with another character of a Kafka parable, Sancho Panza, whom Kafka interpreted as an author of 'a lot of romances of chivalry and adventure' who thereby managed to divert from himself his demon 'whom he later called Don Quixote', sending him out on the 'maddest exploits' that lacked a real object and did not do anyone any harm: 'Sancho Panza, a sedate fool and clumsy assistant, sent his rider on ahead; Bucephalus outlived his. Whether it is a man or a horse is no longer so important, if only the burden is removed from the back' (ibid.: 140). The purpose of studying without a clue, of reading ancient tomes that no longer mean anything to us, is precisely to remove the burden of their continuing presence and significance from our backs, to free us from the self-slanderous guilt by twisting loose from one's capture in the apparatuses of law and tradition (see Lewis 2013). Revealing 'the sickness of tradition' (ibid.: 143) is the sole possibility to regain one's own health. This is why Agamben concludes his reading of Kafka with the claim that 'the new advocate' studies the law 'only on the condition that it no longer be applied' (Agamben 2010: 36).

And this is exactly what Agamben does himself in this pains-takingly detailed archaeology of the Western political tradition. Agamben's critics discussed above are entirely correct in noting the sense of gravity produced by Agamben's account of the persistence of, for example, the logic of sovereignty, the state of exception or the 'anthropological machine' throughout the history of the West. Where they are mistaken is in taking this sense of gravity as Agamben's final word on the subject, whereby the sole effect of his archaeology would be the experience of entrapment within the inescapable tradition. In fact, as we shall demonstrate on many occasions in this book, the effect of Agamben's reading of the tradition is its dispersion or even dissipation into a multiplicity of historical accidents. By demonstrating the sickness of the tradition Agamben's political thought seeks to remove its burden from our backs, affirming the possibility of another politics, no longer grounded in the tradition, not even negatively by attempting to overcome it from within.

This is why despite the gloomy and even morbid nature of the subject matter of his books, Agamben's thought cannot be subsumed under the tragic logic. The persistent attempts of the critics to do so only result in the understandable perception of his critical pathos as excessive and hyperbolic. If, on the other hand, our interpretation is correct and the mood of Agamben's philosophy is primarily comic, the hyperbolic character of his criticism only seeks to make us drop the burden of the tragic tradition off our backs sooner than later. To return to Brodsky's understanding of tragedy, the stakes of Agamben's thought do not consist in the endless mourning of the death of the hero but rather in the redemption of the chorus, in halting the very possibility of the repetition of the bloodbath by stopping the performance of the tragedy.

Evidently, this does not mean that for Agamben the entirety of the Western tradition is simply to be negated. In full accordance with our idea of the comic, Agamben's politics is ultimately a matter of redemption, reclaiming and reappropriation. As we shall argue in Chapter 5, Agamben's political thought belongs to the wider 'messianic' turn in continental philosophy which seeks to mobilise the heritage of Judeo-Christian messianism for emancipatory and egalitarian politics. While we shall focus on Agamben's understanding of redemption in detail below, we may introduce its basic logic with the help of the Bucephalus parable. The law that is studied and not applied is posited by Benjamin as a 'gate to justice' (note that it is not *itself* justice), which in the context of the 'New Advocate' immediately brings to mind the 'gates to India' to which Bucephalus's erstwhile master once 'pointed the way'. The age in which Bucephalus lives is the age of exhaustion and expiry, where there is no longer anyone resembling Alexander the Great who could blaze a trail to India. Yet the absence of heroes does not seek to make these times any less violent: the swords are abundant and the art of murder well developed, yet it seems to have lost its point, since the 'gates to India' have 'receded'. This account of the age resonates with Agamben's description of our contemporary 'politics' as a nihilistic machine whose tasks have long been abandoned but which continues to run on empty, though no less violently than before.

> [We] are witnessing the incessant though aimless motion of the [governmental] machine, which, in a sort of colossal parody of theological *oikonomia*, has assumed the legacy of the providential governance of the world; yet instead of redeeming our world, this machine is leading us to catastrophe. (Agamben 2009c: 24)

For Agamben, it is only the halting of this machine that will ultimately permit the fulfilment of what it once promised, be it freedom, equality, community or justice, in the same manner as the impracticable law, the 'gate to justice', might well be the very same 'gate to India' that Bucephalus's contemporaries have long lost sight of (cf. Agamben 1998: 58). Yet what is left when the machine of government is halted? We have seen that the very form of the subject is a result of the interaction of living beings with the apparatuses that order them, which logically entails that halting the governmental machine would result in the disappearance of the subject as we know it, leaving us with the living being as such.

Yet, this being is, to say the least, an arcane and enigmatic figure. After all, our knowledge of human and other beings is entirely dependent on a myriad of apparatuses that constitute them in various positive ways and it is very difficult to imagine what a living being 'as such', devoid of any positive predicates, might be. Yet this is precisely the task that Agamben's entire philosophical project sets itself. Starting from the 1970s Agamben has attempted to elucidate this figure in various domains and contexts and in this book we shall trace his account of a life beyond the apparatuses in the domains of language, statehood, history and humanity. At this stage, we shall only introduce the immediate answer that Agamben gives to the question of what remains after the halting of the governmental machine: 'the Ungovernable, which is the beginning and, at the same time, the vanishing point of every politics' (Agamben 2009c: 24. See also Agamben 2011: 65). Beyond the apparatuses and the forms of subjectivity that they produce there is the excess of living being that can never be subsumed under them. While this excess does not in itself constitute a political subject, it testifies to the fact that the apparatuses are never all there is, which is precisely why a comic ending to their tragic operation remains possible.

The Limbo

While Agamben's break with the tragic logic appears indisputable, the comic character of his thought should not be overstated. Agamben is evidently not a utopian thinker affirming an infinite wealth of possibilities of a new and better politics. The argument for comedy as the fundamental attunement of Agamben's thought must therefore be qualified in three ways.

Firstly, while for Agamben the overcoming of the tragic logic is certainly possible, more often than not it takes place in circumstances that we would in ordinary language pronounce to be very tragic indeed. Many commentators have noted Agamben's 'morbid obsession with the dehumanized and disenfranchised' (Kearney 2009: 154), his fascination with abject figures from Bartleby to the bandit, from porn stars to the camp inmate, from the fetishist to the anorexic. This fascination is not due to Agamben's eccentricity but reflects a principled methodological focus on those sites or subjects, where the reversal of tragedy into comedy may take place. One of the most regularly cited phrases in Agamben's work is a line from *Patmos*, a hymn by the German Romantic poet Friedrich Hölderlin: 'where danger grows, grows also saving power'. As we recall from the fragment on moods, the desolate experience of the exhaustion of our 'epochal' traditions is simultaneously the mark of a true beginning of our 'word'. While the tragic logic of politics would focus on the dangers necessarily contained in every claim to 'saving power', Agamben rather affirms the saving power arising amidst the hyperbolically extreme danger. His reading of the Western political tradition explicitly asserts that Western politics is moving 'from bad to worse', producing at best a vacuous nihilism and at worst a genocidal totalitarianism. And yet precisely the current exhaustion of this tradition, its self-destructive running on empty, opens a possibility of a transformation so radical that it would leave this tradition behind, whereby the misfortunes and horrors of our tragic history are overcome. This theoretical standpoint calls for a methodological focus on extreme situations and settings as sites, where a comic reversal of the abject condition of the 'state of exception' or the 'ban' into a state of 'happy life' is most likely.

Secondly, this reversal itself does not take the form of a grand transformation of the 'unhappy' condition into a 'happy' one. Agamben frequently cites Benjamin's claim in the essay on Kafka that the coming of the Messiah would not radically change the world by force but would 'only make a slight adjustment within it' (Benjamin 1968: 134). This 'slight adjustment', after which 'everything will be as it is now, just a little different' (Agamben 1993a: 53), is best exemplified by a story presented by Benjamin in the same essay.

> [In] a Hasidic village Jews were sitting together in a shabby inn one Sabbath evening. They were all local people, with the exception of one person no one knew, a very poor ragged man. All sorts of things were discussed, and then it was suggested that everyone should tell what wish he would make if one were granted him. One man wanted money, another wished for a son-in-law, a third dreamed of a new carpenters' bench. After they had finished, only the beggar in his dark corner was left. Reluctantly and hesitantly he answered the question: 'I wish I were a powerful king reigning over a big country. Then, some night while I was asleep in my palace, an enemy would invade my country. Roused from my sleep, I wouldn't have time even to dress and I would have to flee in my shirt. Rushing over hill and dale and through forests day and night, I would finally arrive safely right here at the bench in this corner. This is my wish.' The others exchanged uncomprehending glances. 'And what good would this wish have done you?', someone asked. 'I'd have a shirt', was the answer. (Benjamin 1968: 134–5)

This parable is not merely comic in the conventional sense but illustrates the logic of comic reversal that we shall trace below in various domains of Agamben's political thought. The 'net result' of the wish fulfilment is admittedly meagre, even though we need not underestimate the importance, even a salvific one, of a shirt for the one lacking it: 'Seek for food and clothing first, then the Kingdom of God shall be added unto you' (Hegel cited in Benjamin 1968: 254; cf. Vatter 2008: 63). Yet, despite ultimately returning to one's place, the beggar arguably travels quite a long way, assuming the sovereign power of a king and then losing the possibility of its exercise, ultimately ending up in the position of the opposite of the sovereign, with the consolation prize of the shirt. What is formed in these travels is what Agamben terms a 'zone of indistinction' between sovereign and rabble, which for him is the mark of a truly messianic politics. The beggar *does* become king, yet while in the tragic logic his becoming king would come at the cost of transforming someone else into a beggar, thus perpetuating the tragic story of sovereign power, in the comic version the very logic of sovereignty is suspended so that all the sovereign gets for his troubles is the shirt, which levels his difference from the beggar. It is this transformation that constitutes the 'messianic displacement that integrally changes the world, leaving it at the same time almost intact' (Agamben 2000: 79). While Agamben certainly differs from numerous representatives of the tragic logic in vesting his hope in such a messianic displacement, he also emphasises its minimal, almost imperceptible character.

Finally, we ought to emphasise that the relation between the comic and the tragic is not a binary opposition between two distinct states of affairs but rather between two perspectives on or attunements to the same situation. The comic mood is a modified way of dealing with the tragic that liberates us from its burden. The relation between the two moods is eloquently summed up in Agamben's moving fragment on Elsa Morante, an Italian author and Agamben's long-time friend. Noting that Morante's work is usually associated with the tragic tradition that has never been dominant in the Italian literature since Dante's *Divine Comedy*, Agamben nonetheless defines her work as an 'antitragic tragedy', 'as if inside tragedy there were another tragedy that resisted it' (Agamben 1999a: 132). To illustrate this point Agamben uses the example of the children of limbo that is central to his own theorisation of political community that we shall address in Chapter 3.

> [The] limbo is the place not of innocents but rather of those who have no other guilt than natural guilt, of those infants who could not have been submitted to the punishment of language. The baptism of the Verb cancels this natural guilt but it cancels it only through another, more atrocious punishment. But in Elsa it is as if, at a certain point, the creature from limbo lifted its fragile arm against the historical tragedy of a language in a hopeless gesture, in a silent confrontation whose outcome cannot easily be understood. (Ibid.: 132)

The liberation from natural guilt through baptism comes at the cost of one's subjection to language, history and politics, one's subsumption under the historical apparatuses whose reproduction resigns one to the perpetual replay of tragedy. Yet does not the resistance against this secondary punishment, which is indeed fragile, hopeless and difficult to understand, leave us in the tragic logic, which, after all, is based precisely on the idea of natural guilt? It is here that Agamben undertakes an intricate yet crucial reversal that points to a comic resolution of the 'antitragic tragedy'.

Since the children of limbo have no guilt other than the original sin, they cannot be consigned to hell and their only punishment is the 'perpetual lack of the vision of God' (Agamben 1993a: 4). However, since these children were not baptised and therefore lack any supernatural knowledge, implanted at baptism, they cannot *suffer* this lack, or even perceive it as such. Thus, Agamben argues, what was intended as privation turns into a natural joy for the inhabitants of limbo:

> Irremediably lost, they persist without pain in divine abandon. God has not forgotten them, but rather they have always already forgotten God, and in the face of their forgetfulness, God's forgetting is impotent. Like letters with no addressee, these uprisen beings remain without a destination. Neither blessed like the elected, nor hopeless like the damned, they are infused with a joy with no outlet. (Ibid.: 5)

Thus, limbo, which at first appeared to be a tragic place, is transformed into a site of the definitive taking leave of tragedy, whereby natural guilt is neutralised without being converted into personal guilt:

> These beings have left the world of guilt and justice behind them: the light that rains down on them is that irreparable light of the dawn following the *novissima dies* of judgment. But the life that begins on earth after the last day is simply human life. (Ibid.: 6)

It is this striking image of a simply human 'happy life' (2000: 114) that Agamben's political thought affirms as an ever-present potentiality of the human condition that survives the 'last day' of history and flourishes in its aftermath. Through a 'fragile', 'hopeless' and often barely understandable confrontation with the logic of tragedy at work in the Western political tradition, he seeks *not* to resolve the problems that have plagued political thought in its tragic mode but to leave these problems behind in a 'tiny displacement' that would integrally transform our condition. Let us recall that the distinction between comedy and tragedy is based on the difference with regard to the ending: while tragedy leads from a happy beginning to an unhappy end, comedy begins with various misfortunes and ends in the restoration of happiness. The motto of comic politics is thus 'all's well that ends well': while the tragic logic knows the end to be unhappy and seeks to hold off its inevitable arrival, perpetuating our condition, the comic logic finds the possibility of happiness at the end and *only* at the end, and therefore welcomes and accelerates it, eager to start a new life after the last day.

It is this distance from the tragic logic of both classical and modern political thought that makes Agamben's work simultaneously alluring and difficult, resulting in frequent misreadings or no less frequent 'non-readings', whereby Agamben is simply excluded from the purview of political philosophy. In contrast, this book will proceed on the assumption that Agamben's comic overcoming of the Western political tradition is among the most provocative as well as most promising avenues in contemporary political thought and certainly deserves more than a cursory misreading or a curt dismissal.

Of course, our initial formulation of the fundamental mood of Agamben's political thought leaves more questions than it answers. Our presentation of the comic mood was largely based on concepts and examples from the domains that are quite distant from what we would conventionally characterise as the 'political sphere': Dante, Kafka, Bucephalus, Sancho Panza, limbo, and so on. Is this political thought or, more precisely, *how* is this thought political? How is it capable of intervening in the more conventionally defined political sphere and what effects does its intervention produce? In the following chapters we shall consider precisely these questions. We shall begin by outlining a general logic of comic politics, which consists in rendering apparatuses of government inoperative, and elucidating the idea of inoperativity with a series of paradigms. We shall then trace the operation of this logic in the four key domains of Agamben's work: language, statehood, history and life, demonstrating the persistence of the same logic in these different domains.

Note

1. This dualism *ipso facto* excludes such intermediate forms as tragicomedy, which historically referred to a tragedy with a happy ending that usually combined the elevated pathos of tragedy with the lighter comic moments. Evidently, from a strictly dualistic perspective a tragedy with a happy ending is simply a comedy, insofar as its tragic tribulations find

a happy resolution in the end (just as a tragedy with lighter themes or moments is still a tragedy if its ending is unhappy). Given the importance of the theme of ending in Agamben's work, we shall rely on this dualistic approach to interpret the mood of Agamben's thought as comic, even though the conventional notion of tragicomedy might be more appropriate to describe his works.

Chapter 2

The Sabbatical Animal:
The Politics of Inoperativity

In this chapter we shall elaborate the logic of Agamben's comic politics. In contrast to tragedy, comedy affirms the possibility of happiness, but only at the end. The figure of the ending, of coming or bringing to an end, is thus central to Agamben's work yet acquires a very specific meaning in it. The 'happy end' of Agamben's politics does not consist in the teleological fulfilment of a process or the destruction or elimination of an object but rather in becoming or rendering something *inoperative*, neutralising its force and making it available for *free use*. Inoperativity is the central concept of Agamben's thought, marking the continuity of his philosophical project from the earliest work onwards. Drawing on Agamben's reading of Aristotle, we shall reconstitute his original formulation of this problematic and its linkage with the Aristotelian concept of *potentiality*. We shall then elucidate the functioning of the logic of inoperativity by analysing a series of *paradigmatic* examples from diverse spheres: the glorious body in Christianity, the Sabbath in Judaism, the religious hymn, the empty throne, etc. We shall conclude with a discussion of arguably the most famous and extreme example of inoperativity in Agamben's work, Melville's Bartleby.

The Worklessness of Man

While numerous passages on the coming politics and happy life in Agamben's texts are frequently dismissed in the secondary literature as naive utopianism at odds with the clinical detachment of his critical analyses, this dismissal is due to the misunderstanding of the logic of comedy, for which happiness is possible *but only at the end*. This accounts for Agamben's preoccupation with *endings*: suspension, deactivation, closure, halting are all privileged figures in Agamben's work. In order to understand Agamben's politics it is thus necessary to engage with the question of what the idea of the end means in his work: is it a matter of fulfilment, negation, summation, elimination, interruption, etc? In this chapter we shall address this question, focusing on the neologism central to Agamben's work from his earliest writings onwards: inoperativity (*inoperosità*). For Agamben, the way to bring things to the end consists neither in the teleological fulfilment of a process of development (the end as completion or accomplishment) nor in the merely negative act of the destruction or elimination of an object (the end as termination or cessation). Instead, it is the process of becoming or rendering something *inoperative*, deactivating its functioning in the apparatus and making it available for free use. Happy life is thus made possible by neutralising the multiple apparatuses of power to which we are subjected, including our own identities formed within them.

In our elucidation of the concept of inoperativity in this chapter we shall rely on Agamben's own method, which he terms *paradigmatic*. The notion of paradigm was introduced in Thomas Kuhn's seminal *Structure of Scientific Revolutions* (1970b), where it was used to distinguish 'normal science', characterised by the cumulative growth of knowledge, from 'revolutionary science', arising due to the growth of various anomalies to which no solution could be found by normal-scientific means. While normal science is characterised by the presence of what Kuhn termed a paradigm, within which science unfolds as a 'puzzle-solving' activity, in revolutionary periods the paradigm itself is put in question and challenged by alternatives. Yet what is this paradigm? The use of the term in Kuhn is ambiguous to say the least – according to Masterman (1970) the term is used in the *Structure of Scientific Revolutions* in twenty-one senses. Nonetheless, it is possible to group these many usages into two categories identified in Kuhn's later work. On the one hand, the notion of paradigm refers to widely shared background assumptions, principles, methods or practices of a scientific community that Kuhn later proposed should be termed 'disciplinary matrix' (Kuhn 1970a). In this sense, we might speak of the 'comic paradigm' of Agamben's thought as the fundamental mood at work in various domains of his thought or treat the concept of inoperativity as paradigmatic for Agamben's political philosophy as such. On the other hand, Kuhn also used the notion of the paradigm in the more restricted sense of a single exemplar of a problem-solution (for example, a formula, a method, a model) that guides scientific research in the absence of explicit rules.

In this latter sense, the concept of paradigm has an affinity with the Foucauldian concept of the apparatus, discussed in the previous chapter. Such famous figures of Foucault's studies as the panopticon or the confessional (1977, 1990a) are precisely singular examples that permit to grasp rationalities of power and forms of knowledge in the absence of explicit rules of their functioning. In his methodological essay 'What is a paradigm?' Agamben undertakes an operation similar to his radical generalisation of the concept of the apparatus, tracing the genealogy of the term back from Foucault and Kuhn through Kant and Heidegger all the way to Plato and Aristotle (Agamben 2009b: 1–32). In Agamben's definition, the paradigm is an example that illuminates the set to which it belongs, a 'singular object that, standing equally for all others of the same class, defines the intelligibility of the group of which it is a part and which, at the same time it constitutes' (ibid.: 17), Thus Foucault's panopticon or Agamben's own famous figures of the *homo sacer* and the *Muselmann* are concrete historical phenomena whose significance nonetheless goes beyond their immediate historical context or domain, since they also establish a 'broader problematic context' (ibid.: 17).

Paradigms thus obey a complex logic: insofar as they illuminate something beyond themselves, their normal denotative use must be suspended in order to enable the constitution of a new ensemble. As opposed to induction (the move from particular to the universal) and deduction (the move from the universal to the particular), the paradigmatic method moves from one particular to another in the absence of a universal principle or a general rule, in the manner of Kant's aesthetic judgment or the use of an example in grammar (ibid.: 21). For instance, the word 'paradigm' may itself be used paradigmatically as an example of an English noun, for which its own specific denotation must be suspended. And yet 'it is precisely by virtue of this nonfunctioning and suspension that it can show how the syntagma [of other English nouns] works and can allow the rule to be stated' (ibid.: 24). This is precisely the function of the numerous paradigmatic figures that we encounter in Agamben's works – *homo sacer*, the *Muselmann*, the porn star, Bartleby, angels – are all used in the paradigmatic manner, making intelligible the wider ensemble from which they stand out due to the suspension of their own denotation. While Agamben's key concepts are often introduced in an elliptical, arcane or esoteric manner, their intelligibility is established through the proliferation of such examples. In this chapter we shall briefly introduce the theoretical concept of inoperativity and proceed to elaborate it through a consideration of a series of paradigmatic examples in Agamben's works.

The concept of inoperativity was derived by Agamben from Alexandre Kojève's notion of *désoeuvrement* or 'worklessness', whose formulation in the context of the problematic of the end of history we shall address in Chapter 5. While Kojève's work is arguably the most important reference for Agamben's concept of inoperativity, he was undoubtedly also influenced by the use of the concept of *désoeuvrement* in later French philosophy, most notably in Maurice Blanchot's (1988) and Jean Luc Nancy's (1991) reinterpretations of the idea of community. Another source of the concept may be found in the political praxis of the period, i.e. the Autonomist Marxist movements in Italy in the late 1970s, one of whose key ideas was 'refusal of work' (see Thoburn 2003: 103–38), which evidently did not refer to mere valorisation of idleness but rather sought to overcome the set of relations and identities formed around work in capitalist society.[1]

As Leland de la Durantaye suggested, inoperativity remains one of the most enigmatic and misunderstood concepts in Agamben's entire *oeuvre* (2009: 18–20). Difficulties begin at the stage of translation. How should the Italian *inoperosita* be translated into English? In most translations of Agamben, the term is translated as 'inoperativity', even though some translators also opt for 'inoperativeness' (Agamben 1998: 62), 'inactivity' (2005a: 64) or 'inoperability' (2000: 141). While in this book we shall go along with the predominant translation, we must emphasise that in Agamben's work this term is given an idiosyncratic technical sense, which may indeed make a loan word or a neologism like 'inoperosity' (Negri 2012; Prozorov 2009a, 2009b, 2009d) more appropriate. While the standard use of 'inoperativity' in English denotes either the absence of action and failure to function (inoperative as out-of-order, defective, invalid, etc.) or the absence of utility (inoperative as useless, unworkable, out of service, etc.), Agamben applies the concept to refer to a specific kind of action that, moreover, does not minimise but rather augments the possibilities of use. As we shall demonstrate repeatedly throughout this chapter, to affirm inoperativity is not to affirm inertia, inactivity or apraxia, let alone dysfunctionality or destruction, but rather a form of praxis that is devoid of any telos or task, does not realise any essence and does not correspond to any nature. It is this form of praxis that for Agamben manifests the originary feature of the human condition: 'Because human beings neither are nor have to be any essence, any nature, or any specific destiny, their condition is the most empty and the most insubstantial of all' (Agamben 2000: 94–5).

Agamben's thesis of the constitutive inoperativity of the human being is inspired by his reading of a passage from Aristotle's *Nicomachean Ethics* (I, 7, 1097b22–1098a18). While for Aristotle human beings may have a task or a function that arises out of the particular activity in which they are engaged (as sculptors, flute players, shoemakers, etc.), it is difficult to conceive of a task that would apply to humans *qua* humans, leading to the question of whether man as such is not essentially 'workless', without any tasks to achieve. While this possibility was eventually dropped by Aristotle in favour of identifying 'the work of man' with life according to the *logos*, it continued to haunt the entire history of philosophy from Averroes through Dante to Hegel and Bataille (Agamben 2007c: 6–9; 2005b: 99–104; 1998: 60–2). The problem of inoperativity reaches its most extreme manifestation with the (late-)modern condition that Agamben refers to as nihilism and dates back to World War I.

For Agamben, modern nihilism renders void all established values and discloses the absence of any historical tasks to which humanity must devote itself. While the originary inoperativity of the human being was for centuries veiled by religion or political ideology, the advent of nihilism entails its coming to the foreground of social life:

> [T]oday, it is clear for anyone who is not in absolutely bad faith that there are no longer historical tasks that can be taken on by, or even simply assigned to, men. It was in some ways evident starting with the end of the First World War that the European nation-states were no longer capable of taking on historical tasks and that peoples themselves were bound to disappear. (Agamben 2004b: 76)

And yet, the apparatuses of states, nations and peoples have survived the nihilist disclosure and continue to exist in the present. In Agamben's reading, they were only able to do so by positing life itself as the supreme task of the human being and reorienting government towards the protection, fostering and augmentation of life as such. While 'traditional historical potentialities – poetry, religion, philosophy, which from both the Hegelo-Kojèvian and Heideggerian perspectives kept the historico-political destiny of peoples awake, have long since transformed into cultural spectacles and private experiences', 'the only task that still seems to retain some seriousness is the assumption of the burden of biological life, that is, of the very animality of man' (ibid.: 76–7). This is the phenomenon of modern biopolitics, which is central to Agamben's diagnosis of our tragic political predicament and which we shall analyse in detail in

Chapter 4. The apparatuses of government take life as their object not merely in order to colonise and control it, but primarily because in the condition of nihilism they have no other object and are at the risk of unravelling due to the expiry of all positive historical projects. In contrast to this setting of life itself to work, Agamben's politico-philosophical project advances a radical affirmation of the inoperativity of the human being as the pathway to a new politics that leaves the exhausted apparatuses behind:

> [Politics] is that which corresponds to the essential inoperability of humankind, to the radical being-without-work of human communities. There is politics because human beings are *argos*-beings that cannot be defined by any proper operation, that is, beings of pure potentiality that no identity or vocation can possibly exhaust. Politics might be nothing other than the exposition of humankind's absence of work as well as the exposition of humankind's creative semi-indifference to any task, and might only in this sense remain integrally assigned to happiness. (Agamben 2000: 141–2)

In its abandonment of all tasks, the idea of inoperativity goes beyond the ethico-political models that supplant the external imposition of the 'work of man' with freely chosen forms of self-fashioning, most notably the 'work on the self' that is the centrepiece of a Foucauldian reconstruction of ethics as an aesthetics of existence. The Foucauldian ethics certainly does away with any external task to which human activity is subjected, but retains the overall work-oriented and teleological vision of human praxis – it is important to recall that one of four dimensions of a Foucauldian ethics is precisely telos (Foucault 1990b: 25–32). In contrast, what is at stake in Agamben's idea of inoperativity is dispensing with the work-oriented vision of human existence as such.[2] Yet, as we shall see in the following section, the absence of tasks or work proper to the human being is not understood as a privation but, on the contrary, is conceived as the precondition for any meaningful freedom.

Inoperative Potentiality

At this point we must introduce the concept that is closely intertwined with the idea of inoperativity, i.e. potentiality. Similarly to the former, Agamben develops this concept through an engagement with Aristotle, specifically with his account of potentiality in *De Anima* and *Metaphysics*. For Aristotle, something is potential not simply because it is capable of being, but, more importantly, because it has the capacity *not* to be (see Agamben 1993a: 35–8; 1998: 45–7; 1999b: 249–50). In contrast to the 'material' or 'possible' potentiality of, for example, a child who cannot write but may potentially become a poet, 'perfect potentiality' is only accessible through the image of a poet who already *can* write poetry but does *not* do so (Agamben 1999b: 247). To be worthy of the name, potentiality must retain its potential for being 'impotential', for *not* passing into actuality. Thus, potentiality necessarily 'maintains itself in relation to its own privation, its own *steresis*, its own non-Being' (ibid.: 182). Yet it is evidently not equivalent to non-Being as such, but rather consists in the paradoxical 'existence of non-Being, the presence of an absence' (ibid.: 179). While this understanding of potentiality might at first glance appear esoteric, it is precisely this potential 'not to' that is constitutive of human existence as such:

> [Beings] that exist in the mode of potentiality are capable of their own impotentiality; and only in this way do they become potential. They *can* be because they are in relation to their own non-Being. Human beings, insofar as they know and produce, are those beings who, more than any other, exist in the mode of potentiality. This is the origin of human power, which is so violent and limitless in relation to other living beings. Other living beings are capable only of their specific potentiality: they can only do this or that. But human beings are the animals that are capable of their own impotentiality. (Ibid.: 182)

In this statement, Agamben relies on the understanding of the human condition characteristic of the philosophical anthropology of the 1920s, represented by such authors as Max Scheler, Helmuth Plessner and Arnold Gehlen, and highly influential for such philosophers as Heidegger. This strand of thought, which, as we shall see in Chapter 6, Agamben gradually distanced himself from, interprets the uniqueness of the human condition not in terms of any positive principle (rationality, conscience, language, etc.) but rather in terms of its radical openness and indeterminacy, the separation from one's immediate environment, the 'neotenic' incompleteness and absence of specialisation. In contrast to animals whose potentiality is restricted to the specific possibilities prescribed by their genetic code, human being are constitutively lacking in such prescriptions, retaining throughout their lives the possibility of being otherwise than they are. Thus, human potentiality is never exhausted in actuality but rather 'passes fully into it [and] preserves itself as such in actuality' (ibid.: 183). For Agamben, it is precisely this actual existence of the possible that defines human freedom:

> Here it is possible to see how the root of freedom is to be found in the abyss of potentiality. To be free is not simply to have the power to do this or other thing, nor is it simply to have the power to refuse to do this or other thing. To be free is to be capable of one's own impotentiality, to be in relation to one's own privation. This is why freedom is freedom for both good and evil. (Ibid.: 182–3)

From this perspective, the assessment of the degree of freedom in any given society can never be content with assessing potentialities to do something, offered to its citizens, but must also take into account the potentialities 'not to' that remain available to them. For Agamben the difference between classical authoritarian systems and contemporary capitalist democracies consists in the fact that the former tended to target one's 'positive' potentiality, impeding beings from doing what they can (speak freely, protest, associate, revolt, and so on), while the latter operate much more insidiously by separating beings from their potentiality not to do something. 'Those who are separated from what they can do can, however, still resist; they can still not do. Those who are separated from their own impotentiality lose, on the other hand, first of all the capacity to resist' (Agamben 2010: 44). While prohibition to do something leaves open the possibility of transgression, the negation of potentiality 'not to' makes freedom meaningless, even though it tends to act precisely in the name of its augmentation. The perception that everything is possible – that I can do this and that – merely conceals one's subjection to the apparatuses that feed on that very potentiality in setting human beings to work in actuality:

> The idea that anyone can do or be anything – the suspicion that not only could the doctor who examines me today be a video artist tomorrow but that even the executioner who kills me is actually, as in Kafka's Trial, also a singer – is nothing but the reflection of the awareness that everyone is simply bending him- or her self according to the flexibility that is today the primary quality that the market demands from each person. (Ibid.: 44–5)

In contrast to this augmentation of possibilities in the name of flexible adaptation to what is, Agamben's politics of inoperativity seeks to restore and radicalise freedom by suspending the operation of the apparatuses, thus making room for the potential through opening existing realities to new forms of use. By rendering the apparatuses inoperative or, which often amounts to the same thing, by becoming inoperative within them, one reclaims one's potentiality 'not to' and hence enhances one's freedom. Thus, potentiality and inoperativity are quite simply two sides of the same coin of freedom: to be able to do something is *not to have to* do something (anything) else. 'The only coherent way to understand inoperativeness is to think of it as a generic mode of potentiality that is not exhausted in a *transitus de potentia ad actum*' (Agamben 1998: 62). The inoperative is neither the inactive nor the useless but rather consists in the activity that restores potentiality to beings and things, making them usable in new ways.

Glory

Let us now elaborate this idea of inoperative potentiality through a series of examples from various thematic fields of Agamben's work. Indeed, such examples may easily be found in every field that Agamben has investigated since the 1970s, making inoperativity the central concept that endows Agamben's work with strong coherence despite the dazzling diversity of his concerns. Whether it is a matter of investigating the theme of courtly love in the Provencal poetry of the twelfth century (Agamben 1993b: 129–31) or the most recent biometric technologies (2010: 52–4), the spectre (2010: 37–42) or the tick (2004b: 45–8), Kafka's Joseph K (2010: 20–31) or Orson Welles' Don Quixote (2007b, 93–4), it is always a matter of accentuating the originary status of inoperativity and potentiality and their relation to the positive apparatuses that govern our existence.

Perhaps the most striking example of inoperativity in Agamben's work comes from the sphere of theology and pertains to the idea of the 'glorious body' after the resurrection. The question that preoccupied medieval theologians, including Aquinas, concerned the appearance of this glorious body and specifically its organs of vegetation and procreation that have no reason for existence after the resurrection, such as the stomach, intestines, penis, vagina, and so on (2010: 97–103). At first glance, the organs in question would appear to be patently useless if the functions that they served were no longer practicable in the new condition. Yet their remaining present despite becoming useless would contradict the understanding of the glorious body as 'perfect nature', in which nothing can exist in vain. The intricate solution was to divorce the *existence* of the organs from their *function*:

[The] organ or instrument that was separated from its operation and remains in a state of suspension, acquires, precisely for this reason, an ostensive function; it exhibits the virtue corresponding to the suspended operation. Just as in advertisements or pornography, where the simulacra of merchandise or bodies exalt their appeal precisely to the extent that they cannot be used but only exhibited, so in the resurrection the idle sexual organs will display the potentiality or the virtue of procreation. The glorious body is an ostensive body whose functions are not executed but rather displayed. Glory, in this sense, is in solidarity with inoperativity. (Ibid.: 98)

Thus the post-resurrection body is inoperative in the sense of the suspension of its functions except the ostensive one. Yet to what extent does it also become potential, open to new forms of use? It is here that Agamben introduces the idea of *glory* as the device to limit the potentiality of the inoperative by restricting its use to pure exhibition: 'The eternally inoperative organs in the bodies of the blessed do not represent another use for those organs. There is perhaps nothing more enigmatic than a glorious penis, nothing more spectral than a purely doxological vagina' (ibid.: 99).

This argument parallels Heidegger's famous distinction between the two modes of being: being-ready-to-hand (*Zuhandensein*), which characterises tools or equipment available for use in accordance with their function, and being-present-at-hand (*Vorhandensein*), which characterises the same tools when they are broken, lost or otherwise unusable, when their presence becomes conspicuous, obtrusive and obstinate (Heidegger 1962: 102–7; see also Harman 2002). While in the former mode tools are operative in accordance with their pre-scribed function, in the latter they are inoperative without thereby becoming available for any new use; they are conspicuously *there* without being of any use to us. While for Heidegger this mode of being characterises beings and things as they become the objects of scientific investigation, abstracted and alienated from the world, for Agamben this useless inoperativity characterises beings and things that are captured and confined within a certain apparatus, where either they are removed from use or this use is restricted and regulated. What remains is only the ostensive function fortified by the idea of glory. It is precisely glory that immobilises potentiality by isolating inoperativity in a special 'sacred' sphere where it can be marvelled at but never used:

the sexual organs and the intestines of the blessed are only the hieroglyphs or the arabesques that divine glory inscribes onto its own coat of arms.

The earthly liturgy, like the celestial one, does nothing other than incessantly capture inoperativity and displace it into the sphere of worship. (Agamben 2010: 100)

What would be the alternative to this capture? How can one use the present-at-hand? With reference to Alfred Sohn-Rethel's observations of Neapolitans in the 1920s, Agamben argues for the possibility for inoperativity to become an 'opening, the "open-sesame" that leads to a new possible use' (ibid.):

> According to Sohn-Rethel, a Neapolitan only begins to really use technical objects at the moment when they no longer function. An intact thing that functions well on its own irritates Neapolitans, so they usually avoid it. And yet, by shoving a piece of wood in the right spot, or by making a slight adjustment with a smack of the hand at the right moment, Neapolitans manage to make their apparatuses work according to their desires. (Ibid.: 99)

Thus, rather than subject the inoperative object to the separation into a privileged sphere of pure manifestation, this object must be explored with regard to the new potentialities that the suspension of its canonical functions may open up:

> A new use of the body is possible only if it wrests the inoperative function from its separation, only if it succeeds in bringing together within a single place and in a single gesture both exercise and inoperativity, economic body and glorious body, function and its suspension. Inoperativity is not inert; on the contrary, it allows the very potentiality that has manifested itself in the act to appear. It is not potentiality that is deactivated in inoperativity but only the aims and modalities into which its exercise has been inscribed and separated. And it is this potentiality that can now become the organs of a new possible use. (Ibid.: 102)

What sort of new use may the body be subjected to? Agamben's examples of such use include 'amorous desire and so-called perversion', 'which use the organs of the nutritive and reproductive functions and turn them – in the very act of using them – away from their physiological meaning, towards a new and more human operation' (ibid.: 102). Perversion and fetishism as one of its forms are characterised by the logic diametrically opposed to that of glorious ostentation: whereas in the former case an object acquires glory at the cost of losing all its potentiality, in the latter case potentiality is augmented through sacrificing all the insignia of glory (or, perhaps, attaining real glory for the first time):

The naked, simple human body is not displaced here into a higher and nobler reality: instead, liberated from the witchcraft that once separated it from itself, it is as if this body were now able to gain access to its own truth for the first time. In this way the mouth truly becomes a mouth only if it is about to be kissed, the most intimate and private parts become a place for shared use and pleasure, habitual gestures become the illegible writing, whose hidden meaning the dancer deciphers for all. The glorious body is not some other body, more agile and beautiful, more luminous and spiritual; it is the body itself, at the moment when inoperativity removes the spell from it and opens it up to a new possible common use. (Ibid.: 102–3).[3]

Let us briefly consider other examples in order to illuminate the relation between inoperativity, potentiality and glory. While any holiday exemplifies inoperativity in the sense of the suspension of work, a particularly good example would be the Sabbath, insofar as this holiday celebrates not the activity of divine creation but rather its cessation, whereby 'on the seventh day God abstained from all work'. It is to sanctify this divine inoperativity that the observing Jews abstain from numerous activities on the Sabbath yet, crucially, do not become completely inactive (see Agamben 2011: 239–41). The activities proscribed during the Sabbath are those directed towards production, construction or some positive function. In contrast, festive behaviours, including the consumption of meals, are permitted and encouraged. Yet, what makes the behaviours in question festive is precisely the suspension or neutralisation of any relationship to positive productivity:

> what is done becomes undone, rendered inoperative, liberated and sus-pended from its 'economy', from the reasons and aims that define it during the weekdays. If one eats, it is not done for the sake of being fed; if one gets dressed, it is not done for the sake of being covered up; if one walks, it is not done for the sake of going someplace; if one speaks, it is not done for the sake of communicating information. (Agamben 2010: 111)

We thus arrive at the formula of inoperative praxis as any action liberated from its 'proper' or canonical function or telos.

And yet, similarly to the isolation of the 'glorious body' into the separate sphere of worship, the celebration may be easily separated into a privileged sphere of solemn ritual or liturgy that neutralises the possibilities of use that its inoperative character enables. This 'recodification' of inoperativity (ibid.: 112) in terms of glory is well illustrated by various secular and religious rituals of acclamation that Agamben analyses in his *The Kingdom and the Glory* (2011) and *Highest Poverty* (2013). These liturgical rituals, whose model is the *hymn*, are usually devoid of positive signified content other than the praise they confer. In this suspension of the signifying or communicative function, the hymn serves as a special case of the more general phenomenon of poetry, which Agamben approaches as 'a linguistic operation that renders language inoperative' (Agamben 2011: 250). Poetry takes place when language deactivates its communicative function and, as it were, 'rests within itself, contemplating its own power of speaking' (ibid.: 251). The example of the poem demonstrates once again that inoperativity is not equivalent to inactivity: the poetic use of language evidently involves much more 'work' than our everyday use of language. What is rendered inoperative in poetry is not speaking but its specific function and contents, whose suspension amplifies the potentiality for the use of language in non-canonical ways. However, specific forms of poetry, such as the religious hymn, capture and confine this excess of potentiality in the determinate form of the glorification of the divinity (or secular authority), where inoperative language is not open to new use but solely exhibits its own presence-at-hand:

> At the point where it perfectly coincides with glory, praise is without content; it culminates in the *amen* that says nothing but merely assents to and concludes what has already been said. [This] turning in the void of language is the supreme form of glorification. The hymn is the radical deactivation of signifying language, the word rendered completely inoperative and, nevertheless, retained as such in the form of liturgy. (Ibid.: 237)

Play and Profanation

While Agamben only began to theorise inoperativity explicitly in the 1990s, the logic designated by this concept was central to his earliest books of the late 1970s, such as *Stanzas* and *Infancy and History*, where the relation between inoperativity and glory is addressed in terms of the opposition between ritual and play. Drawing on the work of Benveniste and Lévi-Strauss, Agamben distinguishes between *ritual*, which fixes and structures the chronological time of the calendar through its orderly recurrence, and *play*, which changes and destroys it (Agamben 2007a: 77). In contrast to a sacred ceremony, which combines the form of the ritual with mythical content, play is constituted by the disjunction between the two, transmitting either the pure form of the ritual (as a 'game') or the mere content of the myth (as 'word play'). 'The power of the sacred act lies in the conjunction of the myth that tells the story and the rite that reproduces and stages it. Play breaks up this unity' (2007b: 75). In this manner, the sphere of play is presented by Agamben as 'the topsy-turvy image of the sacred' (2007a: 77), which 'frees and distracts humanity from the sphere of the sacred without simply abolishing it' (2007b: 76). As we have argued with regard to inoperative praxis, play is evidently still a matter of activity and use, yet of a different, non-canonical and non-utilitarian one. 'Children, who play with whatever old thing that falls into their hands, make toys out of things that belong to the spheres of economics, war, laws and other activities that we are used to thinking of as serious' (ibid.: 76) Agamben explicitly links this playful mode of use to Benjamin's interpretation of Kafka's Bucephalus the New Attorney, where, as we recall, the law that was studied but not practised was the 'gate to justice'. Similarly, 'the powers of economics, law and politics, deactivated in play, can become the gateways to a new happiness' (ibid.; see also Lewis 2013).

Thus, for all its diversion from canonical functions, for Agamben play is a very serious matter indeed, functioning as the method of arriving at the comic 'happy ending'. This is even more so given the fact that in contemporary societies 'play is in decline everywhere' (ibid.). While this statement might appear counter-intuitive, given the permanent proliferation of television game shows, computer and mobile phone games and the generally 'playful' turn in social communication, Agamben argues that what is often at stake in this proliferation is the very opposite of the inoperative intention of play:

> At parties, in dances and at play, [man] desperately and stubbornly seeks exactly the opposite of what he could find there: the possibility of reentering the lost feast, returning to the sacred and its rites, even in the form of the inane ceremonies of the new spectacular religion or a tango lesson in a provincial dance hall. (Ibid.: 77)

Just as ritual can be rendered inoperative through play, various conventional forms of play can be transformed into joyless rituals that function as new forms of liturgy, secular, to be sure, but, in Agamben's terminology, not at all profane.

The difference between the secular and the profane is crucial for Agamben's return to the theme of play in his later work on *profanation*. Agamben defines profanation as the overcoming of the separation of an object into a separate, 'sacred' sphere that opens it to free use in a myriad of non-canonical ways, augmenting its potentiality for use by rendering its prescribed functions inoperative (ibid.: 73–4). In this sense, profanation is constitutively opposed to religion and, more generally and originally, glory, which 'removes things, places, animals or people from common use and transfers them to a separate sphere' (ibid.: 74). Yet profanation should also be distinguished from secularisation, which 'leaves intact the forces it deals with by simply moving them from one place to another' (ibid.: 77). Whereas secularisation *relocates* the sacred object from one domain to another while retaining the principle of its separation from free use, profanation *dislocates* the line that separates the object from the possibility of free use. 'Both are political operations: the first guarantees the exercise of power by carrying it back to a sacred model; the second deactivates the apparatuses of power and return to common use the spaces that power had seized' (ibid.).

In other words, secularisation maintains the logic of glory that contains the inoperativity of beings in a separate sphere but transfers this sphere from the divine to the earthly. It is therefore anti-religious in its content but not in its form, while profanation targets precisely the separating form of religion without necessarily being hostile to its content:

> *Religio* is not what unites men and gods but what ensures they remain distinct. It is not disbelief and indifference towards the divine that stand in opposition to religion, but negligence, that is, a behaviour that is free and 'distracted' before things and their use, before forms of separation and their meaning. (Ibid.: 75)

Yet, as the examples of children, fetishists and perverts demonstrate, the negligence or distraction concerns not the profaned object itself, but rather the conditions defining its use, the conditions that must be rendered inoperative to enhance the potentiality of the unconventional use of the object, whereby it becomes what Agamben terms a 'pure means', 'a praxis that, while firmly maintaining its nature as a means, is emancipated from its relationship to an end: it has joyously forgotten its goal and can now show itself as such, as a means without an end' (ibid.: 86).

The contrast between religion and profanation leads Agamben to the elaboration of Benjamin's famous account of capitalism as a religion. In Agamben's reading, capitalism is characterised by a paradoxical coincidence of absolute profanation and absolute consecration. The familiar process of 'all that is solid melting into air', of the

44

liquidation of traditions, identities and forms of life under the aegis of the absolutisation of exchange value evidently marks the moment of a thoroughgoing profanation of all things sacred, whereby objects, phenomena or practices become pure means. Yet this profanation is immediately recuperated by the re-sacralisation of every object in the form of the commodity (see Agamben 1993b: 31–62; 2000: 75–6). The commodity, relegated to the separate sphere of consumption, is withdrawn from the potentiality of free use, since in order to be consumed it must first be possessed as property. In contrast, for Agamben 'use is always a relationship with some thing that cannot be appropriated; it refers to things insofar as they cannot become objects of possession' (Agamben 2007b: 83). Thus capitalism consecrates the objects that it has itself profaned in the form of commodities, whose use value and even exchange value have been eclipsed by the 'exhibition value' with which they are endowed in the apparatuses of advertising (Benjamin 1968: 225; Agamben 2007b: 90):

> If the apparatuses of the capitalist cult are so effective, it is not so much because they act on primary behaviours but because they act on pure means, that is, on behaviours that have been separated from themselves and thus detached from any relationship to an end. In its extreme phase, capitalism is nothing but a gigantic apparatus for capturing pure means, that is, profanatory behaviours. Pure means, which represent the deactivation and rupture of all separation, are in turn separated into a special sphere. (Agamben 2007b: 87–8)

In this manner, capitalism does not simply profane the sacred or sacralise the profane but rather sacralises its own profanation, thereby fortifying the reign of modern nihilism, in which the dissolution of traditional forms of life does not lead to creative experimentation with their residue but rather leaves humanity suspended in the sheer negativity it exposed: 'The pure means, suspended and exhibited in the sphere of the media, shows its own emptiness, speaks only its own nothingness, as if no new use were possible' (ibid.: 87–8).

This nullification of profanatory potential is exemplified most starkly by the apparatus of pornography. In his brief history of the pornographic genre Agamben notes the tendency towards the transformation of the sexual acts of the models into pure means or 'gestures' that no longer communicate any determinate content. As the models in pornographic images increasingly demonstrate to the spectator their awareness of his or her gaze, their own expressions become brazenly indifferent, 'showing nothing but the showing itself (that is, one's absolute mediality)' (ibid.: 90). It is precisely this profane mediality that is recuperated by the apparatus of pornography in a representation that may be consumed in masturbatory activity but never brought to use as such (see Prozorov 2011):

> What it captures is the human capacity to let erotic behaviours idle, to profane them, by detaching them from their immediate ends. But while these behaviours thus open themselves to a different possible use, which concerns not so much the pleasure of the partner as a new collective use of sexuality, pornography intervenes at this point to block and divert the profanatory intention. The solitary and desperate consumption of the pornographic image thus replaces the promise of a new use. (Agamben 2007b: 91)

Thus, from the bodies of the resurrected to the feasts of the faithful, from church liturgy to the pornographic film, we observe the same logic: any object or practice may be rendered inoperative through the suspension of its canonical function, yet this inoperativity either becomes a gateway to a new use or is confined in a separate sphere, exposed and glorified in its sheer presence without the possibility of use.[4] The strategies of play and profanation that seek to enhance the potentiality for use are thus opposed by the strategies of ritualisation and glory that neutralise this potentiality by making the inoperative sacred.

The Empty Throne

What is it that makes inoperativity sacred, or, more correctly, what is it about the inoperative that leads to its separation into a sacred sphere? In his *The Kingdom and the Glory* Agamben demonstrates that in both Judaism and Christianity inoperativity is the attribute of none other than God himself, both before creation and after the work of creation is done. As our example of the Sabbath shows, 'it is not the work of creation that is considered sacred, but the day on which all work ceases. Thus, inoperativity is the name of what is most proper to God' (Agamben 2011: 239). Secondly, as we have seen in the example of the glorious body, inoperativity is extended to the mode of being of the blessed after the Resurrection, in which all activity is ceased. 'It is what remains after the machine of divine *oikonomia* has reached its completion and the hierarchy of angel ministries has become completely inoperative. Paradise not only knows no government but also no writing, reading, no theology and even no liturgical celebration' (ibid.: 239). What takes the place of all of the above is glory, 'the eternal amen in which all works and all divine and human words are resolved' (ibid.: 239).

Thus, what glory simultaneously acclaims and conceals is the fact that '[at] the beginning and the end of the highest power there stands a figure not of action and government but of inoperativity' (ibid.: 242). Moreover, on the basis of his systematic exploration of the analogies between divine and earthly government (the method that Carl Schmitt (1985a) famously termed 'political theology'), Agamben demonstrates the presence of the very same inoperativity at the heart of earthly sovereignty.

> [Glory], both in theology and in politics, is precisely what takes the place of that unthinkable emptiness. And yet, precisely this unsayable vacuity is what nourishes and feeds power. That means that the centre of the governmental apparatus is, in reality, empty and, nevertheless, this inoperativity is so essential for the machine that it must at all costs be adopted and maintained at its centre in the form of glory. (Agamben 2011: 242)

This brings us to yet another striking example of inoperativity, alongside the resurrected body or the brazen face of the porn star: the *empty throne*, whose adoration has ancient roots going back to the Upanishads. In both secular and religious usage the empty throne is a prime symbol of power in its own right, not as a seat occupied by the sovereign (see Kishik 2012: 23–4). Indeed, in its very inoperativity the throne precedes the very existence of the sovereign and will persist after its demise:

> The throne is a symbol not of regality but of glory. Glory precedes the creation of the world and survives its end. The throne is empty, because [glory] is in its innermost self-inoperativity and sabbatism. The void is the sovereign figure of glory. (Agamben 2011: 245)

Similarly to the above-discussed figures of the glorious body, the religious hymn and the pornographic image, the figure of the empty throne captures the inoperativity that characterises the human condition as such in the separate sphere of sovereign power, which, ironically, ensures that human beings are, at every moment of their existence, at work:

> Human life is inoperative and without purpose, but precisely this *argia* and this absence of aim make the incomparable operativity of the human species possible. Man has dedicated himself to production and labor, because in his essence he is completely devoid of work, because he is the Sabbatical animal par excellence. (Ibid.: 245–6)

As long as the inoperativity of the human being is isolated and restricted to that which is not (or not merely) human, be it God or the sovereign, it is possible to subject human beings to various apparatuses that mobilise their existence for various historical tasks.

> The governmental apparatus functions because it has captured in its empty centre the inoperativity of the human essence. This inoperativity is the political substance of the Occident, the glorious nutrient of all power. For this reason festival and idleness return ceaselessly in the dreams and political utopias of the Occident and are equally incessantly shipwrecked there. They are the enigmatic relics that the economic-theological machine abandons on the water's edge of civilization and that each time men question anew, nostalgically and in vain. Nostalgically because they appear to contain something that belongs to the human essence, but in vain because really they are nothing but the waste products of the immaterial and glorious fuel burnt by the motor of the machine as it turns and that cannot be stopped. (Ibid.: 246)

At first glance, in modern societies the apparatus of glory has been in decline since the demise of absolute monarchies, albeit with a notable revival during the 1930s in totalitarian regimes. And yet Agamben argues that practices of glorification and acclamation survive in contemporary democracies in new forms: referendum, public opinion or, to recall Guy Debord's (1994) work that was a major influence on Agamben's thought, the 'society of the spectacle', in which commodities assume the mediatic form of an image.

> What was confined to the spheres of liturgy and ceremonials has become concentrated in the media and, at the same time, through them it spreads and penetrates at each moment into every area of society, both public and private. Contemporary democracy is a democracy that is entirely founded upon glory, that is, on the efficacy of acclamation, multiplied and disseminated by the media beyond all imagination. (Agamben 2011: 256)

Irrespectively of whether the logic of acclamation at work is 'conservative' in its presupposition of the substantial unity of the acclaiming 'people' or 'liberal' in the dissolution of the people in social communication, we observe the same principle of government by acclamation or consent, which establishes states of consensus that reproduce our subjection to the apparatuses of government. The question that defines Agamben's politics is whether it might be possible to stop this machine and affirm the inoperativity of the human condition *outside* the apparatuses of glory that isolate it in the spheres of religion or sovereignty, nationalism or public opinion, etc.

While examples of a captured, confined and glorified inoperativity, separated from every possibility of use, are indeed abundant in both historical and contemporary politics and religion, it is rather more difficult to conceive of concrete exemplars of inoperativity that is not restricted to a particular sphere but rather generalised throughout the social realm. It is as if the inoperative could only attain positive appearance by being subjected to yet another operation, that of manifestation, acclamation or glorification. How can we envision a pure means that is not immediately sacralised, a non-signifying speech that does not glorify, an emptiness that is not represented by the throne? While we shall analyse Agamben's response to this question in various domains of his thought in the remainder of the book, at this point it would be helpful to complement the sweeping genealogical and political-theological arguments with a discussion of a concrete subject of inoperative praxis, a literary figure that embodies the fundamental orientation of Agamben's political thought.

Bartleby

Having analysed a series of examples of inoperativity in Agamben's work, let us conclude this chapter by addressing what is arguably the most well-known and controversial paradigm of inoperative praxis in his entire textual corpus, the protagonist of Hermann Melville's (1986) novella *Bartleby the Scrivener*. Bartleby has become a privileged figure in contemporary continental philosophy as an object of commentaries by, among others, Deleuze (1997), Derrida (1995), Hardt and Negri (2000) and Žižek (2006) (see Deines 2006). While all these authors found something to affirm in this intriguing character, Agamben arguably transformed him into an emblem of his entire philosophy.

Bartleby, a scribe at a Wall Street legal office, abruptly begins to refuse the requests and demands of his superior with a blank formula 'I would prefer not to', forgoing any explanation of this refusal. The preference 'not to' gradually spreads from secondary tasks to his main work of copying, ultimately extending to his refusal to leave the premises of his office after being fired and his refusal to eat in the prison where he ends up for vagrancy. Bartleby's preference 'not to' is striking in its absolute passivity: his refusal of the authority of his superior or the police is not accompanied by any attempt to assert some alternative preference, to resist or to escape his confinement, in which he eventually perishes. Bartleby does not refuse something in favour of something else but rather affirms a simple *absence of preference* as such. His refusal is thus a refusal of nothing in particular or perhaps a refusal of all things particular. In Gilles Deleuze's reading, Bartleby is

> the man without references, without possessions, without properties, without qualities, without particularities: he is too smooth for anyone to be able to hang any particularity on him. Without past or future, he is instantaneous. I PREFER NOT TO is Bartleby's chemical or alchemical formula, but one can read inversely I AM NOT PARTICULAR as its indispensable component. (Deleuze 1997: 74; see also Deleuze and Guattari 1988: 369–73)

Defined neither by any particularity nor any 'insipid generality' (Agamben 1993a: 2), Bartleby is what Deleuze terms an 'original', a singular being that simultaneously affirms the possibility of a new kind of universality:

> To give birth to the new man or the man without particularities, to reunite the original and humanity by constituting a society of brothers as a new universality. If man is the brother of his fellow man, it is not because he belongs to a nation or because he is proprietor or shareholder, but only insofar as he is Man, when he has no consciousness of himself apart from the proprieties of a 'democratic dignity' that considers all particularities as so many ignominious stains that arouse anguish and pity. (Deleuze 1997: 84–5)

Yet, the 'new universality' in question is not obtained by subsuming particular identities under general laws but is constituted by a battle on two fronts: 'against the particularities that pit man against man and nourish an irremediable mistrust; but also against the Universal or the Whole, the fusion of souls in the name of great love or charity' (ibid.: 87). As we shall argue in detail in the following chapter, the political community that Agamben envisions is precisely a community of originals or singularities who have nothing either particular or general about them, who neither affirm a particular trait as an exclusive criterion for membership nor subsume all such traits under a pseudo-universal identity. Yet Bartleby does not seem to be a good example of any communitarian praxis. Although Deleuze calls him 'a new Christ or the brother to us all' (ibid.: 90), Bartleby does not affirm brotherhood or promise salvation; he neither overturns the existing order in the manner of the Russian proletariat nor establishes a new order elsewhere in the manner of the American 'universal immigration'. In fact, Bartleby does not do anything at all that could be construed as politically or socially significant. It is therefore not in his *actions* that his importance to Agamben, Deleuze and other continental philosophers must be sought, but solely in his *being*. 'Pure, patient passivity, as Blanchot would say. Being as being, and nothing more' (ibid.: 71).

Agamben elaborates and complicates this formula with the help of a technical term from the philosophy of the Skeptics, *ou mallon* (no more than). In his 'pure, patient passivity', Bartleby inhabits a suspended state on the threshold 'between Being and Nothing'; he exists 'no more' than he does not (Agamben 1999b: 256). While this mode of being appears to be a privation, it accords with Agamben's concept of potentiality discussed earlier in this chapter. 'What shows itself on the threshold between Being and non-Being, between sensible and intelligible, between word and thing, is not the colourless abyss of the Nothing but the luminous spiral of the possible. To be able is *neither to posit nor to negate*' (Agamben 1999b: 257; emphasis original). Dwelling on the threshold between Being and Nothing in the mode of 'no more than' is not a matter of choosing being over nothing or nothing over being but of affirming one's being-able by suspending its exhaustion in the act. By neither positing nor negating but simply preferring not to, suspending the operation of all the apparatuses that seek, obstinately and vainly, to govern his existence, Bartleby affirms the intimate co-belonging of potentiality and inoperativity.

This approach separates the idea of potentiality from the themes of will and necessity that have obscured its meaning throughout the history of philosophy:

> [P]otentiality is not will, and impotentiality is not necessity. To believe that will has power over potentiality, that the passage to actuality is the result of a decision that puts an end to the ambiguity of potentiality (which is always potentiality to do and not to do) – this is the perpetual illusion of morality. (Ibid.: 254)

This illusion is traced by Agamben to medieval theology, which distinguished between *potentia absoluta*, God's potentiality to do anything whatsoever, and *potentia ordinata*, by which God can only do what is in accordance with his will.

> [Will] is the principle that makes it possible to order the undifferentiated chaos of potentiality. A potentiality without will is altogether unrealizable and cannot pass into actuality. Bartleby calls into question precisely this supremacy of the will over potentiality. If God (at least *de potentia*

ordinata) is truly capable only of what he wants, Bartleby is capable only without wanting, he is capable only *de potentia absoluta*. (Ibid.: 255)

This dissociation of 'absolute potentiality' from will does not thereby resign it to non-existence, whereby the possible becomes impossible. What is at stake is rather precisely the passage of potentiality into actuality *as* potentiality, the real existence of possibility as such.

> [Potentiality] does not remain actualized of a lack of will. One could say of Bartleby that he succeeds in being able (and not being able) absolutely without wanting it. Hence the irreducibility of his 'I would prefer not to'. It is not that he does not *want* to copy or that he does not *want* to leave the office; he simply would prefer not to. The formula that he so obstinately repeats destroys all possibility of constructing a relation between being able and willing, between *potentia absoluta* and *potentia ordinata*. This is the formula of potentiality. (Ibid.: 255)

Why does Agamben go to such lengths to affirm the paradoxical and counter-intuitive idea of 'being capable without wanting'? While the theological distinction between *potentia absoluta* and *potentia ordinata* appears arcane, Agamben's argument is crucial for understanding his politics of inoperativity. The limitation of potentiality by will (*potentia ordinata*) produces a familiar image of politics as the voluntarist project of affirming some specific possibilities over others, exhausting potentiality in the new vision of actuality, a 'better world' or a 'bright future'. In contrast, the radical dissociation of potentiality from will makes it possible to conceive of a politics that renders the existing order of things inoperative not in order to replace it with an actual alternative from the past or the future. Instead, this politics would venture to restore potentiality to all that has *not* been actualised, the possible worlds that have been willed out of existence and demand to be restored to their possibility (Agamben 2005b: 39). This is not a matter of the creation of something new but of what Agamben terms the 'decreation' of reality, whereby 'what could not have been but was becomes indistinguishable from what could have been but was not' (Agamben 1999b: 270). Decreation evidently does not refer to the destruction of the world (and it is notable that Bartleby refrains from destructive actions as much as he does from productive ones), but rather to its return to its potentiality not to be, whereby it exists in the 'no more than' mode, on par with the infinite plurality of possible worlds as something whose existence is in no way necessary, as something that can *not be*: 'the actual world is led back to its right not to be; all possible worlds are led back to their right to existence' (ibid.: 271).[5] This dwelling in pure potentiality constitutes what Agamben terms Bartleby's 'experiment *de contingentia absoluta*' (ibid.: 261).

What are we to make of Bartleby's experiment? The reason why Agamben's reading of Bartleby has led to so many confusions and misreadings is his idiosyncratic use of paradigms, whereby the exemplary function is often assigned to extreme, excessive or hyperbolic cases. As we have discussed, a paradigm is an example that stands out from the ensemble which it nonetheless illuminates, its particular denotation suspended to enable its exemplary function. Yet, while 'to suspend' is a good paradigm of a regular verb in the English language because it shares key characteristics with other such verbs, can we say the same of Bartleby and the inoperative political community that Agamben affirms? Evidently, in his extreme passivity, his emaciated, catatonic and anorexic state, Bartleby is not a typical representative of this community though he might certainly be among its members. The same goes *a fortiori* for two more famous paradigms that we shall address in detail in Chapter 4: *homo sacer* and the *Muselmann* that are held to exemplify the condition of the subject of biopolitical sovereignty. While it is certainly possible to find analogies or structural similarities between Bartleby and the various subjects of inoperative and profanatory politics who seek a new use of their lives, bodies and faculties, for example body artists, fetishists, lovers, children or experimental scientists, it appears that Bartleby's stance (just as the *homo sacer*'s peril or the *Muselmann*'s suffering) is so extreme as to disable the paradigmatic function. Bartleby certainly is a subject of inoperative politics, yet this does not mean that its other subjects resemble or *must* resemble Bartleby: why could not the subject of profanation that renders an apparatus inoperative to open whatever is confined in it to a free and common use actually *prefer* this profanation to the continuing sacralisation of the beings in question?[6] At stake here is not the resonance of the figure of Bartleby with Agamben's concept of inoperativity, which is beyond doubt: Bartleby does not express any particular identity, vocation or tasks but deactivates all of them, does not venture to transform the order of things but rather to suspend it, does not engage in voluntarist revolt but rather practises radical immobility without a positive preference, and so on. The question is simply whether this hyperbolic example succeeds in its function of elucidating a wider ensemble of subjects and practices or stands alone as an extreme case whose extension to the wider domain is controversial or outright dubious.

Agamben's critics have interpreted his paradigmatic use of Bartleby as an indication of his excessive radicalism and pessimism, which only finds an elusive spark of redemption in utter abjection and suffering, with which it is preoccupied to such an extent that some critics termed his approach 'pornographic' (Bernstein 2004; see also La Capra 2007, Hegarty 2005, Mills 2008: 136; cf. Prozorov 2011). According to these accounts, if there is such a thing as 'Bartleby-politics' (cf. Žižek 2006: 342–3, 381), it must be a politics that is from the outset resigned to failure (Power 2010; Whyte 2009). In the remainder of this section we shall address Alain Badiou's critique of Agamben's 'politics of weakness', which specifically singles out Bartleby as the example of what is wrong with Agamben's politics. In his *Logics of Worlds* Badiou contrasts his own affirmative project, characterised by a militant activism in pursuit of universal truths, with Agamben's valorisation of weakness.

> [Agamben's] recurrent theme is being as weakness, its presentational poverty, power preserved from the glory of its act. Likewise, in politics, the hero is the one brought back to its pure being as a transitory living being, the one who may be killed without judgment, the *homo sacer* of the Romans, the *muselmann* of the extermination camp. Agamben, this Franciscan of ontology, prefers, to the affirmative becoming of truths, the delicate, almost secret persistence of life, what remains to one who no longer has anything; this forever sacrificed 'bare life', both humble and essential, which conveys everything of which we – crushed by the crass commotion of powers – are capable of in terms of sense. (Badiou 2009: 558–9)

This interpretation of Agamben is easily understandable from the activist-militant perspective of Badiou's politics of truth and is shared by a number of other critics sharing this orientation.[7] However, the evident differences may obscure a more subtle yet also more fundamental proximity between the two authors. After all, Badiou's 'being' is also characterised by a certain 'presentational poverty', which is testified by Badiou's recourse to the void (the empty set) as the 'proper name of being' (Badiou 2005a: 52–9). Moreover, Badiou's politics is characterised by the ascent of 'pure being' to appearance within positively structured 'worlds' that ruptures their transcendental order in the manner that resonates with Agamben's deactivation of historical apparatuses of government (Badiou 2009: 357–80). Expressing themselves in utterly different idioms, Agamben and Badiou arguably share the ontological understanding of politics as the process of the affirmation of pure being against the historically contingent apparatuses of government.

The key difference between the two authors thus pertains not to *being* but to *action*, Agamben affirming inoperativity and Badiou calling for the militant activity of the subject. Yet, as we have argued in this chapter, Agamben's inoperativity is *not* equivalent to mere passivity but rather consists in a specific kind of activity, which, insofar as it subtracts one's existence from the positive hold of the apparatuses of government, affirming its potentiality before and beyond any actualisation, definitely resonates with the actions of Badiou's subject that brings the inexistent objects of his world to maximal existence within it (see Badiou 2005a: 391–409; 2009: 321–4, 451–76). We must therefore understand the difference between Agamben and Badiou as primarily a difference in style, tonality or, most precisely, *mood*, in the methodological sense espoused in this book. It is not so much that Agamben affirms weakness while Badiou affirms strength, but that in contrast to Agamben Badiou remains tied to the tragic paradigm of politics and, specifically, to the *tragic hero*, which accounts for his distaste for the key figures of Agamben's thought, particularly Bartleby.

In *Logics of Worlds* Badiou picks Bartleby as an example of the negation of a truth by its subject in the form of betrayal: 'One can, like the office clerk Bartleby in Melville's eponymous novella, "prefer not to". But then a truth will be sacrificed by its very subject. Betrayal' (Badiou 2009: 400). It is indeed possible to betray a truth, just as, for Agamben, it is possible to close oneself off from one's inoperative potentiality and enter the state of the 'deficit of existence' that, similarly to Badiou (2001a: 71), he bluntly calls 'evil' (Agamben 1993a: 43). But what does Bartleby have to do with any of it? The fact is that Bartleby did not betray anything or anyone, since his preference not to *was* his truth that he actually upheld faithfully until his death. Moreover, this truth is not so far from Badiou's own idea of truth as indiscernible, generic and universal (2005a: 327–54) – recall that for both Agamben and Deleuze, Bartleby is a personification of a singular life beyond all particular predicates, which points to a 'new universality' of 'originals'.

Be that as it may, Badiou's own examples of political subjects are furthest away from Bartleby: Spartacus, the French Communards, Mao, and so on (2009: 24–7, 51–7, 64–5, 493–503). Badiou offers grand examples from the history of emancipatory and revolutionary politics (slave uprising, peasant revolt, proletarian revolution), which are all based on the transhistorical invariant that he terms 'the communist hypothesis' of radical equality (Badiou 2010). In contrast, Agamben's political subjects tend to be rather less than grand and heroic, even as they might also traverse some of these grand-political sequences: Bartleby, Kafka's Joseph K and K the land surveyor (Agamben 2010, 20–35), Tiananmen protesters (1993a: 85–6), Anna Akhmatova (1999b: 177–8), and so on. Yet what paradoxically aligns Badiou with Agamben is the fact that all of his grand-political sequences have ended in failure, be it in the form of defeat, betrayal or the perversion of original goals. Despite the best intentions of Spartacus, the Communards or the Russian revolutionaries, grand emancipatory politics ended in various versions of the tragic logic that Agamben seeks to overcome: a move from a happy beginning to a sorrowful end, in which the subjective innocence of political subjects ends up overshadowed by the objective tragic consequences of their actions.

There is, however, an important exception to Badiou's commitment to tragic politics, which is none other than Badiou himself as a political subject. Badiou's own micro-political engagement in the now-defunct Organisation Politique (OP) (Badiou 2001a: 95–119; Hallward 2003: 43–5, 227–42) was characterised by action at a distance from the state, the refusal to take part in elections and the renunciation of all figures of political representation. Badiou's Organisation was completely uninterested in instituting a new political system but was solely concerned with undermining the existing order on the basis of the axiomatic affirmation of equality. This approach is quite different from Spartacus, Mao or any other heroic leaders of constituent power that Badiou discusses in his works on politics. Indeed, in its combination of utter radicalism and practical modesty, axiomatic tone and strategic ineffectiveness, Badiou's own politics is, dare we say, somewhat Agambenian. While as a philosopher of politics Badiou prefers grand examples of tragic instances of emancipatory and revolutionary politics, in his own activity as a political subject *he is a lot like Bartleby*, repeatedly 'preferring not to' run in elections, read mainstream press, act in accordance with any managerial rationality or the imperative of profit, etc. (Badiou 2008: 43–50).

Despite the decidedly insignificant role that the OP played in 'grand' French politics, its strategic weakness did not appear to bother Badiou in the slightest, instead animating his commitment to cultivating a distance to all systemic and strategic politics. Similarly,

Agamben's 'weak' subjects seem to have internalised failure to such an extent that they ironically manage to succeed in their doomed ventures against all odds. Since their task is not the production of a new order, apparatus or world but the affirmation of potentiality subtracted from every actual positive form, their victory is wholly contained in their 'I can' as such. Thus, true to the comic mood of his philosophy, Agamben does not share the widespread pessimistic reading of the ending of *Bartleby*:

> The creature is finally at home, saved in being irredeemable. This is why in the end the walled courtyard [of the prison] is not a sad place. There is sky and there is grass. And the creature knows perfectly well 'where it is'. (Agamben 1999b: 271)

The last sentence alludes to Bartleby's reply to the narrator who tries to rouse him from his passivity by reminding him that he is in the Tombs, a Manhattan jail that is also, ironically, known as the Halls of Justice: 'I know where I am.'

What does this typically Agambenian elliptic finale actually mean? The first thing to note is that in these lines Bartleby appears as a 'creature', whose relevant surroundings are strictly natural ('sky and grass') – a living being not subsumed by any of the apparatuses he struggled to evade, including the apparatus of the prison which can only confine someone who would *prefer* to get out, which is of course not Bartleby's preference. Thus, Bartleby stands precisely for the Ungovernable that remains when the apparatuses are suspended and the living being emerges as such, not in its originary natural purity, which is no longer attainable, but in a necessarily scarred or wounded state. Recalling our discussion of Agamben's reading of Morante in Chapter 1, we are dealing with an experience that is certainly tragic (Bartleby's imprisonment, Akhmatova's son's confinement in the camps, the peril of *homo sacer*, the degradation of the *Muselmann*) but obstinately resists tragedy from within tragedy, leading to a reversal that is comic, even if, as in the case of Bartleby, it comes at the price of the subject's own being.

While the example of Bartleby is indeed best grasped as hyperbolic rather than paradigmatic, it illuminates most starkly the ethico-political principle at the heart of the logic of inoperativity: the apparatuses of government ought to be resisted and deactivated not merely because of some specific or positive potentialities that they restrict, limiting our preferences *to* be or do something, but primarily because of the generic potentiality they capture and confine, our preference *not to* be or do something, which is the condition of any possible experience of freedom. It is because the apparatuses capture our potentiality for inoperativity and mobilise our existence for their positive projects of government that they must themselves be rendered inoperative, their expropriating and dominating force deactivated. Inoperativity is thus not merely the *end* or telos of Agamben's politics, i.e. something to be recovered or rediscovered as the outcome of political praxis, but is also its *method*, insofar as the originary inoperativity that defines the human condition as potential can only be reclaimed for free use by rendering inoperative the plurality of the apparatuses that set human beings to work. In the following chapters we shall see how this method is deployed in the key domains of Agamben's politics.

Notes

1. See Franchi 2004 for the more detailed genealogy of the concept. See also Murray 2010: 44–8; De la Durantaye 2009: 18–20; Mills 2008: 120–3.
2. Thus Agamben's *inoperosita* has a much wider reference than Georges Bataille's concept of *désoeuvrement*, which refers to the 'disengaged' negativity that could never be recuperated by the dialectic and reabsorbed into the positive order of things. For Bataille (2001), inoperative experiences of this kind include various extreme and excessive experiences of eroticism, violence, luxury and so on. Nothing could be further from Agamben's concept of inoperativity, which is entirely at odds with any pathos of extremity but pertains solely to the deactivation of the 'work' involved in the most mundane areas of our existence. The pathos of sovereign negativity is entirely alien to Agamben, who considers it both useless and tasteless. On the differences between Agamben and Bataille see Agamben 1998: 61; 2005b: 124; 2000: 7.
3. See Clemens 2010 on the importance of the category of fetishism to Agamben's work, not only in terms of substance but also in terms of method. See also Chiesa and Ruda (2011: 372) for a similar argument with relation to perversion. Agamben's preoccupation with nonconventional forms of use certainly does exemplify a fetishist disposition, which is for him a necessary precondition for any genuinely experimental and innovative politics. A new world is possible not *ex nihilo* but by subjecting what *is* to a new kind of use. Agamben has shown interest in perversion and fetishism from his earliest work onwards; see, for example, Agamben 1993b: 146–7.
4. Chiesa and Ruda (2011: 171) choose to distinguish between the 'negative' inoperativity manifested in the apparatuses of glory, the state of exception and so on, and the 'positive' inoperativity of the messianic

reappropriation of potentiality. Yet it is important to recall that it is the *same* inoperativity that is at stake in both cases, the originary inoperativity of the human condition. What may be negative and positive is rather the *relation* one establishes to it, which may be that of sacralisation or profanation.

5. While it is crucial to Agamben's thought, the concept of decreation is used less frequently than that of inoperativity. Aside from the reference to decreation in the essay on Bartleby, the term only appears in a 1998 essay on the work of the contemporary artist Cy Twombly (Agamben 2006). In this essay Agamben interprets Twombly's sculpture as a caesura that manifests within the work of art its 'inactive core', irreducible to artistic practice. The gesture of decreation points to the possibility of art entering a standstill, 'almost thunderstruck, falling and risen at every moment' (Agamben 2006: 15). Agamben borrows the concept of decreation from Simone Weil's political thought (Weil 1952: 78–83; see De la Durantaye, 2009: 23), yet whereas Weil used it to designate a process of desubjectivation, liberation from the self that at the same time opens up to the world, Agamben's use is somewhat different. His idea of decreation pertains to a dual process of the reversal of modal categories, whereby what is necessary becomes contingent and may even be relegated to inexistence, while what was impossible becomes possible: 'what happened and what did not happen are returned to their originary unity in the mind of God' (Agamben 1999b: 270). In the terms of Pauline messianism, in a decreated world what was something comes to nought while what did not exist comes to existence. Decreation does not mark the birth of a new world but the 'slight adjustment' in this world here that renders the existing apparatuses of its government inoperative, making the world potential again.

6. We shall return to this problem in the concluding chapter of this book, where we identify Agamben's refusal of the very question of will as the most problematic aspect of his political thought.

7. See also Negri 2012, Power 2010, Chiesa 2009, Nedoh 2011. While we shall show that Badiou's criticism is often misdirected, his designation of Agamben's approach as 'Franciscan' is arguably correct. In fact, Agamben has recently devoted a whole book to Franciscan monasticism (Agamben 2013), tracing in its techniques and practices the model for a mode of inoperative existence that he terms 'form-of-life', which we shall address in detail in Chapter 4. For a more positive assessment of Agamben's notion of decreation see Sumic 2011.

Chapter 3

Speaking the Unspeakable:
Inoperative Language

In the following four chapters we shall elaborate this ethos at the key sites of Agamben's politics: language, statehood, history and humanity. We shall begin with language, which might appear a somewhat counter-intuitive starting point for investigating politics. Nonetheless, it is precisely in his early works on language, culminating in the 1982 book *Language and Death*, that Agamben developed many of the arguments subsequently elaborated in the *Homo Sacer* series and the latter can hardly be understood in isolation from the former. Neither the logic of the sovereign ban nor the concept of bare life is intelligible without first engaging with Agamben's account of the experience or the event of language that transforms the creature, the 'living being', into a *speaking being*. Thus, prior to analysing Agamben's most famous and controversial political claims we shall dwell on the ontological level and pose the question of the being of language. We shall first outline Agamben's isolation of the dimension of *speakability* or communicability that is at work in every speech act yet is itself devoid of any signification. It is this event of language as simultaneously potential and inoperative that both conditions the possibility of speech and itself remains unspoken in it, functioning as the ineffable or *negative foundation* of language. We shall then proceed to Agamben's confrontation with this logic of negative foundation in *Language and Death*, where it is generalised from a strictly linguistic puzzle or paradox to an ethico-political predicament of human existence that has only been fully unveiled in the modern condition of nihilism. We shall discuss Agamben's attempt to overcome this predicament at the site of language in an analysis of his notion of *infancy* and his extension of this solution to the realm of the political community, defined in terms of *whatever being* and modelled on the experience of the inoperative potentiality of language. In the remainder of the chapter we shall address the political implications of this understanding of

60

community, specifically its universal character and its criticism as utopian and unrealisable.

The Thing Itself

In the preceding chapter we have outlined the formal logic of inoperativity and elaborated it in a series of paradigms. Yet there remains a question of what the content of the inoperative is. Since, as we have argued, inoperative praxis does not destroy the thing but rather suspends its canonical function and enables its free use, this content cannot be void, yet neither can it consist in any positive predicate of the object or practice, since it is precisely the latter that are deactivated. Evidently, the sole content of the inoperative is the sheer *existence* of a thing or a phenomenon. An unusable tool has lost its recognisable functions, its relations to other tools, its place in the overall context of the workshop but it still exists as an object, for which a new use can be found. A law that is no longer applied retains its semantic content even when wholly devoid of force. A body whose physiological functions have been suspended is nonetheless there as an object of ostentation or a new, perverse use. Thus it is precisely inoperativity that grants us access to the essence of the phenomenon, which, as it is for Heidegger (1962: 67), is entirely contained in sheer existence. Thus, the inoperativity of a thing gives us access to the *thing itself*, yet this thing itself is not some hidden essence of the thing but rather the sheer facticity of its existence, attested to by language.

Agamben's idea of the thing itself was developed in a series of articles from the early 1980s onwards, of which the two most important are 'The Thing Itself' and 'The Idea of Language'. In the former text, Agamben reinterprets the theory of forms in Plato's Seventh Letter, focusing on the 'thing itself' as the fifth element of all thought besides the name, referent, the denoted object and true knowledge (Agamben 1999b: 31). In the Letter Plato is rather elusive about this fifth element, claiming that it 'does not admit of verbal expression' but may be 'suddenly brought to birth in the soul' when one has 'dwelled for a long time close to it' (Plato cited in Agamben 1999b: 29). While this evasive presentation gave rise to the interpretation of the thing itself as something esoteric or outright mystical, Agamben offers a different interpretation that is at once simple, almost literal, and highly intricate. Rather than being something that transcends language, the thing itself only exists within language even if, for now, it remains unspeakable within it. In the terms that we shall encounter repeatedly in the remainder of the book, it is *included* in language (i.e. it is nothing extra-linguistic) but solely in the mode of its *exclusion* (i.e. as unspeakable).

Yet what is this unspeakable thing? In Agamben's complex exegesis which we shall not reproduce here (see Agamben 1999b: 31–7) he arrives at a striking conclusion: the thing itself is nothing other than the thing's own 'being-said in language, which language can only presuppose but never express' (ibid.: 32). While a linguistic statement tells us something about the thing it speaks of (e.g. 'the rose is red' predicates a colour to the rose), it simultaneously effaces the fact of its speaking of it, transforming it into an ineffable presupposition. 'Sayability itself remains unsaid in what is said and in that about which something is said, [and] knowability itself is lost in what is known and in that about which something is known' (ibid.: 33). Indeed, if we were to try to bring this 'sayability' to speech by transforming it into a name, to which predicates may be assigned and about which discourse is possible, we would only succeed in 'hypothesising' it, turning the thing itself into a thing like any other:

> [The] thing itself is not a thing; it is the very sayability, the very openness at issue in language, which, in language, we always presuppose and forget, because it is at bottom its own oblivion and abandonment. The presuppositional structure of language is the very structure of tradition; we presuppose, pass on and thereby – according to the double sense of the word *traditio* – betray the thing itself in language, so that language may speak about something. The effacement of the thing itself is the sole foundation on which it is possible for something like a tradition to be constituted. (Ibid.: 35)

The significance of this claim cannot be overestimated. What Agamben targets here is nothing less than the logic of the constitution of any apparatus, linguistic or otherwise. For any positive order to be constituted and sustained as a 'tradition', something must be betrayed and this something is the sheer speakability and knowability of the thing caught up in it. This theoretical constellation provides with an initial matrix that will be gradually elaborated in the theory of sovereign power and bare life in *Homo Sacer*.

If the thing itself remains unsaid in actual discourse and a discourse about it is only possible by transforming it into a thing, what could possibly be done to overcome this structure of tradition/ betrayal? For Agamben, the task of philosophy is to come with speech to help speech, so that, in speech, speech itself does not remain presupposed, but instead comes to speech. At this point, the presuppositional power of language touches its limit and its end; language says presuppositions as presuppositions and, in this way, reaches the unpresupposable and unpresupposed principle that, as such, constitutes authentic human community and communication. (Agamben 1999b: 35)

The stakes of Agamben's ontological investigation of language are thus evidently raised: it is no longer a matter of addressing a problem proper to the particular domain of the linguistic, but, since human beings are conventionally defined as speaking beings, a matter of accounting for the conditions of possibility of the 'authentic human community'. Agamben's wager is that if we succeed in bringing speakability to speech and removing the ineffable from language we will be able to conceive of a human community that is similarly devoid of presuppositions and hence of exclusions and restrictions that throughout history have produced conflict and violence.

Yet what kind of discourse would be adequate to the task of bringing speakability to speech? In the article 'The Idea of Language' Agamben addresses the discourse of revelation, arguing that what is revealed in it is never any particular content about the world, language or whatever else but rather the sheer fact '*that* the world is, that language exists' (ibid.: 41; emphasis original). Thus revelation seeks precisely to reveal within language the thing itself that remains unspoken in it. In Agamben's interpretation this is the meaning of the famous prologue to the Gospel of John: 'in the beginning was the word and the word was God'. If the word is in the beginning, it cannot presuppose or refer to anything beyond or before itself but only reveals itself as devoid of any presupposition or foundation: 'the proper sense of revelation is therefore that all human speech and knowledge has as its root and foundation an openness that infinitely transcends it' (ibid.: 41). What is at stake in revelation is thus the experience of language as such, not in the sense of meaningful speech but in the sense of its sheer existence as a 'voice that, without signifying anything, signifies signification itself' (ibid.: 42). It is this non-signifying voice that, in Agamben's reading, was equated with God in the Gospel of John and that in the aftermath of the 'death of God' in modern nihilism reveals itself as the pure event of language:

For the first time we are truly alone with language, abandoned without any final foundation. We are the first human beings who have become completely conscious of language. For the first time, what preceding generations called God, Being, Spirit, unconscious appear to us as what they are: names of language. (Ibid.: 45–6)

This unprecedented consciousness of language is both an extremely dangerous and a radically promising situation, in full accordance with the 'Hölderlin principle' of the simultaneous growth of danger and saving power. The danger of the complete unveiling of language consists in the nihilist reduction of this unveiling to pure Nothingness that would then function as the final negative presupposition of language and human existence: '[nihilism] interprets the extreme revelation of language in the sense that there is nothing to reveal, that the truth of language is that it unveils the Nothing of all things' (ibid.: 46). Here Agamben interprets nihilism in the Heideggerian vein: nihilism is not merely the affirmation of the Nothing (for example, the foundational status of the non-signifying voice) but the *secondary negation* or nullification of this Nothing, whereby the nothing-as-foundation becomes converted into mere absence of foundation (cf. Heidegger 1961: 217).

Agamben's own response to the unveiling of language does not seek to overcome nihilism in a facile and vain manner by re-founding language on some positive presupposition – any attempt at such negation of nihilism would itself be supremely nihilistic. Instead, he affirms the possibility of appropriating the presuppositionless character of language as the 'non-foundation' of all human community and praxis.[1] In the following section we shall address the logic of this appropriation of the negative foundation in an analysis of Agamben's *Language and Death*.

The Voice

Language and Death is a short yet remarkably dense text that illuminates the ontological background to Agamben's subsequent turn to explicitly political issues in *The Coming Community* and the *Homo Sacer* series. Similarly to the articles analysed in the previous section, in this book Agamben targets the presuppositional structure of language that resigns it to the logic of negative foundation, whereby the foundation of language (or community, social praxis, and so on) is found in something excluded from or unspeakable within it. Agamben argues that this negativity is not the effect of late-modern efforts to overcome metaphysics by, for example, Heidegger or Derrida, but rather its fundamental feature that has only fully come to light in the conditions of modern nihilism. Similarly to the idea of inoperativity discussed in the previous chapter, the logic of negative foundation is both originary for the Western tradition and contemporary in its ultimate unveiling under the conditions of nihilism.

Language and Death begins relatively innocuously with an analysis of the function of indicative pronouns in Hegel (*diese* or 'this') and Heidegger (*da* or 'there'), demonstrating the centrality of negativity for the two philosophers even on the terminological level. When we use the pronoun 'this' to refer to any given object, the object itself is never fully reached by us but only approximately grasped by an abstract pronoun that, moreover, has no concrete reference of its own but depends entirely on the situation of discourse. By the same token, the pronoun *da* in Heidegger's famous notion of *Dasein* refers to the 'there' into which one is always thrown and in which one exists as one's own possibility, the 'ownmost' possibility being one's own death, and is entirely devoid of all positive content. Rather than refer, belatedly and vainly, to the unnamed object, the sole reference of these two pronouns is to the *instance of discourse* when they are enunciated: 'indication is the category within which language refers to its own taking place' (Agamben 1991: 25).

Agamben elaborates this paradoxical status of pronouns with reference to the work of such twentieth-century linguists as Roman Jakobson and Émile Benveniste, who famously described deictic pronouns as 'indicators of the utterance' or 'shifters' whose sole reference is to the very existence of discourse (ibid.: 23–5). Shifters articulate the passage from language as a sign system to actual speech or, in Agamben's terminology, from the *semantic* to the *semiotic*. Thus pronouns and other shifters refer to the thing itself that, as we have seen, consists in the sheer speakability or being-called: 'prior to the world of meanings, they permit the reference to the very event of language, the only context in which something can be signified' (ibid.: 25).

This function of shifters leads Agamben to assert the intimate co-belonging of linguistics and metaphysics, which will prove highly important for his subsequent direct transfer of his argument to the terrain of community and politics. The linguistic utterance, i.e. the act of putting language into action in speech, corresponds exactly with the metaphysical concept of being:

That which is always already indicated in speech without being named is, for philosophy, being. The dimension of meaning of the word 'being', whose eternal quest and eternal loss constitute the history of metaphysics, coincides with the taking place of language; metaphysics is that experience of language that, in every speech act, grasps the disclosure of that dimension and in all speech experiences above all the 'marvel' that language exists. (Ibid.: 25)

Thus, Agamben is able to recast Heidegger's ontological difference between being and beings as the difference between the pure taking place of language and the signified content of this experience. What transcends particular contents of speech is nothing but the event of language coming to speech as such: 'the opening of the ontological dimension (being, the world) corresponds to the pure taking place of language as an originary event, while the ontic dimension (entities, things) corresponds to that which, in this opening, is said and signified' (ibid.: 26).

Yet what does it mean to indicate the instance of discourse? Evidently, the utterance is only indicated by the fact of being spoken, i.e. its existence is attested to by the voice that speaks it. Yet, the concept of the voice at work here is rather more complicated than mere sound (*phone*). Mere natural or animal sound can never indicate the instance of human discourse, unless it is supplemented and thereby negated by the 'intention to signify' that precedes every concrete act of signification. What takes the place of voice as sound is a fictitious concept that Agamben terms the Voice, now capitalised to accentuate its difference from voice as mere natural sound. The Voice is characterised by a double negativity. Firstly, as the indicator of the taking-place of language, it is characterised by the removal of the voice as natural sound (*phone*) and the anticipation of signification (*logos*) and is thus located in the gap between the having-been and the not-yet. This is why it can only be posited as fictitious: as neither sound nor language, it is never really *there*. Secondly, for this very reason the Voice cannot itself be spoken in a discourse whose existence it indicates (ibid.: 84). Thus Agamben concludes that

> language is and is not the voice of man. If language were immediately the voice of man, as braying is the voice of the ass and chirping the voice of the cicada, man could not experience the taking place of language or the disclosure of being. But if, on the other hand, man radically possessed no voice (not even a negative Voice), every shifter and every possibility of indicating the event of language would disappear equally. (Ibid.: 84–5)

For Agamben, it is this 'originary negativity' of the Voice that is at work in all Western metaphysics, functioning as the resolution of the problem of the relation between *physis* and *logos*, nature and culture: 'Man is the living being who removes himself and preserves himself at the same time – as unspeakable – in language; negativity is the human means of *having* language' (ibid.: 85; emphasis original). By the same token, the relation between human nature and social or political life, which we shall address in the following chapter, has in the Western political tradition been construed in terms of the simultaneous negation of natural life (*zoe*) as a condition for acceding to political life (*bios*) and the entry of this natural life into the political order *in the negated form* that Agamben terms 'bare life'. Even in more specialised fields of knowledge such as ontology or linguistics it is easy to recognise analogues to the Voice in the form of respectively Being as the transcendence of beings and the phoneme as the insignificant particle that makes signification and discourse possible (Agamben 2007a: 66–7). Every human experience is stuck in negativity and thus remains close to death: 'to experience death as death signifies, in fact, to experience the removal of the voice and the appearance, in its place, of another Voice, which constitutes the original negative foundation of the human word' (Agamben 199: 86). In the final chapter of *Language and Death*, the proximity of all experience to death stops being a theoretical matter and acquires decidedly ominous overtones that would only be strengthened in the *Homo Sacer* books. Agamben traces the operation of the logic of negative foundation in the practice of sacrifice in primitive societies, whereby a radically ungrounded violent action, usually murder, becomes converted into an unspeakable foundation of a positive social order, grounding the existence of particular communities and traditions (ibid.: 104–6). If the Voice originally dwells in the negative place of death, it should not be surprising that in concrete social practices death will come to take the place of the Voice.

It is now clear that the stakes of Agamben's enterprise in *Language and Death* far exceed the narrowly exegetic task of accounting for the status of pronouns in Hegel and Heidegger but rather pertain to the fundamental ontopolitical logic of Western culture that founds human existence on the negation of human nature. The 'thing itself' at work in language, its sheer communicability prior to every act of signification, is in this logic rendered ineffable and transformed into a mystical foundation of actual speech acts, particular communities and forms of life – mystical insofar as it is informulable in the positive discourses that it founds. Thus, any attempt to break the link between language and death must proceed through the liquidation of every figure of the Voice, 'eliminating the unsayable from language' (Agamben 2007a: 4) or the 'liquidation of the mystical' (1991: 91). 'Only if language no longer refers to any Voice [...], is it possible for man to experience a language that is not marked by negativity and death' (ibid.: 95). The final pages of *Language and Death* thus lay out the programme that Agamben's more explicitly political writings will subsequently take up:

> A completed foundation of humanity in itself should signify the definitive elimination of the sacrificial mythologeme and of the ideas of nature and culture, of the unspeakable and the speakable, which are grounded in it. In fact, even the sacralisation of life derives from sacrifice: from this point of view it simply abandons the naked natural life to its own violence and its own unspeakableness, in order to ground in them every cultural rule and all language. The ethos, humanity's own, is not something unspeakable or *sacer* that must remain unsaid in all praxis and human speech. Neither is it nothingness, whose nullity serves as the basis for the arbitrariness and violence of social action. Rather, it is social praxis itself, human speech itself, which have become transparent to themselves. (Ibid.: 106)

If one is looking for a concise summary of *Homo Sacer*, one need not look any further. Yet, prior to considering this and other explicitly political texts in detail, let us first address the way Agamben attempts the 'definitive elimination' of the logic of negative foundation at the original site of language. Admittedly arcane, these ideas will be helpful for grasping the movement of Agamben's thought from ontology, linguistics and poetry to politics.

Infancy

If the logic of negative foundation is at work in the entire ontopolitical tradition of the West, including the critical attempts to overcome it, how is it to be confronted? What would an experience of language devoid of the presuppositional structure of negative foundation look like? How is it possible to bring the ineffable 'thing itself' to speech without consigning it to negativity?

If the negative foundation of the Voice is produced by the 'removal' or negation of the 'animal voice' or natural sound, then a self-evident solution would be to refrain from this negation and return to the natural immediacy of language akin to the braying of the ass or the chirping of the cricket. The comic overcoming of our tragic dwelling in negativity and in proximity to death would then end by the reversal of the constitutive practice of *anthropogenesis* or the formation of the human being, whereby language would be posited immediately as the voice of the human being, akin to the natural sounds emitted by animals. Indeed, as Agamben claimed in *The Sacrament of Language*, a late work that revisits the main concerns of *Language and Death*,

> it is perhaps time to call into question the prestige that language has enjoyed and continues to enjoy in our culture, as a tool of incomparable potency, efficacy and beauty. Considered in itself, it is no more beautiful than birdsong, no more efficacious than the signals insects exchange, no more powerful than the roar with which the lion asserts his dominion. (Agamben 2009a: 71)

Nonetheless, the problem with any claim for the return to the originary condition, be it that of language or community, is that it ignores the irrevocable loss of the origin: we are always already thrown into language marked by a scission between the Voice and speech, the natural sound always already removed. Moreover, it is this very removal that makes it possible for human beings to stand in the disclosure of being and hence pose the ontological question in first place. 'We can only think if language is not our voice, only if we reach our own aphonia at its very bottom' (Agamben 1991: 108). To seek to return to the voice before the Voice would be to sacrifice the very capacity to access the event of language, let alone bring it to speech. It is the negative structure of language itself that makes properly human action and experience possible by opening up the void between language and speech where the human subject emerges. It is therefore within this negative structure that the ethico-political resolution to the problem of negativity must be sought.

> The decisive element that confers on human language its peculiar virtue is not in the tool itself but in the place it leaves to the speaker, in the fact that it prepares within itself a hollowed out form that the speaker must always assume in order to speak. The human being is that living being that, in order to speak, must say 'I', must 'take the word', assume it and make it his own. (Agamben 2009a: 71)

While in such later texts as *The Open* that we shall consider in Chapter 6 Agamben would rethink this privilege accorded to human beings, in *Language and Death* and other works of the 1980s it remains a crucial mark of the difference between animals and humans that does not permit any simple return to the animal voice. Instead of the nostalgic approach that vainly calls for a return to the origin that we never had or could not possibly remember ever having, Agamben opts for a different understanding of the origin. The 'transcendental origin' has been a key concept in Agamben's methodology since the 1978 book *Infancy and History* (2007a) and found its most sustained treatment in the 2009 essay 'Philosophical Archaeology' (2009b). In these texts the origin is no longer understood as a cause chronologically separate and prior to the object but rather as something constitutive of and coextensive with it.

> What we must renounce is merely a concept of origin cast in a mould already abandoned by the natural sciences themselves, one which locates it in a chronology, a primary cause that separates in time a before and an after. Such a concept of origins is useless to the human sciences whenever what is at issue is not an 'object' presupposing the human already behind it, but is instead itself constitutive of the human. The origin of a 'being' of this kind cannot be *historicized* because it is itself *historicizing*, and itself founds the possibility of there being any history. (Agamben 2007a: 56)

Instead of the chronological concept of the origin Agamben affirms the dimension of 'transcendental history' as the zone of indistinction between the diachronic and the synchronic, whereby the origin is not something that has occurred once in the past but rather that which *keeps occurring* in the present and thereby renders intelligible that of which it is the origin. To return to the examples of *Language and Death*, the removal of the animal voice that founds human language was not a datable past event that happened once and is now consigned to memory or oblivion; on the contrary, it keeps happening over and over, in every act of speech. Agamben's favourite example of the transcendental origin is the Indo-European root, 'reinstated through philological comparison of the historical languages, a historically unattested state of the language, yet still real' (ibid.: 57; see also Agamben 2009b: 109–10). Other examples include 'the child of psychoanalysis exerting an active force within the psychic life of the adult, or the big bang which is supposed to have given rise to the universe but continues to send toward us its fossil radiation' (Agamben 2007a: 57).[2]

In Agamben's early work on language the paradigm of such a transcendental origin is the experience of *infancy*. In the conclusion to *Language and Death*, Agamben speaks elliptically of 'infantile dwelling in language' (1991: 92) as an alternative to the nihilistic and lethal logic of the Voice. What does 'infancy' stand for in this context? In an earlier collection of essays, *Infancy and History*,

Agamben defined infancy as the experience of the human being's entry into language, which logically presupposes its not-having language at that point (hence, *in-fancy*, 'not speaking'). While this condition evidently characterises the human infant at a certain developmental stage, the idea of the transcendental origin leads Agamben away from the specifically neo-natal experience of the acquisition of language towards the generalisation of infancy as the *threshold* of every act of speech, the experience of not-having language to begin with and having to enter into language as a condition of becoming a subject, which Agamben defines as the enunciator, the one who says 'I'.

If subjectivity is linguistically produced and if language is not given from the outset, then it is precisely infancy, the condition immediately prior to the entrance into language, that offers us the 'originary' experience of being human that need not be sought in the receding depths of childhood as yet another version of the mystical foundation. It is only human language that is not immediately given to its speakers – animals are, in Agamben's early anthropocentric interpretation, always already *inside* language and hence incapable of *entering* it: 'Man, instead, by having an infancy, by preceding speech, splits this single language and, in order to speak, has to constitute himself as the subject of language – he has to say "I"' (Agamben 2007a: 59). Thus only human language is split between the *semiotic* dimension of a closed and self-referential system of signs existing prior to the speaker and the *semantic* dimension of actual discourse.[3] It is this split that accounts for the already discussed scission between nature and culture or history: if one were always already within language, one would be always united with one's nature and there would literally be no place where the discontinuity of history could enter. Thus, contrary to the traditional belief since Aristotle, a human being is not an animal *possessing* language but rather an animal originally *deprived* of it and having to enter it, thereby effecting the transition from the semiotic into the semantic. Agamben does not define the human condition in terms of plenitude or 'added value' (animal *plus* language) but rather in terms of lack, as the originary being-without-language that must be overcome through a subjectivating practice of entry into language.

Yet, in a typical Agambenian reversal, this lack ultimately is converted into a new kind of plenitude, not an actual plenitude of possessing *more* than the animal but the plenitude of potentiality that the animal lacks as such. Indeed, we may easily recognise the concept of potentiality addressed in the previous chapter in the logical structure of the experience of infancy. The human being does not possess language as such but rather a *faculty* of language, a potentiality for speech that logically presupposes its obverse, the potentiality not to speak, to remain in infancy. The passage from language to discourse and from a natural being to a human subject remains radically contingent and hence a matter of freedom, which is not grounded in any positive aspect of the human condition, but, somewhat paradoxically, in the possibility *not* to become human, to remain outside discourse.

Insofar as infancy marks the contingent passage of language into discourse, the point at which language exists in the mode of the pure intention to signify without any actual signification, the potentiality of (not) speaking that pertains to the 'infant' subject has its correlate in the inoperativity of language itself, whose signifying function is suspended and which, at this moment, refers only to itself, to the 'pure fact that one speaks, that language exists' (2007a: 6). Agamben terms this simultaneous experience of potentiality and inoperativity of language *experimentum linguae*, 'in which the limits of language are to be found not outside language, in the direction of its referent, but in the experience of language as such, in its pure self-reference' (2007a: 5–6). Evidently, such an experiment takes place whenever our use of language is not exhausted by its signified content, i.e. when the communicative function of language is rendered inoperative in the act of speech that does not thereby fall silent, but in accordance with our discussion of the relation between inoperativity and potentiality in Chapter 2, is opened up to new forms of use. Evidently, poetry serves as the best example for such an experimental use of language that explores its potentialities beyond the signifying function (Agamben 2011: 234–9; see more generally 2009a: 43–61, 93–101).

Yet it is important to emphasise that the poetic experimentation with language remains only one particular example of the *experimentum linguae*, whose significance is far more general. The experience of language as such, prior to and beyond all signification, is not only accessible in particular types of speech acts but in literally *every* act of speaking by reflecting on and problematising the sheer potentiality of signification that conditions it. If infancy has as its locus the threshold between the semiotic and the semantic, the threshold where language comes to life, then this coming to life may be experienced by occupying and dwelling, however momentarily, on this threshold. It is this experience of occupying the threshold of speech that provides a resolution of the problem of negative foundation. The thing itself, the sheer existence of language, is no longer included in it in the negative mode of exclusion, but is brought to speech in the very passage from language to discourse, the originary experience of language which has nothing esoteric or mystical about it but is available to all speaking beings in every act of speech. In the place of the Voice, the place of negativity and death, now stands the human being that has appropriated this space as its ethos and the site of its freedom.

It is somewhat paradoxical that the example Agamben chooses to illustrate the exclusively human phenomenon of infancy belongs to the animal realm. The *axolotl*, a Mexican albino salamander, remains in the neotenic or infant condition throughout its life, maintaining for its entire duration the characteristics typical only for the larval stage of amphibians alongside normally adult ones (Agamben 1995: 95). While the axolotl is, for Agamben, an exception among animals, who are otherwise tied to a genetic code and the finite possibilities inscribed in it, this exceptionality is the rule for human beings, even if it remains concealed by the apparatuses of government, law or culture that expropriate our potentiality and tie us to particular environments, codes, functions and specialisations. This potentiality may nonetheless be reclaimed by rendering these apparatuses inoperative, whereby the human being appears as such, in its 'transcendentally originary' status as an eternal infant

> ecstatically overwhelmed, cast out of himself, not like other living beings into a specific adventure or environment, but for the first time into a *world*. He would be truly listening to being. His voice still free from any genetic prescription, and having absolutely nothing to say or express, sole animal of its kind, he could, like Adam, *name* things in his language. (Ibid.: 96–7)

This invitation to reclaiming infancy must appear particularly tempting, since the sole alternative consists in continuing to dwell in proximity to negativity and death for no reason. The condition of modern nihilism has thoroughly desacralised every mystical version of the unspeakable foundation so that all that remains as the negative foundation is simply *nothing,* not an alluring and tempting Nothing that we could marvel at but a mere nullity devoid of any possible significance. Yet, in a characteristic comic reversal, Agamben suggests that this experience of nullity is the condition of possibility of the overcoming of nihilism and the human appropriation of the nothing-ness of its foundations as its ethos:

> Perhaps in the age of absolutely speakable things, whose extreme nihil-istic furour we are experiencing today, the age in which all the figures of the Unspeakable and all the masks of ontotheology have been *liquidated*, or released or spent in words that merely show the nothingness of their foundation; the age in which all human experience of language has been redirected to the final negative reality of a willing that means nothing – perhaps this age is also the age of man's in-fantile dwelling in language. (Ibid.: 92; emphasis original)

In the condition of modern nihilism the choice we are facing is between sticking to the mysticism of the ineffable, whose vacuity has been completely exposed, and the inoperative potentiality attained in the *experimentum linguae*. By opting for the latter, by occupying the place of the Voice with our own infancy we do not merely access a new, more fundamental and originary experience of language but, insofar as it is the faculty for language that distinguishes the human being, a different mode of being human, a new understanding of the human community. In the remainder of this chapter we shall focus on the implications of Agamben's *experimentum linguae* beyond the sphere of language proper.

Whatever Being

We have seen that Agamben's theorisation of the experience of language operates with a systematic analogy between language and community. Just as language may be brought to speech as self-referential and presuppositionless, so the community that Agamben invokes in his 'language-oriented' works of the 1980s and comes to theorise explicitly in the 1990 book *The Coming Community*, is con-ceived as devoid of any presuppositions or predicates:

> [Only] because man finds himself cast into language without the vehicle of a voice, and only because the *experimentum linguae* lures him, gram-marless, into that void and that aphonia, do an ethos and a community of any kind become possible. So the community that is born of the *experi-mentum linguae* cannot take the form of a presupposition, not even in the purely 'grammatical' form of a self-presupposition. The first outcome of the *experimentum linguae*, therefore, is a radical revision of the very idea of Community. The only content of the *experimentum* is that there is language; we cannot represent this, by the dominant model in our culture, as *a* language. It is, rather, the unpresupposable non-latency in which men

have always dwelt and in which, speaking, they move and breathe. For all the forty millennia of *Homo Sapiens*, man has not yet ventured to assume this non-latency, to have the experience of his speaking being. (Agamben 2007a: 10)

This statement is a good illustration of the logic of comic affirmation reconstituted in the previous chapters. On the one hand, the 'experiment' that Agamben proposes is a matter of a radical overcoming of the way the elementary human faculty of having language has been treated in philosophy, culture and speech itself. On the other hand, in accordance with the messianic logic of a 'slight adjustment', what is at stake in the experiment is not the revelation of any esoteric wisdom but the sheer fact of there being language at all, the fact that for all its apparent self-evidence has not been brought to speech as such for the forty millennia of human existence. An unkind commentator might counter that if during forty thousand years no one bothered to bring the sheer speakability of language to speech, it is probably because it is so trivial as not to merit talking about. Yet, for Agamben this non-signifying experience turns out to be extremely significant, not merely because of what it reveals to us about language itself but because of its implications for rethinking the politics and ethics of human life as such. Recalling Wittgenstein's famous statement that the most appropriate expression for the miracle of the existence of world is the existence of language, Agamben adds that if this is so, then 'the correct experience for the existence of language is human life, as ethos, as ethical way. The search for a *polis* and an *oikia* befitting this void and unpresupposable community is the infantile task of future generations' (ibid.: 11).

Just as Agamben treats language as more than *a* language (a particular sign system) but rather addresses it in its sheer being (the inoperative potentiality of signification), so it is possible to speak of a political community that goes beyond particular communities, for example states, nations or peoples, which, just as individual languages, get very little attention from Agamben. Instead, Agamben focuses on two elementary 'facts', *factum loquendi* and *factum pluralitatis*, the fact of language and the fact of multiplicity or plurality, that the respective sciences of language and politics both presuppose and efface as negative foundations.

We do not have the slightest idea of what either a people or a language is. It is well known that linguistics can construct a grammar – that is, a unitary system with describable characteristics that could be called language – only by taking the *factum loquendi*, a fact that is still inaccessible to science – for granted. [In turn,] political theory must presuppose, without the ability to explain it, the *factum pluralitatis* – with which I would like to indicate the simple fact that human beings form a community – whereas linguistics must presuppose, without questioning it, the *factum loquendi*. The simple correspondence between these two facts defines modern political discourse. (Agamben 2000: 66)

Just as the *factum loquendi* is negated and maintained in this negated state as the foundation of particular languages, so the *factum pluralitatis*, which refers to the sheer existence of the multiplicity of (human) beings with no criterion of belonging or exclusion, is converted into the ineffable foundation for multiple communities structured precisely according to these criteria. And yet the phenomenon of nihilism, already well familiar to us, makes sure that these particular communities can no longer maintain the illusions of either consistency or closure. For Agamben, the ultimate symptom of the falsity of all particular communities or 'peoples' is their dependence on the power of the state: 'All well-meaning chatter notwithstanding, the idea of a people today is nothing other than the empty support of state identity and is recognized only as such' (ibid.: 67). Just as the people without a state makes no sense and has no rights, so a language lacking 'state dignity' (Catalan, Basque, Gaelic) is treated as a dialect or a jargon. Yet this only means that in the absence of state support, 'all peoples are Gypsies and all languages are jargons' (ibid.: 68), there being nothing in particular languages and communities themselves to authorise any greater dignity. In Agamben's reading, then, particularism in language and politics only serves to subject the potentiality of human existence to apparatuses and traditions that are already devoid of all sense:

> The plurality of nations and the numerous historical languages are the false callings by which man attempts to respond to his intolerable absence of voice: or, if one prefers, they are the attempts, fatally come to nothing, to make graspable the ungraspable, to become – this eternal child – an adult. Only on the day when the original infantile openness is truly, dizzyingly taken up as such, will men be able finally to construct a history and language that are universal and no longer deferrable, and stop their wandering through traditions. This authentic recalling of humanity to the infantile soma is called thought – that is, politics. (Agamben 1995: 98)

In this manner, Agamben's philosophy of language is directly and immediately converted into political thought, or, rather into 'thought as politics'. If the *factum loquendi* can be brought to speech in any speech act whatsoever in the experience of infancy, then the *factum pluralitatis*, which lies at the foundation of every particular community, may also be 'taken up as such' as the sole substance of a community that has abandoned all presuppositions:

> There can be no true human community on the basis of a presupposition – be it a nation, a language, or even the a priori of communication of which hermeneutics speaks. What unites human beings among themselves is not a nature, a voice or a common experience in a signifying language; it is the vision of language itself and therefore the experience of language's limits, its *end*. A true community can only be a community that is *not presupposed*. (Agamben 1999b: 47; emphasis original)

Agamben's explicit theorisation of this community begins with the introduction of two key notions: 'being-thus' and 'whatever being'. While both concepts continue to puzzle many commentators, our preceding discussion makes them instantly recognisable as ontological equivalents of the 'thing itself' of language. Whatever being is *a* being that appears solely in its *being*, subtracted from all its positive predicates, be they gender, colour, profession, political or sexual preferences. Since, in Kant's famous expression, 'being is not a real predicate' (Kant 2008 [1781]: 504; cf. Heidegger 1998: 337–63, 1962: 127), the subtraction of a being from all real predicates leaves it with nothing but its being itself, the sheer facticity of its existence.

> Exposure, in other words being-such-as, is not any of the real predicates (being red, hot, small, smooth, etc.), but neither is it other than these (otherwise it would be something else added to the concept of a thing and therefore still a real predicate). That you are exposed is not one of your qualities, but neither is it other than them (we could say, in fact, that it is none-other than them). (Agamben 1993a: 96)

We must emphasise that in their exposure 'whatever beings' do not discard or destroy their positive predicates, just as the ecstatic character of the existence of *Dasein* in Heidegger consists in 'exiting' from itself *without* 'abandoning' itself (Heidegger, 1995: 365). Yet even though these beings retain their predicates, they are no longer definable through them: being-thus is 'neither this nor that, neither thus nor thus, but *thus*, as it is, with all its predicates (all its predicates is not a predicate)' (Agamben 1993a: 93). In other words, whatever beings undergo neither a deprivation (of the old identity) nor a transformation (into a new one), but solely the exposure of the sheer fact *that* they are in the absence of any identification of *what* they are.

By virtue of this becoming inoperative of all particular identities, the members of this community share nothing else but the very fact of their being, their being-as-they-are, whatever they are.

In 1986 Jean-Luc Nancy, a philosopher perhaps closest to Agamben among contemporary continental thinkers, published a book entitled *Inoperative Community* (1991). Although Agamben's *The Coming Community*, published four years later, does not refer explicitly to Nancy's work, there are numerous parallels with Nancy's argument, particularly with regard to the idea of inoperativity as the key to the overcoming of the dangers of exclusion, violence and totalitarianism that the very notion of community became associated with during the twentieth century. Both Nancy and Agamben emphasise the need to separate the idea of community from anything like a political project that would realise its essence by dominating, excluding or eliminating the inessential, the false or the alien. Evidently the community of whatever being, whose members' positive identities are deactivated, can only be inoperative, since there is no longer anything in which its 'work' or 'task' could be grounded. For both Agamben and Nancy, this inoperative condition marks not the end but the very beginning of *ethical* life, which, to be worthy of the name, must be entirely dissociated from any teleological tasks and identitarian predicates.

> There is no essence, no historical or spiritual vocation, no biological destiny that humans must enact or realise. This is the only reason why something like ethics can exist, because it is clear that if humans were or had to be this or that substance, this or that destiny, no ethical experience would be possible – there would be only tasks to be done. (Agamben 1993a: 42)

The only possible ethical injunction that could be formulated in the inoperative community is to persist in 'being (one's own) potentiality, of being (one's own) possibility' rather than to actualise (and hence exhaust) this potentiality in the form of a positive identity, which would be equivalent to a passage into a 'deficit of existence' (ibid.: 44).

The immediately political stakes of this ethics of inoperative potentiality are made explicit in 'Tiananmen', the moving concluding fragment of *The Coming Community*:

> Whatever singularity, which wants to appropriate belonging itself, its own being-in-language, and thus rejects all identity and every condition of belonging, is the principal enemy of the State. Wherever these

singularities peacefully demonstrate their being in common, there will be a Tiananmen, and sooner or later tanks will appear. (Ibid.: 86)

For Agamben, what is absolutely threatening to the state, what the state 'cannot tolerate in any way' is not any particular claim for identity, which can always be recognised or conceded, but rather the possibility of human beings co-belonging in the absence of any identity: 'A being radically devoid of any representable identity would be absolutely irrelevant to the State' (ibid.: 85). Contrary to the Hegelian emphasis on the struggle for recognition that continues to define most contemporary political theories, the key political problem for Agamben is not the recognition of an identity but rather the affirmation of the radical heterogeneity or *non-identity* between the state (or any other apparatus of government) and the inoperative community of whatever beings:

> The novelty of the coming politics is that it will no longer be a struggle for the conquest or control of the State, but a struggle between the State and the non-State (humanity), an insurmountable disjunction between whatever singularity and the State organization. This has nothing to do with the simple affirmation of the social in opposition to the State that has often found expression in the protest movements of recent years. Whatever singularities cannot form a *societas*, because they do not possess any identity to vindicate any bond to belonging for which to seek recognition. (Ibid.: 86)

Thus Agamben posits as the key antagonism of contemporary politics a conflict between the governmental logic of the state and other apparatuses that capture human existence and transform its potentiality into a set of positive identities and the generic 'whatever community', whose only foundation is the *factum pluralitatis* of being-in-common and which never attains an institutional form. This antagonism may therefore not be formulated in the classical terms of the friend-enemy distinction, posited by Schmitt (1976) as the essence of the political. While the latter distinction presupposes a strong degree of symmetry between friend and enemy, which must be homologous or commensurable figures for their enmity to make sense, the antagonism between apparatuses and the inoperative community is radically asymmetric, pitting the indiscernible community of whatever being against the apparatuses, whose very *modus operandi* consists in discernment and identification (see Prozorov 2009c). Moreover, the community of whatever being does not seek inclusion into or recognition by these apparatuses, not even the formation of the alternative apparatus of its own, but rather affirms its *non-recognition of itself* in the apparatuses that capture it. While in the Hegelian logic only the universalisation of recognition may guarantee political pacification under the aegis of the 'universal homogeneous state', for Agamben the possibility of peace rather lies in something like a universalised non-recognition:

> [There] is not and can never be a sign of peace, since true peace would only be there, where all the signs were fulfilled and exhausted. Every struggle among men is in fact a struggle for recognition and the peace that follows such a struggle is only a convention instituting the signs and conditions of mutual, precarious recognition. Such a peace is only and always a peace amongst states and of the law, a fiction of the recognition of an identity in language, which comes from war and will end in war. Not the appeal to guaranteed signs or images but the fact that we cannot recognise ourselves in any sign or image: that is peace in non-recognition. Peace is the perfectly empty sky of humanity; it is the display of non-appearance as the only homeland of man. (Agamben 1995: 82)

The parallel with the experience of language permits us to understand this somewhat surprising claim: just as in *Infancy and History* and *Language and Death* the ethos of human beings was located not in some particular signified content but in the pure potentiality for signification that carries no determinate content, so the political ethos (dwelling place or 'homeland') of humanity is similarly not this or that form of community or mode of organisation, characterised by reciprocal recognition, the assignment of rights and duties and the specification of responsibilities but rather the being-in-common of all human beings irrespective of all of the above. The universality of the coming community is not the universality of the Hegelian-Kojèvian 'universal homogeneous' state, arrived at through the painstaking mediation of particularities in the struggle for recognition. Instead, it is the universality *immediately* attained by subtraction from all particularity and the suspension of the struggle for recognition: once there is no particularity to recognise, the struggle loses its point (cf. Prozorov 2013b).

Generic Universality

Agamben's understanding of universality is complex and deserves to be addressed in some detail. As we have done throughout this chapter, we may grasp Agamben's concept of the universal with the help of his studies of language – in this case, the idea of a 'universal language'. Agamben was particularly influenced by Benjamin's early essay 'On Language as Such and on the Language of Man' (Benjamin 1978: 314–32), where Benjamin discusses the idea of a pure language irreducible to any actually existing particular languages. While the latter remain subjected to the communicative function (that is the 'work' of language) and hence are reduced to mere signs, pure language would be strictly self-referential, no longer mediated by meaning, a language 'that does not mean anything but simply speaks' (Agamben 1999b: 54). It would therefore signify nothing but its own existence and refer only to its own communicability, to its 'thing itself' that Benjamin terms 'expressionless word' (cited in Agamben 1999b: 53). For both Benjamin and Agamben, *all* languages express this communicability, yet in every particular language it remains crowded out by particular signified content:

> All historical languages, Benjamin writes, mean pure language. It is what is meant in every language, what every language means to say. On the other hand, however, it itself does not mean anything; it does not want to say anything, and all meaning and all intention come to a halt in it. We may thus say that all languages mean to say the word that does not mean anything. (Agamben 1999b: 53)

Similarly, particular human communities (nations, states, cultures) seek to express the sheer *factum pluralitatis* of human multiplicity, which nonetheless remains ineffable in them, concealed by particular positive content of these communities that serves as the condition of belonging to them and exclusion from them. Yet the universal community that the *factum pluralitatis* affirms does not itself express anything, has no determining predicate or positive content, but simply exposes the being-in-common of all beings. Just as the universal language extinguishes all linguistic meaning but simply speaks, the universal community liquidates every determinate aspect of belonging and simply exists.

How can this expressionless, non-signifying universality become accessible? Evidently, it is not a matter of an actual establishment or production of the universal, be it a language or a community. Neither Benjamin nor Agamben advocate the establishment of a positive universal language, a new Esperanto, since any such language would be taken up by the signifying function, its universality thereby negated as a negative foundation of a new linguistic hegemony. Yet neither is it a matter of simply positing pure language as an ever-receding Ideal or regulative idea not subject to actualisation. Similarly, Agamben's 'coming community' is neither an actually existing positive entity (the sum total of all human beings, the state of all states, and so on) nor a vapid idea of the forever deferred unification of humanity. Just as universal language only works in and through particular languages, rendering them inoperative and undermining their signifying function, the universal community is accessible only within a myriad of particular ones as the subtraction from their particularities, the unworking of their identities and the deactivation of their vocations.

From this perspective, Agamben's political thought clearly belongs to what might be termed the 'new universalist' turn in continental thought that also characterises, in different ways, the work of Badiou, Nancy, Rancière and Žižek (see Prozorov 2009c; 2013). After decades of discredit in (post)structuralist philosophies of difference, continental philosophy has increasingly come to reassess and rehabilitate the notion of universality. Of course, this reassessment should be distinguished from a simple reaffirmation of familiar liberal-cosmopolitan or Marxist universalisms. Perhaps, in order not to be confused with any such reaffirmation, Agamben has consistently resisted the label of universalism, unlike other participants in this turn, such as Badiou, who has enthusiastically adopted it. A brief consideration of the debate between Agamben and Badiou on the universalism of St Paul, the object of their two books, would help us clarify Agamben's stance on universalism.

In his 1997 book *St. Paul: The Foundation of Universalism* Badiou offers a stinging critique of the contemporary terrain of particularistic 'identity politics', which he views as a necessary complement of the pseudo-universality of capitalism and seeks to overcome with a radically universalist politics of truth, the paradigm of which he finds in Pauline epistles. Badiou reinterprets Pauline texts from his own ontological perspective, finding in Paul the examples of his categories of the event, intervention, fidelity and truth. Bracketing off the narrowly religious content of Paul's epistles and dismissing it brusquely as a 'fable' (Badiou 2001b: 4), Badiou reconstructs something like a formal model of Pauline universalism, arising from the event of Christ's resurrection, which is important solely as a starting point for the procedure that it launches:

> Paul's general procedure is the following: if there has been an event, and if truth consists in declaring it and then in being faithful to this declaration, two consequences ensue. First, since truth is eventual, it is singular. It is neither structural, nor axiomatic, nor legal. No available generality can account for it, nor structure the subject who claims to follow in its

wake. Consequently, there cannot be a law of truth. Second, truth being inscribed on the basis of a declaration that is in essence subjective, no preconstituted subset can support it; nothing communitarian or historically established can lead its substance to the process of truth. Truth is diagonal relative to every subset; it neither claims authority from, nor constitutes any identity. It is offered to all, or addressed to everyone, without a condition of belonging being able to limit their offer or this address. (Badiou 2001b: 14)

Thus the truth that Paul affirms is a singular universality, an effect of the rupture of the event in a given world that carries universally valid consequences that cannot be restricted by any conditions of belonging. The 'body of truth', constituted by the subjective fidelity to the event, does not, in Paul's famous words, discern between Jews and Greeks, men and women, free persons and slaves, and so on. The Christian subject is constituted by one's intervention into the situation that declares the occurrence of the event and one's subsequent fidelity to it. The subject of truth is wholly indifferent to the particular words or situations in which the subjective process unfolds, remaining 'subtracted from the organization of subsets prescribed by the State' (ibid.: 15).

Agamben's *The Time that Remains*, published in Italian three years after the publication of Badiou's book, explicitly rejects the designation of Pauline messianism as universalist. In Agamben's reading, rather than offer a truth 'for all' (the conventional understanding of universalism), Paul rather affirms the non-coincidence of 'all' with themselves, whereby the particularistic division into Jews and Greeks, men and women, and so on is divided once more according to a new criterion, the distinction between 'flesh' (apparent, superficial belonging valid only in the eyes of the law) and 'breath' (genuine belonging on the basis of fidelity). We thus end up with a figure of the 'remnant' that does not fit in the opposition of Jews and non-Jews, a 'non-non-Jew' who is not under the positive law of a particular community but rather under the law of the Messiah.

> At this point one can measure the distance that separates the Pauline operation from modern universalism – when something like the humanity of man is taken as the principle that abolishes all difference or as the ultimate difference beyond which further division is impossible. (Agamben 2005b: 52)

While Badiou's reading of Paul emphasises his indifference to differences, whereby particularities become tolerated as the sites traversed by universality, which must always be affirmed locally within a situation (Badiou 2001b, 98–9), Agamben goes beyond what appears to him to be a mere benevolent or condescending 'tolerance': what the Pauline division does is render the operations of the law and other apparatuses that establish and sustain difference inoperative so that

> [all] that is left is a remnant and the impossibility of the Jew or the Greek to coincide with himself, without ever providing [one] with some other identity. You see why it makes no sense to speak of universalism with regard to Paul, at least when the universal is thought of as a principle above cuts and divisions and the individual as the ultimate limit of each division. (Agamben 2005b: 53)

The problem, nonetheless, is that the universal is *not* thought that way by Badiou. As a singularity that is not anticipated, prescribed by or subsumed under any law, it is clearly not 'above' cuts and divisions, but rather itself consists in the subtractive cut that separates one from the identities prescribed by the positive order that Badiou terms 'the state of the situation'. Secondly, as a subjective process that does not pre-exist the declaration of the event, universality cannot be localised within any particular subset, be it a group or an individual. Badiou's 'for all' is not identical to what Agamben terms 'modern universalism', which posits a difference (humanity) that abolishes all differences, but rather consists in the subtraction from all differences that resembles the messianic division that produces the figure of the remnant. Badiou's political subject, subtracted from its 'intra-worldly' determinations, is best grasped precisely as a 'non-non-Jew' (Greek, man, woman, and so on), the second negation negating the first and making it irrelevant.

Thus the differences between Badiou and Agamben on the question of universalism appear to be overstated. Interestingly, this is also the view of Badiou himself, who, as we have seen in the previous chapter, is otherwise quite explicit about his disagreements with Agamben:

> [I] know that Agamben's reading of Paul is very different from mine, but is this difference really a contradiction? I ask because, in fact, the question of separation belongs to the question of universalism. There is not, in my view, necessarily a contradiction between the two. In Paul there is an interplay between separation and universalism. For Paul, there is certainly a kind of separation necessary for his universalism because we have separated ourselves from the old man. We have, out of this separation, a newness of life. But it remains a universalism because there is no limit

to this separation, there is no closure. Instead, [Paul] proposes something that is open to everybody, a collective determination, the realization of a separation in a universal field. So, naturally, there is, for Paul, in the process of universalism, something like division but this is a division internal to the subject itself. So I perfectly understand that universalism can take the form of a separation. There is always something like an intimate division when universalism takes the form of a separation. But there is never the pure opposition of universalism and separation because there is something like the becoming-separate of a universalism. (Badiou 2005c: 39–40)

We may therefore conclude that while Agamben's insistence on the difference of his construction of Pauline messianism from 'modern universalism' is certainly understandable, Badiou's singular universalism is much closer to his own reading, particularly in the wider context of Agamben's writings on the universal language and its correlate in the open and non-exclusive community of whatever singularities. Indeed, just as Agamben's 'coming community', Badiou's community 'without conditions of belonging' that subtracts itself from all particular 'communitarian' and 'historically established' forms consists entirely in the *factum pluralitatis* of the being-in-common of the sheer multiplicity of beings. Similarly, Agamben's notion of 'whatever being' is strictly analogous to Badiou's more technical concept of the 'generic' subset of the situation emerging in the practices of fidelity to the event. The generic subset is *indiscernible* within the situation, i.e. it cannot be individualised by any of its positive predicates.

> [It] contains a little bit of everything [but] *only* possesses the properties necessary to its existence as multiple in its material. It does not possess any particular, discerning, separative property. At base, its sole property is that of consisting as pure multiple, of being. Subtracted from language, it makes do with its being. (Badiou 2005a: 371)

As we have seen, the same logic of the subtraction from all positive, particular content underlies Agamben's *experimentum linguae* and its political correlate of the community of whatever being.

While in our interpretation Agamben's political thought clearly belongs to the new universalist turn in continental philosophy, we must reiterate that this universalism is fundamentally heterogeneous to the more familiar hegemonic or imperialist forms. Just as universal language is not to be attained by forcibly changing the ways people communicate and making them all speak some new language, so a universal community is never attained by unification or integration of particular communities but rather by subtraction, separation and division that traverse every subject, be it an individual or a group. Agamben's universalism does not merely *not* contradict pluralism but rather proceeds through a thoroughgoing pluralisation that leaves nothing identical with itself.

The Thick of It

In conclusion, let us consider the criticism of this generic reinterpretation of community that is as easy to anticipate as it is difficult to counter. Isn't the idea of a radically non-exclusive community defined by no positive predicate and sharing nothing than exposed existence so hopelessly utopian as to be politically vacuous? This is indeed the approach of many of Agamben's critics (Passavant 2007; Toscano 2011; Chiesa and Ruda 2011; Sharpe 2009), for whom the very transfer of ideas from linguistics or ontology to politics is problematic. It might be all very well to affirm the pure experience of language in poetry or contemplate the appearance of things in their being, but what is the political significance of the being-in-common of humanity, a fact as self-evident as it is apparently useless? Even if we were to agree with this understanding of community, where would it take us in the world that continues to be structured by particular communities, just as our speech still possesses some signified content?

An Agambenian response to this accusation would, not surprisingly, be based on Hölderlin's dictum introduced in Chapter 1: 'where danger grows, grows also saving power'. Agamben's interpretation of our current predicament as an epoch of nihilism, characterised by the devaluation of all values, the exhaustion of all teleologies, the vacuity of all vocations, logically entails not only that the pure experiences of language and existence, *factum loquendi* and *factum pluralitatis*, that have been concealed by the logic of negative foundation, are now coming to light. It also entails that they are the *only* things that are coming to light in the times devoid of revelation and characterised by the utmost vanity and banality of speech:

> when the ethical connection that united words, things and human actions is broken, this in fact promotes a spectacular and unprecedented proliferation of vain words on the one hand, and, on the other, of legislative apparatuses that seek obstinately to legislate on every aspect of that life on which they seem no longer to have any hold. (Agamben 2009a: 71)

While Agamben's paradigms tend to focus on its more morbid and violent aspects of politics (refugee camps, anti-terrorist legislation, biometrics, surveillance, and so on), his general interpretation of the contemporary situation is rather less dramatic, emphasising less the violence than the senselessness of the apparatuses of government in the age of nihilism. The proliferation of 'vain words' and 'legislative apparatuses' that seek and fail to capture life is furthest away from the image of the malevolent or out-of-control Leviathan that Agamben is often accused of invoking. While it was indeed the thesis about the concentration camp as the paradigmatic space of modern politics that made Agamben famous, his general diagnosis of modern politics as destined to nihilism and his resolution of the problem of nihilism through the reappropriation of inoperativity and potentiality are not tied to the paradigm of the camp and, furthermore, would arguably be least suitable for a politics structured according to such a paradigm: it is difficult to see how play, profanation or even Bartleby's cultivated apathy would be effective political strategies in the camp or, more generally, in a violently repressive regime akin to Nazism or Stalinism, in which political action as such becomes an impossibility (cf. Arendt 1973: 437–59, 468–74). While the camp and the phenomenon of totalitarianism evidently emerge in the age of modern nihilism, they are too extreme to exemplify modern nihilism as such. Since Agamben's above-discussed preference for hyperbolic examples accounts for numerous misunderstandings and excessive criticism of his affirmative solutions,[4] a more 'typical' example of contemporary nihilistic politics of vain words and ceaselessly legislating apparatuses would be helpful for appreciating the effectivity of his politics of inoperativity.

A good paradigm of Agamben's account of the nihilism of contemporary politics is offered by the British satirical television series *The Thick of It* (2005–12), created by Armando Iannucci, which depicts the inner workings of a department of the UK government and its relations with the party spin doctors, the opposition and the media. The political world constructed in the series is entirely devoid of any sense: neither the government nor the opposition demonstrates anything like a positive transformative or regulatory agenda and the praxis of government is revealed as a mix of ad hoc measures designed for often miscalculated media effects, nice-sounding yet utterly meaningless 'initiatives' and ridiculous blunders arising from the ineptitude of everyone involved in the running of things. While the inner workings of the department, staffed by a succession of possibly well-meaning but hopelessly maladroit ministers and morally dubious advisors, exemplify Agamben's thesis on the ultimately 'anarchic', i.e. ontologically unfounded character of all apparatuses of government (2011: 62–7), the sovereign function of the negative foundation of the political order is presented, in a parodic form, by the government's Director of Communications, Malcolm Tucker, whose task is to oversee the department's activities and correct its all too frequent blunders through media spin. Yet while he is universally feared in the manner of Hobbes's Leviathan who keeps 'all in awe', the violence that Tucker exercises largely takes the form of verbal abuse in the form of exceptionally eloquent swearing and threats that keep the system running, albeit running on empty.

The brilliance of the *The Thick of It* does not merely consist in the parodic desublimation of the activity of government, which loses all trace of transcendence, seriousness or importance. Iannucci makes an important step forward in depicting the world of government as not merely incapable of redeeming its promises, whatever they are, but as *itself* badly in need of redemption: the ministers, the advisors, the secretaries and, ultimately, the fearsome Malcolm Tucker himself, are manifestly miserable in the apparatus that they sustain and in which they are themselves caught up. To recall Agamben's reading of Kafka, addressed in Chapter 1, the only happy ending we could imagine for the series is the redemption of the 'anonymous crowd of judges, lawyers and guardians indiscriminately packed together in dusty corridors or stooped beneath oppressive ceilings' (Agamben 1995: 85). Whenever we encounter the criticism of Agamben's allegedly excessive criticism of contemporary politics, his insufficient appreciation of democracy or the rule of law, we would do well to recall the world of *The Thick of It* and ask ourselves if there is any point in letting this travesty go on.

What would it mean to stop the machine of vain words and impotent government? Nihilism apparently resigns us to speech that has nothing to say and praxis that has nothing to do. Yet this very evacuation of linguistic and political content makes the 'infantile' community of whatever being not only an attractive but also a *realistic* option; after all, it is not like there was anything *else* around, aside from vain words and apparatuses gone mad in the desire to regulate for no reason. In full accordance with Hölderlin's maxim, it is the utter destitution wrought by nihilism that makes ontically possible the community whose ever-present ontological potentiality was *always* (for the proverbial forty millennia!) covered over by particular languages and communities:

> [For] the first time it is possible for humans to experience their own linguistic being – not this or that content of language, but language itself. Contemporary politics is this devastating *experimentum linguae* that all over the planet unhinges and empties traditions and beliefs, ideologies and religions, identities and communities. (Agamben 1993a: 82)

The experiment of rendering language and community inoperative is *already* at work in modern nihilism; the question is rather whether the inoperativity unveiled in it is opened to free and profane use that enhances the potentiality of human existence or is separated into a new sacred sphere and subjected to the glorification of its own nullity and senselessness. Agamben's political thought is thus not a utopian discourse on the brighter future entirely divorced from the present, but an affirmation of the possibilities already at work in this present, the injunction to seize them and the warning about the dangers of not doing so.

> If instead of continuing to search for a proper identity in the *already improper and senseless form of individuality*, humans were to succeed in belonging to this impropriety as such, in making of the proper being-thus not an identity and individual property but a singularity without identity, a common and absolutely exposed singularity – if humans could, that is, not be thus in this or that particular biography but be only *the* thus, their singular exteriority and their face, then they would for the first time enter into a community without presuppositions and without subjects. (Agamben 1993a: 64; emphasis original)

It is from the perspective of this choice between sticking to the exhausted tradition and the reappropriation of the potentialities that it confines and feeds on that we must re-engage with the familiar image of Agamben as a shrill and hyperbolic critic of the Western political tradition. As we have seen, Agamben's affirmative vision of the coming community is derived by analogy with the pure experience of the existence of language and its universality is obtained immediately without passing through particular communities, be they states, nations or other political entities populating the Western tradition. Why, then, does Agamben spend so much effort at the painstaking genealogies of this tradition, tracing the minute details in the histories of sovereignty, government or the economy? Agamben's relation to the Western political tradition is similar to Benjamin's famous description of his relation to theology as that of the blotting pad to ink: 'It is soaked through with it. But if it were up to the blotting pad, there would be no more ink' (Benjamin cited in Agamben 1999b: 58). Agamben's affirmation of a community of whatever being that renders inoperative the plurality of particular communities and their apparatuses only takes up the traditions in which these communities have functioned so as to be able to find ways to render them inoperative. If it were 'up to' Agamben, particularistic communities organised into states founded on the logic of sovereignty would simply vanish into thin air, sucked into the void, into which their sense and content have already disappeared. Yet, as it is *not up to* Agamben, since even the apparatuses running on empty cannot be simply wished away, his affirmation of the community based on *factum pluralitatis* must necessarily traverse the existing political landscape, absorbing the tradition that governs it like the blotting pad does the ink, but always from the perspective of the community of whatever being that this tradition presupposes and betrays. It is to Agamben's deactivation of this tradition that we turn in the following chapter.

Notes

1. While in this book we shall frequently resort to the notion of reappropriation to describe Agamben's political strategy, this term might appear problematic in the context of his philosophy. This is due to its etymological link with the notions of 'the proper' and 'property', both of which are quite alien to Agamben's lexicon, in which it is rather the 'common' (or 'improper') and 'use' (as opposed to possession) that figure prominently (see 1999b: 201–4; 2013: 123–43). At the same time, the idea of appropriation and particularly *re*-appropriation or *re*-claiming is central to Agamben's affirmative politics, which, as we have seen, seeks to wrest away the originary inoperativity and potentiality of human existence from their capture and confinement (*ex*-propriation) in historically contingent apparatuses of government. The notion of reappropriation is thus a legitimate designation of Agamben's strategy, as long as we bear in mind that, firstly, what is reappropriated in it is not the proper (identity, task or voice) but the irreducibly common, indeed universal, attribute of existence, and, secondly, that the reappropriation of inoperativity and potentiality cannot by definition be grasped in terms of possession or property but pertains solely to their return to free use. See Agamben (2013: 123–43) for a detailed discussion of the notion of use in the context of Franciscan monasticism as the key aspect of a form of life beyond both law and property.

2. The affirmation of the origin as transcendental, i.e. irreducible to a chronological moment in the past and instead functional and observable at any moment in the present, is not specific to Agamben's work but is a key characteristic of Italian philosophy in general. In Roberto Esposito's reading (2013: 22–3, 25–8), Italian philosophy differs from its English, French or German counterparts in refusing the gesture of a radical break with the origin, the cleaning of the slate, whereby philosophical thought severs itself from everything natural, mythical or irrational to establish itself as a new beginning on secure, if artificial, foundations. In contrast, Italian philosophy has tended to maintain itself in close relation with the 'pre-philosophical' substrate of tradition, nature or life that is impossible to separate from philosophy proper but which remains at work within philosophy despite remaining heterogeneous to it. The same logic can be traced in the approach of Italian philosophy to history and politics, which, contrary to its Hobbesian or Cartesian counterparts, has been marked by the attention to which various ostensibly natural or vital elements persist within historical and political orders that purport to extricate themselves from them (ibid.: 49–58).

3. The attention to this split between the semantic and the semiotic characterises Agamben's work in its entirety. The most recent example is the theory of *signatures* (2009b: 33–79) that has become the key methodological innovation in his late works (see, for example, Agamben 2011: 3–4). In a historical account of the idea of signatures from Paracelsus to Foucault, Agamben defines them as neither concepts nor signs but rather as a force that 'makes the mute signs of creation efficacious and expressive' (2009b: 43). 'Signs do not speak unless signatures make them speak' (ibid.: 61). Thus, at a most general level a signature is what transforms the semiotic dimension of a system of signs into signifying speech, hence its structural locus is the experience of infancy, in which language begins to *exist* for the first time. Another example from Agamben's later work is his theory of the *oath* (2009a), which he interprets as the condition of possibility of effective signification, whereby the semiotic content of language is endowed with additional performative efficacy in the acts of speech. Signatures, oaths and other performative utterances take place in the gap between the semiotic and the semantic, without which language would be asubjective and immediately effective, devoid of the possibility of perjury, blasphemy or falsity and hence devoid of all potentiality.

4. A somewhat similar criticism has been offered by Paul Passavant (2007), in whose argument Agamben operates with a contradictory concept of the state, split between a neo-Marxist account of the state as a governmental structure ultimately determined by the capitalist economy and a neo-Schmittian account of the state as the autonomous subject of biopolitical sovereignty. As a result, his affirmative politics allegedly becomes incoherent, since it is not clear *which* state it is supposed to

target. Agamben has responded to this criticism in his *The Kingdom and the Glory* (2011), which links the two paradigms of the state, sovereign and governmental or economic. In this book, sovereignty, which was discussed in *Homo Sacer* and *State of Exception* as a mode of power in its own right, is presented as the constitutive outside or negative foundation of positive governmental or economic orders. Agamben interprets government as a 'bipolar' system, in which the transcendence of sovereignty and the immanence of the economy perpetually refer to each other: in the absence of economic government, sovereign power would be incapable of producing positive effects, while in the absence of the transcendent locus of sovereignty, the immanent activity of government would lack a foundation. Thus, the contradiction between sovereignty and economic government does not yield two different concepts of the state but must be located *within* the concept of the state itself as the problematic and fragile attempt to reconcile transcendence and immanence, negativity and positivity, being and action. As Agamben demonstrates in the final chapters of *The Kingdom and the Glory*, such a reconciliation between inoperative sovereignty and the unfounded work of government in the Western tradition takes the form of glory, which, as we have seen in Chapter 2, conceals this inoperativity by the perpetual labour of its acclamation: the 'economic' state perpetually feeds on the inoperativity of the 'sovereign' one, which is in turn only a product of the prior expropriation of the general inoperativity of all human beings (2011: 241–6).

Chapter 4

How to Play with the Law:
Inoperative Statehood

The analysis of Agamben's concept of political community as modelled on the experience of the inoperative potentiality of language has laid the groundwork for the engagement with his best-known political texts in the *Homo Sacer* series. As we shall demonstrate in this chapter, these texts only become fully intelligible on the basis of Agamben's critique of the logic of negative foundation and his programme for the reappropriation of human potentiality. Yet these works are also marked by a complex and erudite re-engagement with the classic works of political philosophy, from Hobbes to Foucault. We shall first address Agamben's reinterpretation of Foucault's notion of *biopolitics* and Schmitt's notion of *sovereignty*, tracing his fusion of the two into the idea of biopolitical sovereignty, whose object and product is *bare life*, the exact correlate of the notion of the Voice in the philosophy of language. We shall then discuss Agamben's resolution of the problem of sovereignty that, in accordance with the general logic of inoperativity, does not take the form of either the takeover or the destruction of the state but rather consists in the *deactivation* of its ordering power. This is what Agamben, following Benjamin, terms the *real state of exception*, i.e. the *reappropriation* of the inoperativity of the law from its confinement in the sphere of sovereignty as a general condition of human existence without any relation to the law or the state. The chapter concludes with the discussion of Agamben's notion of *form-of-life* as the restoration of bare life to its own potentiality.

Biopolitics: Old or New?

The first volume of *Homo Sacer, Sovereign Power and Bare Life*, is initially presented by Agamben as an attempt to 'correct' or 'complete' Foucault's theory of biopolitics (Agamben 1998: 9). This theory, outlined at the end of the first volume of Foucault's *History of Sexuality* (1990a) and developed in a series of lecture courses of the late 1970s (2007, 2008), traces the transformation of the mode of power relations in early modern Europe. In his genealogies of the prison and sexuality, Foucault observes the emergence of the technologies of power that are heterogeneous to the traditional concepts of law and sovereignty and are concerned with normalisation rather than prohibition. He argues that modernity has not been about the liberation from or the weakening of state power, but rather brought about the intensification, multiplication and diversification of power relations beyond the sphere of the state proper. The monarchical power of the sovereign that consisted in the right to decide life and death, to take life or let live was transformed into a 'power over life', a power 'to foster life or disallow it to the point of death' (Foucault 1990a: 138). The correlate of this process in the field of knowledge has been the development of modern social science in the systematic investigation of historical, demographic and social processes within the context of governmental administration, a form of knowledge that differed from both earlier ethical and prudential modes of thinking about politics as an art of good life and the Machiavellian advice to the prince grounded in the idea of autonomy of political reason.

The development of power over life took two distinct forms. The first type of power relations focused on the body as a machine, aiming to optimise its functioning and increase its efficiency and capacity for control. Foucault calls this *disciplinary* technique of producing 'docile bodies' (1977: 135) the *anatomo-politics of the human body*. The second form of power, termed *biopolitics of the population* (1990a: 135), has as its object of knowledge and action the broad range of processes of life that refer to human collectivities, the 'population' with its birth, death and fertility rates, its conditions of life and labour, its movements and transformations. In this manner, 'natural life' enters the domain of state power as an object of political action: 'for millennia, man remained what he was for Aristotle: a living animal with the additional capacity for political existence; modern man is an animal whose politics calls his existence as a living being into question' (ibid.: 143). It is precisely to Aristotle that Agamben returns in order to correct and complete Foucault's diagnosis.

Agamben starts from the distinction between two terms for 'life' in Ancient Greek: '*zoe*, which expressed the simple fact of living common to all living beings (animals, men or gods) and *bios*, which indicated the form or way of living proper to an individual or a group'

(Agamben 1998: 1). From this perspective, to speak of 'a *zoe politike* of the citizens of Athens would have made no sense' (ibid.: 1), since politics only pertained to *bios* as qualified forms of life, while *zoe* in the sense of natural or reproductive life was excluded to the domain of the *oikos* or home (cf. Dubreuil 2008). In these terms, the advent of biopolitics (which it would be more correct to term 'zoopolitics') would consist in the entry of *zoe* into *bios*, or, in Agamben's already famous phrase, the entry of both terms into a 'zone of irreducible indistinction' (ibid.: 9). While agreeing with Foucault that this indistinction defines the loosely defined 'modern' period (from the late eighteenth century onwards), Agamben nonetheless questions, firstly, the reduction of biopolitics *as such* to a historically novel phenomenon and, secondly, its heterogeneity to sovereign power. While Foucault's theory of biopolitics unfolded in the context of his attempt to abandon the 'juridico-discursive' model of power as negative, repressive and centred on the figure of the sovereign, with law as its main instrument, Agamben explicitly starts out from the need to establish the 'intersection between the juridico-institutional and the biopolitical models of power' (ibid.: 6) and finds such an intersection in the figure of bare life.

While we shall return to the concept of bare life throughout this chapter, at this point it is important to strictly differentiate it from *zoe* as natural life (Mills 2008: 64; Murray 2010: 61; De la Durantaye 2009: 202–5; Kishik 2012: 102). While Agamben's text sometimes slips into the identification of two terms (1998: 6), in the logic of his argument bare life does *not* precede politics but is rather its product, a result of the inclusion of *zoe* into *bios* that cannot be identical to *zoe* itself. Rather than being natural, bare life is in a sense always denatured as a result of its inclusion into the political order, even if, as Agamben argues, this inclusion originally took the form of exclusion that left *zoe* at the margins of the polis, 'outside but yet belonging'. To risk a simplistic formula, bare life is what happens to *zoe* when it is included in the bios. Since this inclusion is originary and not merely a modern invention, it cannot amount to anything like a 'new' form of power. Instead of positing biopolitics as the successor to sovereign politics or at least the indicator of its transformation, Agamben argues that biopolitics, and bare life as its object, are produced by sovereign power:

> the inclusion of bare life in the political realm constitutes the original –
> if concealed – nucleus of sovereign power. *It can even be said that the*

production of a biopolitical body is the original activity of sovereign power. In this sense, biopolitics is at least as old as sovereign power. (Ibid.: 6; emphasis original)

This statement clearly runs contrary to Foucault's analysis and has given rise to criticism of Agamben's work as 'ahistorical' and 'ontologizing' (see Connolly 2007; Passavant 2007; Toscano 2011). The most famous of the critics of Agamben's approach to biopolitics was perhaps Jacques Derrida, a philosopher with whom Agamben has critically engaged throughout his career and whose differences from Agamben we shall return to in this book (see De la Durantaye 2009: 184–91; Mills 2008: 44–6; Murray 2010: 29–32; Thurschwell 2005). In his final seminar, *The Beast and the Sovereign* (2009), Derrida subjected Agamben's understanding of biopolitics to a stinging critique, arguing that Agamben overstates the stability of the conceptual distinction between *bios* and *zoe* in the Antiquity so as to strengthen his claim about their subsequent entry into the zone of indistinction. If the distinction was never strictly observable to begin with, then its weakening or collapse could not be posited as the fundamental threshold of modernity, which it is for both Foucault and Agamben (perhaps more so for the former, given his interest in specifically modern techniques of power). In Derrida's derisive reading, Agamben perpetually oscillates between two mutually exclusive claims: the originary or 'ancient' status of biopolitics and its irreducibly modern character:

[If] biopolitics is an arch-ancient thing, why all the effort to pretend to wake politics up to something that is supposedly 'the decisive event of modernity'? In truth, Agamben, giving nothing up, like the unconscious, wants to be twice first, the first to see and announce, and the first to remind: he wants both to be the first to announce an unprecedented and new thing, what he calls this 'decisive event of modernity' [the birth of biopolitics], and also to be the first to recall that in fact it's always been like this, from time immemorial. He is the first to tell us two things in one: it's just happened for the first time, you ain't seen nothing yet, but nor have you seen, I'm telling you for the first time, that it dates from year zero. (Derrida 2009: 330)

In the conclusion to the seminar Derrida makes an uncharacteristically blunt statement regarding Aristotle and his definition of man as *zoon politikon*, which is supposed to end any dispute about the status of biopolitics:

What Aristotle says is that man is that living being who is taken by politics: he is a political living being, and essentially so. In other words, he is zoo-political, that's his essential definition, that's what is proper to him, *idion*; what is proper to man is politics: what is proper to the living being that man is, is politics, and therefore man is immediately zoo-political, in his very life, and it's obvious that already in Aristotle there's thinking of what is today called 'zoopolitics' or 'biopolitics'. Which does not mean, of course, that Aristotle had already foreseen, thought, understood, analysed all the figures of today's zoopolitics or biopolitics: it would be absurd to think so. But as for the biopolitical or zoopolitical structure, it's put forward by Aristotle, it's already there, and the debate opens there. (Derrida 2009: 349)

The sole problem with this statement is that Agamben (though admittedly not Foucault!) ultimately says the same thing. While Derrida spends pages ridiculing Agamben's desire to have it both ways, to have biopolitics as *both* modern and ancient, from the very beginning of *Homo Sacer* Agamben actually separates the two dimensions quite clearly:

> Biopolitics is at least as old as the sovereign exception. Placing biological life at the centre of its calculations, the modern State therefore does nothing other than bring to light the secret tie uniting power and bare life, thereby reaffirming the bond between modern power and the most immemorial of the *arcana imperii*. (Agamben 1998: 6)

As we shall demonstrate in more detail below, the logic at work in Agamben's argument is exactly the same as the one encountered above in his analysis of inoperativity and its revelation under modern nihilism: it is *only* in modern nihilism that the fundamental ontological feature of the human condition, its 'absence of work', has been illuminated. Agamben's argument is therefore closer to Derrida's than to Foucault's original attempt to posit a break, however tentative and incomplete, between the era of sovereign power and the age of biopolitics. What is at stake for Agamben is rather the specific mode of the *implication* of *zoe* in *bios*, which in the times of Aristotle (and the subsequent dozen centuries) was that of *exclusion* but in modernity became that of *indistinction*.

> What characterizes modern politics is not so much the inclusion of *zoe* in the polis, which is, in itself, absolutely ancient – nor simply the fact that life as such becomes a principal object of the projections and calculations of state power. Instead, the decisive fact is that the realm of bare life – which is originally situated at the margins of the political order – gradually begins to coincide with the political realm and exclusion and inclusion, outside and inside, *bios* and *zoe*, right and fact, enter into a zone of irreducible indistinction. (Ibid.: 9)

This is where Agamben famously formulates the paradox of sovereignty in terms of 'inclusive exclusion', which should be perfectly familiar to us from the preceding chapter. The mode of implication of *zoe* in *bios* is exactly the same as that of *phone* in *logos*, i.e. the former serves as the negative foundation of the latter:

> The question 'In what way does the living being have language?' corresponds exactly to the question 'In what way does bare life dwell in the polis?' The living being has *logos* by taking away and conserving its own voice in it, even as it dwells in the polis by letting its own bare life be excluded, as an exception, within it. Politics therefore appears as the truly fundamental structure of Western metaphysics, insofar as it occupies the threshold on which the relation between the living being and the logos is realized. There is politics because man is the living being who, in language, separates and opposes himself to his own bare life and, at the same time, maintains himself in relation to that bare life in an inclusive exclusion. (Ibid.: 8)

There is thus no contradiction between the claim that biopolitics is as old as sovereignty (since the logic of negative foundation marks their originary articulation) and the claim that the ascent of biopolitics to prominence marks the decisive event of modernity (or, more specifically, of modern nihilism). Biopolitics is indeed as old as the hills, yet in modern times something new has happened and is happening to it, i.e. the coming to light of its negativity due to the expiry or devaluation of all positive projects under the condition of nihilism.

From this perspective, we should reconsider the criticism of Agamben's reinterpretation of Foucault's concept of biopolitics as dehistoricising and ontologising. However damaging in the contemporary intellectual context dominated by various forms of historical nominalism, these charges seem to bang on an open door, insofar as Agamben explicitly rethinks the inclusive exclusion of life into the polis as an ontological operation irreducible to particular historical rationalities of government. While Foucault was primarily interested in those rationalities themselves, in their positive difference from sovereign modes of rule, what interests Agamben in the problematic of biopolitics is the overall constellation whereby life is captured in political rationalities. While the *forms* of this capture certainly vary historically and the period from the late eighteenth to early nineteenth century might indeed form an important threshold for this change (as Foucault and the post-Foucauldian scholarship contends), the *fact* of this capture has evidently been there long before Western liberalism, the appearance of statistics, the invention of the population and other relevant categories, and so on (see Ojakangas 2012). It is therefore not very productive to read the difference between Foucault and Agamben as a 'debate' in which one is expected to take sides; this is rather a difference of perspective and different perspectives suit different research problems.

The analysis of Agamben's philosophy of language and community in the previous chapter permits us to understand his move away from the canonical Foucauldian problematic. Insofar as Agamben affirms a strict homology between the oppositions of *phone/logos* and *zoe/bios* and, consequently, the notions of Voice and bare life, biopolitics is *ipso facto* as old as human language. The critics of 'dehistoricisation' are therefore ultimately incorrect: what Agamben traces is indeed a historical event, albeit the one that took place long before European modernity or, for that matter, the Greek polis, but could be dated back to forty millennia ago (Agamben 2007a: 9), i.e. the emergence of the human being as a speaking being. And yet, as we have argued in our discussion of the transcendental origin, this event of anthropogenesis is not simply a one-off historical happening but rather keeps on taking place in every act of speech. Insofar as the entry of life into politics is strictly analogous to the entry of the human being into language, Agamben is furthest away from dehistoricising biopolitics; if anything, he makes it historical through and through, coextensive with the *history of humanity* as such. Just as the entry of the human being into language makes history possible by removing the natural 'voice of man', the inclusive exclusion of bare life into the polis launches politics as a historical process, in which various forms of *bios* are constructed on the basis of bare life as negated *zoe*.

The Sovereign Ban

Let us now elaborate the way bare life functions as the negative foundation of political orders. Since, as Agamben argues, the production of bare life as the biopolitical body is the originary activity of sovereign power, we must investigate the character of that power as well. It is here that Agamben complements Foucault, who famously rejected the very problematic of sovereignty in his call to 'cut off the head of the king in political thought' (1990a: 89), with the reinterpretation of one of the most controversial political theorists of the twentieth century, Carl Schmitt. Due to his association with the Nazi party in the first years after its victory, Schmitt remains a controversial and frequently reviled thinker, often called 'The Crown Jurist of the Third Reich' (see McCormick 1997; Scheuerman 1999; Ojakangas 2006; Slomp 2009). Nonetheless, one can only ignore Schmitt's political thought at one's own peril, since its (often esoteric) influence extends far beyond the historical context of interwar European fascism. In his theories of the political as the friend–enemy distinction, of sovereignty as the decision on exception, his studies of the crisis of parliamentary democracy and the collapse of the inter-state order (1976, 1985a, 1985b, 2003) Schmitt undertook nothing less than a fundamental revaluation of the entire Western political tradition, and while his conclusions may be discomforting, his insights can hardly be ignored.

In *Homo Sacer* Agamben takes up and elaborates Schmitt's theory of sovereignty, illuminating its paradoxical character. For Schmitt (1985a: 1), 'sovereign is he who decides on the exception' or, in more contemporary juridical language, has the power to institute a state of exception or emergency, suspending the existing juridico-political order. This means that the sovereign is simultaneously *inside* the legal order (it is indeed only sovereign *in* that order and never 'as such' or 'in itself') and *outside* it, since its power remains effective even when the validity of the existing legal or constitutional norms is suspended. Schmitt's notion of the sovereign exception thus demonstrates that the exception is never wholly external to that which it takes exception to, i.e. the normal order, but is in fact included into it in the paradoxical mode of the 'internal other' or 'constitutive outside'. Insofar as the sovereign's power extends to suspending the very order that it constitutes and sustains, it logically follows that the sovereign decision could never be subsumed under any positive law, norm or system of rules. The sovereign remains a borderline or threshold figure at the limit of order, at the opening to whatever is outside or beyond it. Yet this opening to the outside remains essential for the very existence of the interiority of order:

> The most proper characteristic of the exception is that what is excluded in it is not, on account of being excluded, absolutely without relation to the rule. On the contrary, what is excluded in the exception maintains itself in relation to the rule in the form of the rule's suspension. The rule applies to the exception in no longer applying, in withdrawing from it. The state of exception is thus not the chaos that precedes order but rather the situation that results from its suspension. (Agamben 1998: 17–18)

Similarly undecidable is the belonging of the exception to the spheres of right and fact: insofar as it is not subsumed under the rule, it appears to be an extra-juridical fact, yet since it only exists by means of the suspension of the rule, it can never be purely factual.

> In its archetypal form, the state of exception is therefore the principle of every juridical localization, since only the state of exception opens the space, in which the determination of a certain juridical order and a particular territory first becomes possible. (Ibid.: 19)

Paradoxically, it is only through the construction of the zone of *anomie* at the heart of the legal order that this order may establish its connection to the life that it governs (Agamben 2005a: 51).

Recalling the context of world politics in the aftermath of the publication of *Homo Sacer*, which was characterised by the explicit invocation of exceptional measures by the US government after the terrorist attacks of 11 September 2001, it is easy to understand why Agamben's reading of sovereign exceptionalism would attract attention. Yet it is crucial to emphasise that, similarly to Schmitt, Agamben does not interpret exceptional measures as an unfortunate remnant of or relapse into authoritarian rule in modern democracies, but rather as a constitutive principle that sustains these democracies themselves. Contrary to the critics of the US government after 9/11 who demanded the return to normal, domestic- or international-law-based instruments of policy, Agamben argued that the hope of any such 'return' is illusory, since the normal is constituted and sustained by the exception which remains at work within it. Even when exceptional or emergency measures are not actualised in policies, they remain potentialities of state action and may indeed be more effective *as* potentialities, capable of regulating conduct by the sheer threat of their actualisation. Doing away with exceptionalism through the fortification of the norm is at best futile and at worst counterproductive, since what is simultaneously fortified is the capacity to act on the basis of the norm's suspension.

Agamben uses Nancy's term 'ban' (Nancy 1993: 43–4) to describe this relationship of inclusive exclusion. What is caught up in the ban is nothing but life itself, in two senses: a life that is exposed to the violence of the power that suspends the law, and the law that by virtue of its suspension itself becomes indistinguishable from life. The life that is caught up in the state of exception is not simply 'let be' as irrelevant to power but is rather abandoned *to* its continuing force yet stripped of the protections that its positive norms may have afforded (Agamben 1998: 28). This is precisely the situation at which life *becomes bare*. Perhaps 'bared life' would be a better term for the object caught up in the sovereign ban, since it would emphasise the violent aspect of being stripped of all protections and abandoned to the force of law whose positive content has been suspended and which is therefore, in Agamben's influential formula, 'in force without significance' (ibid.: 51).

Let us consider this formula in more detail. What does it mean to say that in the state of exception the law remains in force without significance? In *The Time that Remains* Agamben offers three characteristics of this condition. Firstly, it entails an 'absolute indeterminacy between inside and outside', whereby 'the law includes that which it rejected from itself' (Agamben 2005b: 105), so that there is no longer any outside of the law. In this manner, the law coincides with reality itself through its auto-suspension. Secondly, in the state of exception it is impossible to distinguish between observance and transgression of the law. Perfectly innocent actions, like walking, smiling, holding hands or dancing, may be *found* to be transgressive, insofar as the law no longer applies in defining transgression, just as ostensibly transgressive, illegal or violent acts may be found to be in accordance with the suspended law, if they are politically expedient, such as in the case of mob violence against political protesters. 'The law, inasmuch as it simply coincides with reality, is absolutely unobservable, and unobservability is the originary figure of the norm' (ibid.: 105). Finally, insofar as its positive content is suspended and its application is unobservable, the law ends up 'absolutely informulable' (ibid.: 106), no longer accessible in terms of a prescription or a prohibition. Agamben relies on the example of the status of the Weimar Constitution after the suspension of its key articles by the Reichstag Fire Decree of 28 February 1933. These articles, dealing with personal and civil liberties, were simply suspended without being replaced with new regulations, making it impossible to differentiate between the licit and the illicit.

Thus the state of exception cannot be defined in terms of the fullness of positive powers granted to or assumed by the sovereign: it is not a 'pleromatic state of the law, as in the dictatorial model, but a kenomatic state, an emptiness and standstill of the law' (Agamben 2005a: 48). And yet, insofar as in Schmitt's theory the state of exception remains a sovereign prerogative, this state of emptiness remains annexed to the law as the condition of the very possibility of its application to life. It is this paradoxical condition of the 'incorporated void' that Agamben terms the 'original political relation' that founds political communities as we know them. Dismissing every attempt at a social contract theory or the efforts to ground communities in any criterion of belonging or even, as Schmitt does, in the conflict between friend and enemy, Agamben confidently transfers to the political domain his ontological insight discussed in the previous chapter: *the sole foundation of Western politics is negative.* In order to elucidate the significance of this claim let us address Agamben's critique of sovereign power in his commentary on the author most strongly associated with the modern concept of sovereignty, Thomas Hobbes.

State of Nature

Agamben confronts the Hobbesian figure of the state of nature early on in the first part of *Homo Sacer*, devoted to the reconstitution of the logic of sovereignty (1998: 15–29). He questions the familiar thesis of the temporal *antecedence* and spatial *exteriority* of the state of nature to the Commonwealth. According to this reading, the state of nature as the state of war of every man against every man is a pre-political condition, which is negated in the formation of the Commonwealth through the surrender of everyone's natural rights to the sovereign. In contrast, for Agamben the state of nature is not a *precondition* of the institution of sovereignty that recedes into oblivion once the civil order is established, but rather it 'survives' within this order in the form of the state of exception, in which sovereign power finds full manifestation:

> [Sovereignty] presents itself as the incorporation of the state of nature in society, or, if one prefers, as a state of indistinction between nature and culture, between violence and law, and this very indistinction constitutes specifically sovereign violence. The state of nature is therefore not truly external to *nomos* but rather contains its virtuality. Exteriority – the law of nature and the principle of the preservation of one's own life – is truly the innermost centre of the political system and the political system lives off it in the same way that the rule, according to Schmitt, lives off the exception. (Ibid.: 35–6)

Thus, the Hobbesian state of nature may no longer be treated as a pre-political condition but, as the state of exception, becomes the epitome of the political as such. 'The state of nature is not a real epoch chronologically prior to the foundation of the City, but a principle internal to the City, which appears at the moment the City is considered *tanquam dissoluta*, "as if it were dissolved"' (ibid.: 105). Agamben's claim is hardly a deformation of Hobbes's own argument, which, after all, never maintained an absolute spatiotemporal disjunction between the two conditions. Indeed, aside from the reference to the 'savage people of America', Hobbes's famous examples of life in the state of nature do not concern any ancient or prehistoric condition but are resolutely contemporary:

> let him therefore consider with himselfe, when taking a journey he armes himselfe and seeks to go well-accompanied; when going to sleep, he locks his dores; when even in his house he locks his chests; and this when he knows there bee Lawes, and publike officers, armed, to revenge all injuries shall bee done him. (Hobbes 1985 [1651]: 186–7)

These examples invoke the dangers perceived and acted upon by individuals who actually live in the Commonwealth under the protection of the sovereign. Yet they are nonetheless deployed to gain the readers' adherence to the thesis about the 'nasty, brutish and short' (ibid.: 186) character of life in a wholly different condition, defined by the absence of the sovereign. If the state of nature is best illustrated by examples from our everyday existence in the Commonwealth, it can hardly be considered a real historical condition preceding its foundation.

Indeed, even in Hobbes's own argument the state of nature is not presented as a real historical condition. While Agamben has been read as 'dehistoricizing the Hobbesian construction' of the state of nature (Rasch 2007: 101), this construction can hardly be dehistoricised because it was never historical to begin with. As Foucault has demonstrated, the 'war of every man against every man' that characterises the state of nature is manifestly not a real historical condition, but a self-consciously fictitious construct, deployed rhetorically to legitimise the existence of the state:

> [What] Hobbes calls the war of every man against every man is in no sense a real historical war, but a play of presentations that allows every man to evaluate the threat that every man represents to him, to evaluate the willingness of others to fight, and to assess the risk that he himself would run if he resorted to force. Sovereignty is established not by the fact of warlike domination, but, on the contrary, by a calculation that makes it possible to avoid war. For Hobbes, it is a nonwar that founds the State and gives it its form. (Foucault 2003: 270)

Contrary to the familiar image, Hobbes was neither a naturalist nor an essentialist, who posited a pre-political state of nature that subsequent criticism would then reveal to be fictitious. On the contrary, what Hobbes did is consciously produce a *fiction*, whose only semblance to reality is uncannily provided by the exceptional moments of the dissolution of the social order or the dangers that persist even in the ordered Commonwealth. While the criticism that Hobbes anticipated (1985 [1651]: 186–8) accuses him of passing the fiction (the concept of state of nature) for reality (an actual pre-political stage), the situation is exactly the opposite. By generalising the experiences of the crisis of the civil order and synthesising them into an originary condition of human existence, Hobbes turns *reality into fiction*, i.e. transforms the reality of the state of exception into a fiction of the state of nature, in which the sovereign violence that characterises the state of exception is cast as a ubiquitous feature of relations between human beings. It is precisely this operation that permits Hobbes to banish from the 'City' what is originally born in the City itself.

In contrast, Agamben's goal is to restore the state of nature to its status of the product of sovereign power, a contingency that is an *effect* of sovereign decision as opposed to a contingency that *calls* for sovereign decision. Thus, what Agamben does is not dehistoricise Hobbes's state of nature, but rather restore reality to this ahistorical figure by dismantling the spatiotemporal distinction between the state of nature and the Commonwealth and recasting the state of nature as a 'principle internal to the City'. The state of nature is constituted by the sovereign decision that, by treating the civil state as dissolved, suspends the operation of its internal laws and norms that define it as *bios* and thereby reduces the existence of its population to 'bare life'. In this condition, the Covenant is treated as void and the subject is simultaneously abandoned *by* the sovereign, i.e. left without his protection, and abandoned *to* the sovereign's unlimited exercise of violence. In this manner, the fictitious condition of war of all against all gives way to a real, if no less terrifying, condition of the exposure of each and all to the sovereign violence arising from the suspension of the law. As Agamben reminds us (1998: 35), 'in Hobbes the state of nature survives in the person of the sovereign who is the only one to preserve its natural *ius contra omnes*'. Insofar as we establish that the state of nature is not an antecedent epoch, its 'survival' in the figure of the sovereign must be treated as a metaphor that assists Hobbes in the legitimation of sovereign violence manifested most explicitly in the right to punish:

[It] is manifest that the Right which the Common-wealth (that is, he or they that represent it) have to Punish, is not grounded on any concession or gift of the Subjects. For the Subjects did not give the Soveraign that right; but onely in laying down their, strengthened him to use his own, as he should think fit, for the preservation of them all: so that it *was not given, but left to him*, and to him onely; and (excepting the limits set him by naturall Law) as entire, as in the condition of meer Nature, and of warre of every one against his neighbour. (Hobbes 1985 [1651]: 354; emphasis added)

Yet what does it mean for this right to be 'left' to the sovereign if we reject the idea of the temporal antecedence of the state of nature? What we are dealing with here is not a residue from a pre-political era but rather a remainder that is temporally coextensive with the political order in the manner of Agamben's figure of the transcendental origin. Every legal system necessarily inscribes within itself something that is radically heterogeneous to it and cannot be represented in its terms, the 'nothingness', from which the sovereign decision 'emanates' in Schmitt's famous formulation (Schmitt 1985a: 12). Similarly, Agamben argues that

[t]his space devoid of law seems to be so essential to the juridical order that it must seek in every way to assure itself a relation with it, as if in order to ground itself the juridical order necessarily had to maintain itself in relation with an anomie. (Agamben 2005a: 51)

Thus, at the heart of any normative system there resides the ineradicable potentiality of its self-suspension, whereby the rights 'given' to the sovereign (as well as rights given by him to the subjects) are rendered inoperative by the realisation of the originary right that was 'left' to the sovereign. The state of nature is thus nothing other than the inoperative 'being-in-potentiality' of the law (Agamben 1998: 35), its already familiar potential *not to be*, i.e. 'it is what remains of law if law is wholly suspended' (Agamben 2005a: 80). The Hobbesian state of nature is not a prehistoric condition that we have long abandoned for the civil state, but rather a real and contemporary condition of being abandoned *by* this state, of being captured in the sovereign ban.

The stakes of this discussion of the status of the state of nature far exceed any historico-philological concerns. If, as the facile reading goes, Hobbes's sovereign saves us from the war of all against all in the state of nature and protects us by preventing any relapse into that state, then, as William Rasch notes, 'the political, however temporary and flawed it may be, is cherished because it establishes the hope of civil peace. [The] principle of sovereignty is consequently seen as a necessarily imperfect but nevertheless still *necessary* solution to a perpetual problem' (Rasch 2007: 102; emphasis original). However, if we concur with Agamben that 'the problem that Hobbes thinks he solves is in reality the *product* of the political space he creates' (ibid.: 102; emphasis original), then the line of reasoning, espoused by the philosophers of the political from Hobbes to Schmitt and beyond, becomes incongruous if not outright obscene. If the state of nature is the product of the political, then the flaws and imperfections of the political, including the periodic or perpetual relapses into the state of exception, can by definition no longer be justified as 'lesser evils' in comparison with the 'return' to the state of nature, since they *are* nothing but this return itself, the secure Commonwealth being entirely indistinct from the perilous sovereign ban.

Abandoned Life

Having outlined the formal logic of the sovereign ban, whereby the juridical order incorporates within itself the potentiality of its own suspension, let us now address the form of life confined in this ban. Perhaps the most famous of all Agamben's paradigms is the figure of *homo sacer* in Roman law that exemplifies the subject caught up in the ban. According to Pompius Festus, a 'sacred man' is one who has been 'judged on account of a crime' and may not be sacrificed, yet may be killed without committing homicide (Agamben 1998: 71). *Homo sacer* is thus excluded from both human law (as a being that can be killed with impunity) and divine law (as a being that cannot be given over to the gods). Yet, in an already recognisable twist, Agamben interprets this exclusion as simultaneously inclusive: '*homo sacer* belongs to God in the form of unsacrificeability and is included in the community in the form of being able to be killed' (ibid.: 72). This subject is included in the political order as wholly exposed to the potentiality of violent death that, moreover, carries no sacrificial sense whatsoever but is perfectly senseless.[1] *Homo sacer* is thus the embodiment of bare life produced in the sovereign ban and may be grasped in terms of the inversion of the definition of the sovereign: 'the sovereign is the one with respect to whom all men are potentially *homines sacri*, [while] *homo sacer* is the one to whom all mean act as sovereign' (ibid.: 84).

At first glance, the figure of *homo sacer* has as little contempo-rary relevance in Western democracies as the figure of the sovereign existing on the outer limits of the law. Yet, in Agamben's argument, modern democracy did not abandon either the logic of sovereignty or bare life as its object, but rather 'shattered it and disseminated it into every individual body, making it what is at stake in political conflict' (ibid.: 124). While the complicated genealogy of this process is beyond the scope of our book, we may simply recall such land-mark events as the writ of *habeas corpus* in late seventeenth-century England, the French Declaration of the Rights of Man and Citizen in 1789, the rapid increase in the number of refugees and the state-less in the aftermath of World War I, the rise of humanitarianism and the discourse of human rights in the post-World War II period, and so on. Every step in the democratic dissemination of sovereignty throughout the social body was accompanied by the subjection of individual bodies as 'bare lives'.

> [The] principle of nativity and the principle of sovereignty are now irrevo-cably united in the body of the 'sovereign subject' so that the foundation of the new nation-state may be constituted. What lies at the basis of the modern state is not man as a free and conscious political subject, but, above all, man's bare life, the simple birth that as such is invested with the principle of sovereignty. (Ibid.: 128)

The sovereign and *homo sacer* may well coexist in the same person who may be both the bearer of inalienable human rights and the object of governmental interventions that put its very existence at stake: '[he] who will appear as the bearer of rights and the new sov-ereign subject can only be constituted as such through the repetition of the sovereign exception and the isolation of bare life in himself' (ibid.: 128). The sovereign subject of rights becomes the abject bearer of bare life whenever the recognition of these rights by the state is suspended in the state of exception, which, as we have seen, remains a potentiality of every existing political order.

The emblematic case here is that of refugees and the stateless who, having lost or forgone the citizenship of their states without gaining the citizenship of another state, find themselves abandoned by the law to purely arbitrary sovereign violence. Agamben follows Hannah Arendt in interpreting the plight of the refugees as the proof of the vacuity of the very idea of human rights. Refugees are perfect corre-lates of the 'rights of man', since they are by definition deprived of all rights *other* than human rights. Yet rather than benefit from the only rights for which they are eligible, they are abandoned to the power that does not recognise them as subjects of rights and, for this reason, as properly 'human' (see Arendt 1973: 267–302; Agamben 1998: 126–34; 2000: 16). The figure of *homo sacer* is thus not an archaic remnant from the dark ages of autocracy but is only fully coming into its own with the democratic dissemination of sovereignty. Just as democracy can easily collapse into totalitarianism,[2] so the sovereign freedoms and rights of the sovereign subject can always be converted into subjection to sovereign power.

The abandonment of the *homo sacer* to sovereign violence finds its institutional form in the concentration camp, which Agamben, famously and scandalously, termed 'the nomos of the modern' (1998: 166). Since this thesis has given rise to numerous misunderstandings and facile criticism of 'jarringly disconcerting claims', 'wild statements' and 'unregulated decisions' (see respectively LaCapra 2007: 133; Laclau 2007: 22; Norris 2005: 273), it is important to be clear about what Agamben intended with it. It is evidently not a matter of saying that we all live in concentration camps or are all equally likely to end up in them any time soon, even though we ought not to forget that camps of all kinds (refugee camps, special prisons, detention centres, correctional facilities, rehab centres, deportation facilities, and so on) are indeed becoming everyday reality for increasing numbers of people worldwide. Similarly to the notion of *homo sacer*, the camp is one of the hyperbolic paradigms whose problematic status in Agamben's work we addressed in the discussion of Bartleby. If the 'state of exception comes more and more to the foreground as the fundamental political structure and ultimately begins to become the rule', then the *nomos*, i.e. the fundamental spatial order, of modern politics must reflect this shift topologically: 'today it is not the city but rather the camp that is the fundamental biopolitical paradigm of the West' (Agamben 1998: 181). If the exception is everywhere becoming the rule, then it is not surprising that the paradigm of such a politics must be a space in which the indistinction of the rule and the exception, norm and fact, law and life, is absolute and the curse of bare life as the negative foundation of politics becomes fully transparent.

> [The] camp is the structure in which the state of exception is realized *normally*. The sovereign no longer limits himself to deciding on the exception on the basis of recognizing a given factual situation (danger to public safety). The camp is a hybrid of law and fact, in which the two terms have become indistinguishable. Whoever entered the camp moved in a zone of indistinction between outside and inside, exception and rule,

licit and illicit, in which the very concepts of subjective right and juridical protection no longer made any sense. Insofar as its inhabitants were stripped of every political status and wholly reduced to bare life, the camp was also the most absolute biopolitical space ever to have been realized, in which power confronts nothing but pure life, without any mediation. (Ibid.: 170–1)

Thus the camp is the materialisation of the state of exception in its most regular or normal form, of the exception-*as*-rule, which, in Agamben's reading, is the tendency of contemporary world politics. While the claim that the camp is the *nomos* of modernity would evidently be unwarranted if it was read as an attempt to subsume all topologies of modern social or political life (e.g. parliaments, factories, universities, hospitals, and so on) under the model of the camp, it is not entirely illegitimate as a paradigm of modern politics, since it illuminates the structure of the indistinction between the exception and the rule in the most stark and unadulterated manner. It is not that all modern political spaces are camps but rather that the camp illuminates most starkly what all these spaces may become if the tendency towards the indistinction of the exception and the rule is fully actualised in them. Any institutional space, structured according to the principle of the ban, is a variation of the model of the camp, irrespectively of whether mass atrocities are committed there or not (yet).

It is from the same perspective that we should consider the third controversial paradigmatic figure that Agamben presents in *Homo Sacer* and develops in detail in the sequel to that work, *Remnants of Auschwitz*: the *Muselmann*. In the Nazi concentration camps the *Muselmänner* were those inmates who were so weakened and decrepit both physically and mentally that they were perceived as the 'living dead', occupying the limit between humanity and inhumanity. The *Muselmann* exemplifies most starkly the often obscured difference between bare life and natural life: there is nothing natural, animal or instinctual left in the *Muselmann*, his 'nature' being taken away from him along with his 'reason', 'dignity' or any other feature of the positive order of *bios*. And yet the *Muselmann* remains alive, precisely in the sense of bare life obtained by the progressive subtraction of every possible qualification that leaves one alive 'as such', in one's pure being (Agamben 1999c: 41–86). Similarly to the Voice in Agamben's philosophy of language, which is a purely negative figure obtained by the 'removal' or negation of natural or animal sound, bare life is removed as much from nature as it is from culture.

The horror of the camps consists precisely in the fact that they managed to produce, as a real existence, what has hitherto remained an obscene fiction, a life wholly devoid of any attributes. Agamben refers to this real existence of bare life as 'survival', interpreting it as the main effect of the biopolitical capture of life in the state of exception: 'biopolitics [operates] on the disjunction between the organic and the animal, realizing the dream of a vegetative life that indefinitely survives the life of relation, a non-human life infinitely separable from human existence' (ibid.: 154). Whereas for Foucault sovereign power consists in making die and modern biopolitics consists in making live, Agamben's sovereign biopolitics must be grasped as 'making survive': 'biopower's supreme ambition is to produce, in a human body, the absolute separation of the living being and the speaking being, *zoe* and *bios*, the inhuman and the human' (ibid.: 156). The production of this separation evidently cannot be grasped in terms of any instrumental rationality or functional logic. It is not a matter of biopolitics producing a positive form of life cor-relative with the principles of a certain political ideology, such as a liberal, socialist or fascist subject. The separation at work in 'making survive' is so extreme as to ultimately separate the *Muselmann* as its product from the very power that made him or her such, making power itself powerless before a being that has become indifferent to everything. The *Muselmann* is the embodiment of the perversity of biopolitics in the condition of nihilism where the exception becomes the rule and the machine of government is running on empty, no longer distinguishing between making die and making live, between friends and enemies, but ceaselessly and senselessly strips life of all forms and predicates, ending up with a bare life that can no longer even suffer the violence it is subjected to.

The three figures of bare life, *homo sacer* and the *Muselmann* are often equated or treated as homologous, which leads to the criti-cism of Agamben as allegedly equating well-off citizens of Western democracies with concentration camp inmates (cf. Ojakangas 2005; De la Durantaye 2009: 210–11). It is important to stress that the three terms differ in terms of both conceptual scope and the intensity of their connotations. Evidently, bare life is the most general term of all and embraces not merely the lives of ostensible victims but also sovereigns themselves, from Roman emperors to Hitler, whose authority (*auctoritas*) (Agamben 2005a: 74–88; 1998: 172–3, 184) was inscribed in their very bodies, supplementing and exceeding the formal powers (*potestas*) conferred by the law. Other examples of bare life include comatose patients, doctors experimenting on their own bodies, the bandit or the exiled, and so on (Agamben 1998: 181–6). The *Muselmann* is only the most extreme and hyperbolic example of bare life, a life from which *everything* positive has been stripped and all that exists is permanent exposure to death in a space of confinement: '[it] is the final biopolitical substance to be isolated in the biological continuum. Beyond the Muselmann lies only the gas chamber' (Agamben 1999c: 85). *Homo sacer* may then be understood as an errant figure between the extremes of the more 'benign' modes of bare life (such as body artists, experimental scientists, romantic outcasts) and the *Muselmann* as its negative limit. Unlike the camp inmate, the original Roman *homo sacer* was not confined and remained free despite his exclusion and exposure; the literal deformation of life that is actualised for the *Muselmann* remains only potential for *homo sacer*. This is why it would be obscene to say that 'we are all *Muselmänner*', which Agamben never said, but it makes sense to claim, as Agamben does repeatedly, that 'we are all virtually *homines sacri*' (Agamben 1998: 115).

Towards a Real State of Exception

The topology of the state of exception is in Agamben's argument the quasi-transcendental condition of Occidental politics, characterising all Western political orders from the ancient times onwards (for a critique see, for example, Laclau 2007; Fitzpatrick 2005; Deranty 2008). What *does* vary historically is the precise status of the state of exception within the order that it founds. In Agamben's reading, the political history of the West is marked by the gradual *expansion* of the state of exception from a circumscribed area within the political order, which manifested itself in concrete occasions of public tumult, the death of the ruler, anomic feasts, and so on (Agamben 2005a: 65–73) to the entire domain of *nomos* itself:

> [W]hat happened and is still happening before our eyes is that the 'juridi-cally empty' space of the state of exception (in which the law is in force in the figure of its own dissolution, and in which everything that the sovereign deemed *de facto* necessary could happen) has transgressed its spatiotemporal boundaries and now, overflowing outside them, is start-ing to coincide with the normal order, in which everything again becomes possible. (Agamben 1998: 38)

As long as the exception as the constitutive outside of the political order remained marginal, its foundational role could be concealed beneath the veneer of the positive norms instituted by the state, violated only as a matter of 'emergency' or 'necessity'. Yet, in Agamben's argument, starting from World War I (which, for him, is the decisive event of European, and subsequently global, nihilism), the exception and the rule have become increasingly difficult to distinguish (1998: 37–8; 2004b: 76–7). Examples of this indistinction are numerous, ranging from the expansion of administrative regulation in all spheres of life that sidelines parliamentary procedures of law-making to wars and military operations undertaken in blatant disregard of international law. Following Benjamin's famous claim in his 'Theses on the Philosophy of History' about the state of exception becoming the rule (1968: 257), Agamben argues that contemporary world politics is characterised by the tendency towards the *coincidence* of the exception and the rule in the apparatus that can only be compared to a 'killing machine':

> [As] long as the two elements (law and anomie) remain correlated yet conceptually, temporally and subjectively distinct, their dialectic can nevertheless function in some way. But when they tend to coincide in the single person, when the state of exception, in which they are bound and blurred together, becomes the rule, then the juridico-political system transforms itself into a killing machine. The normative aspect of law can thus be obliterated and contradicted with impunity by a government violence that – while ignoring international law externally and producing a permanent state of exception internally – nevertheless still claims to be applying the law. (Agamben 2005a: 86–7)

In an already familiar rhetorical strategy Agamben invokes the image of an apparatus of law under the condition of nihilism, in which all positive content of the law is exhausted and all that remains is its pure force, indistinguishable from sheer violence and yet confined into a separate, pseudo-sacred sphere of legality. Just as in the condition of nihilism the Voice as the negative foundation of language ultimately assumes centre-stage in voiding speech of all meaningful content and leaving it with the quasi-mystical communication of the Nothing itself, so the law entirely consumed by the exception is a machine that keeps running on empty without any positive productivity other than the consumption of the lives it captures within itself.

Yet, if the problem has a familiar ring, then so must the solution. Let us first consider two apparently self-evident but ultimately false solutions to the problem of the sovereign ban. The first consists in the perfection of the legal system in order to banish every trace of the exception from it: if the problem with the law is the potentiality of its suspension, why not make such a suspension impossible? Agamben is scathing about every attempt to resolve the problem of the state of exception by bringing it

> back within its spatially and temporally defined boundaries in order to then reaffirm the primacy of a norm and of rights that are themselves ulti-mately grounded in it. From the real state of exception in which we live, it is not possible to return to the state of law. (Ibid.: 87)

The legal-positivist argument that characterised the liberalism of Schmitt's time as well as many of its contemporary descendants is convincingly refuted by Agamben's radicalisation of Schmitt's decisionism, which demonstrates the dependence of the rule on the exception, whereby every positive right is conditioned by the sover-eign's 'preservation' of the right to punish. Any search for a more effective, 'exception-proof' legal system, a perfect *bios* without the inclusive exclusion of *zoe*, is entirely in vain. Modern nihilism is not a matter of the exception somehow escaping its 'proper' confines and running amok but rather of the illumination of its constitutive status for every form of order.

On the other hand, neither is it possible to return from the ban to a pre-political state of nature, a *zoe* not yet degraded by its negation in the *bios*. If the state of nature *were* temporally antecedent to sov-ereign power, then it could at least be envisioned, however naively, as a site of possible redemption. Nonetheless, there is no passage *back* from *bios* to *zoe* and any attempt at such passage only throws us back into the state of exception and the production of bare life.

> There are not *first* life as a natural biological given and anomie as the state of nature and *then* their implication in law through the state of excep-tion. On the contrary, the very possibility of distinguishing life and law, anomie and nomos, coincides with their articulation in the biopolitical machine. (Ibid.: 88)

Moreover, Agamben's account of human subjectivation in language that we have addressed in the previous chapter clearly demonstrates the impossibility of any return to natural existence. The entrance of the human being into language necessarily involves the 'expropria-tion' of all its pre-linguistic experience as a living being, the removal of the natural *phone* as a condition for the acquisition of *logos*. In exactly the same manner, the political existence of humanity is from the outset accompanied by the 'removal' or crossing out of *zoe*, whose inclusive exclusion as a negative foundation of the political order makes impossible any 'return to nature' other than in the form of an obscene and degrading 'dehumanisation' practised in the concentration camps and other loci of the state of exception. Thus, it is impossible to break out of the state of exception through an unequivocal valorisation of either *bios* or *zoe*, which leads Agamben to assert the ultimate futility of maintaining this dualism:

> [Every] attempt to rethink the political space of the West must begin with the clear awareness that we no longer know anything of the classical distinction between *zoe* and *bios*, between private life and political existence, between man as a simple living being at home in the house and man's political existence in the city. There is no return from the camps to classical politics. In the camps, city and house became indistinguishable, and the possibility of differentiating between our biological body and our political body was taken from us forever. (Agamben 1998: 188)

Yet if this is so, then the state of exception appears almost immutable. It is at this point that Agamben deploys his already familiar 'comic' move of finding the 'saving power' in the conditions of utmost danger, hopelessness or despair. We have no hope of evading the state of exception by opting for the uncontaminated normativity of *bios* or the pure naturalism of *zoe*. The only solution to the problem of the political is to be found within the state of exception and consists in rendering inoperative the entire 'killing machine' of biopolitical sovereignty:

> if it is possible to attempt to halt the machine, this is because between violence and law, between life and norm there is no substantial articulation. Alongside the movement that seeks to keep them in relation at all cost, there is a countermovement that, working in a reverse direction in law and in life, always seeks to loosen what has been artificially and violently linked. (Agamben 2005a: 86)

Following Benjamin, Agamben terms this countermovement 'the real state of exception', as opposed to the 'fictive' state of exception that remains connected to the law and appropriated by the sovereign. This real state of exception would be the precise equivalent of the *experimentum linguae* that speaks the sheer facticity of language and the community wholly contained in the *factum pluralitatis*. In the biopolitical lexicon introduced in this chapter, such a state of exception would evidently consist in rendering inoperative every form of *bios* so as to reclaim and reaffirm the bare life produced and caught up in it.

In *Homo Sacer* the path toward the real state of exception is envisioned in terms of a radical distancing from the law:

> Only if it is possible to think the Being of abandonment beyond every idea of the law (even that of the empty form of law's being in force without significance) will we have moved out of the paradox of sovereignty towards a politics freed from every ban. (Agamben 1998: 59)

This admittedly arcane claim must be understood in the context of Benjamin's seminal essay 'Critique of Violence' in which he distinguished between law-preserving and law-establishing violence as two forms of 'mythic' violence. Law-preserving violence pertains to the order of 'constituted power' and consists in legal, para- or extra-legal measures that sustain the existing law and order of things. Law-establishing violence pertains to the dimension of 'constituent power' and serves to institute a new form of order, which makes it *ipso facto* impossible to subsume under the existing norms and laws (Benjamin 1978: 277–300).

Agamben reinterprets the problem of the relation between the anarchic and revolutionary violence of constituent power and the stabilising and ordering violence of constituted power in the context of his theory of potentiality, discussed in Chapter 2. While the prioritisation of actuality over potentiality would logically entail the complete exhaustion of constituent power in the constituted order that it establishes, the affirmation of constituent power is only thinkable on the basis of the assertion of the ontological primacy of potentiality. Antonio Negri, Agamben's critical interlocutor since the 1970s, ventures precisely such an affirmation, separating constituent power as creative and revolutionary power of the multitude from the constituted power of the state or any other structure of authority.

> [Constituting] power is the act of choice, the punctual determination that opens a horizon, the radical enacting of something that did not exist before and whose conditions of existence stipulated that the creative act cannot lose its characteristics in creating. Sovereignty, on the other hand, arises as the establishment – and therefore, as the end – of constituting power, as the consumption of the freedom brought by constituting power. (Negri cited in Agamben 1998: 43)

Negri's argument belongs to the long series of attempts of the radical-democratic tradition to theorise constituent power in the manner that prevents its exhaustion in the constituted order to which it gives rise, the tradition whose twentieth-century paradigms include Trotsky's 'permanent revolution' and Mao's 'uninterrupted revolution' (Agamben 1998: 41–2). While Negri wishes to dissociate the potentiality of constituent power from the 'actualising' force of sovereignty, Agamben rather finds the ontological structure of sovereignty precisely in the Aristotelian concept of potentiality, which, as we recall, is always potentiality *not to be*. While the conventional reading of sovereignty as supreme law-giving power emphasises the 'positive' dimension of potentiality ('I can'), to be worthy of the name this potentiality must be accompanied by its 'negative' counterpart ('I can *not*'), which refers precisely to the possibility for the sovereign to *suspend* the law that it itself gives, to treat the Commonwealth *tanquam dissoluta*. It is in this suspended state that potentiality can maintain a real existence without passing completely into actuality and this is precisely the way the law exists in the state of exception: 'the sovereign ban, which applies to the exception in no longer applying, corresponds to the structure of potentiality, which maintains itself in relation to actuality precisely through its ability not to be' (ibid.: 46). It is thus impossible to oppose sovereignty as the actualising force of order to the constituent power of the multitude as creative potentiality:

> potentiality and actuality are simply the two faces of the sovereign self-grounding of Being. Sovereignty is always double because Being, as potentiality, suspends itself, maintaining itself in a relation of ban with itself in order to realize itself as absolute actuality. At the limit, pure potentiality and pure actuality are indistinguishable, and the sovereign is precisely this zone of indistinction. (Ibid.: 47)

Thus, sovereign power always already possesses all those features of potentiality and creativity that Negri and other thinkers in the radical-democratic or populist traditions try to reserve for the multitude, the people, the revolutionary party, the councils or other embodiments of constituent power. Agamben's argument sheds light on the problem that has plagued arguably the entire history of revolutionary movements, whose victories have, with important variations, largely led to the reproduction of the sovereign and statist logics that these movements initially targeted. Examples of French, Russian and Chinese revolutions are sufficient to observe how sovereign power recuperates the creative potentialities ostensibly advanced against it. In Agamben's interpretation, this repeated failure of radical politics has to do with its commitment to law and sovereignty in the guise of apparent opposition to them in the form of constituent power.

> Politics has suffered a lasting eclipse because it has been contaminated by law, seeing itself, at best, as constituent power (that is, violence that makes law), when it is not reduced to merely the power to negotiate with the law. The only truly political action, however, is that, which severs the nexus between violence and law. (Agamben 2005a: 88)

The pathway to a post-statist politics thus does not consist in vain attempts to purify constituent power from the constituted order but in severing the link between power (potentiality) and constitution as such, whatever positive form it takes:

> That constituting power never exhausts itself in constituted power is not enough: sovereign power can also, as such, maintain itself indefinitely, without ever passing into actuality. [One] must think the existence of potentiality without any relation to Being in the form of actuality – not even in the extreme form of the ban and the potentiality not to be – and think the existence of potentiality even without any relation to being in the form of the gift of the self and of letting be. This, however, implies nothing less than thinking ontology and politics beyond every figure of relation. (Agamben 1998: 47)

These lines are among the most enigmatic in Agamben's entire *oeuvre*, yet the conclusion to this chapter of *Homo Sacer* provides us with an important clue for their decipherment. Agamben concludes the discussion of potentiality and law with an invocation of none other than Bartleby, whose 'objection' to the principle of sovereignty was 'stronger' than that of Schelling, Nietzsche or Heidegger (ibid.: 48). It is thus inoperativity that emerges as the solution to the ontologico-political problem of the exception. Indeed, we had this solution in our sights all along, since it was embodied in none other than the sovereign itself as the figure that exists in the world in the suspended, exceptional mode of constitutive alterity. The problem is thus not sovereignty *per se*, which, as we have seen, is but a political translation of the ontological concept of potentiality and is therefore at work in any meaningful notion of freedom (see Prozorov 2007), but rather the *confinement* of this inoperative potentiality within the 'sacred' sphere of the law that makes the state of exception always 'fictive', its anomie always already annexed to or subsumed by the *nomos* (Agamben 2005a: 58–9). The inoperative potentiality of the sovereign exception is thereby brought back 'to work' as a form of power in the same way that the glorious bodies of the blessed are delivered from all functions and tasks, except for the ostensive function, the work of glory. Similarly to the glorious body, the feast or the hymn, in politics inoperative potentiality is withdrawn from free common use and embodied in the figure of the sovereign, leaving its subjects to acclaim the glory of that which they were deprived of.

If this fictitious state of exception is to be made 'real', inoperativity must shed every relation to the law, which entails that it is no longer contained within a single sovereign person or institution but is radically generalised throughout the social realm. The empty throne that symbolised the restriction of inoperativity to a single glorified figure must be smashed into pieces that could never form a single whole. The idea of a dispersed or disseminated sovereignty, in which potentiality is no longer restricted to a particular person or structure, recalls Agamben's idea of a universalist community wholly contained in the *factum pluralitatis* of being-in-common without a common identity, task or vocation. It is precisely this 'coming community' of whatever being that is the subject of politics in the real state of exception, a politics that is post-juridical or post-statist without being in a strict sense post-sovereign, since sovereignty in the ontological sense of potentiality, of the sheer affirmation 'I can' (cf. Derrida 2005: 11–13, 23), is not only *not* absent from this community but is universally dispersed within and absorbed by it. The real state of exception thus consists in the *reappropriation* of the sovereignty that characterises our very being, the reappropriation of our potentiality from the ban and, ultimately, the appropriation of our abandonment as such (see Prozorov 2009a).

Thus potentiality without relation to the law is nothing other than inoperative praxis that neither sustains nor institutes a form of order but rather deactivates it, dissolving the relation between law and life, norm and fact, established in the state of exception. In his 'Critique of Violence' Benjamin terms this mode of action that is neither law-preserving nor law-establishing 'divine violence' (1978: 297–300). While this esoteric concept has given rise to numerous divergent interpretations (see Derrida 1992; Žižek 2009: 157–73; Weber 2008: 176–94; Martell 2011; Critchley 2012: 207–45), Agamben understands divine violence as a 'pure means' (2000: 116–18, 57–60; 2005a: 60–4) that has lost every relationship to any end and merely manifests its own pure mediality. Similarly to the already familiar concepts of 'whatever being' and 'being-thus' a pure means is a being wholly exposed in the facticity of its being, subtracted from an identity or function and for this reason available for new forms of use. Divine violence is pure not in the sense of its transcendent or unearthly origin but in the same sense that Benjamin's 'universal language' was pure in being devoid of any signifying content, saying nothing but its own communicability: 'To a word that does not bind, that neither commands nor prohibits anything, but says only itself, would correspond an action as pure means, which shows only itself, without any relation to an end' (Agamben 2005a: 88).

What is divine about this exposure? Evidently, divine violence is not the violence authorised by a divinity or purified of all earthly considerations, but quite simply a mode of praxis that deactivates its tie to the law, rendering it inoperative and thus available for a new, non-instrumental use in the manner we described in Chapter 2 in terms of profanation and play: 'one day humanity will play with law just as children play with disused toys, not in order to restore them to the canonical use but to free them from it for good' (ibid.: 64). While we are conventionally inclined to only accept or forgive violence in the situations where it is 'absolutely necessary', divine violence is on the contrary devoid of any claim to necessity and divorced from every end. What is divine about it is precisely its utter indifference to any end, its non-strategic gratuitousness that contrasts with the calculative deployment of violence by various governmental apparatuses. Yet it would evidently be absurd to understand this gratuitous character of violence as the unconditional 'licence to kill'. While the reference to divinity in Benjamin's formulation is sometimes interpreted in terms of omnipotence, we may rather suggest that it should be understood in the diametrically opposite sense, resonating with the notion of 'weak messianic power' that Benjamin's 'Theses on the Philosophy of History' invoke (Benjamin 1968: 254; cf. Agamben 2005b: 125–37, Santner 2006: 87–95, Dickinson 2011: 84–98; Prozorov 2007: 143–6). Messianic power is 'weak' not only because it is comparatively weaker than sovereign power but because it operates by *weakening* the latter without producing its own form of sovereignty, its power being wholly exhausted in its Bartlebyan 'decreation' of established orders. Divine violence does not seek to defeat sovereign power at its own game of establishing and maintaining the law but rather seeks to put an end to the game itself.

Form-of-Life

What does it mean to live in the real state of exception? What happens to bare life when it is no longer caught up in the sovereign ban but exists with no relation to the law? Is this life still bare? Is it *bios*, *zoe* or perhaps something else entirely? In the final paragraph to *Homo Sacer* Agamben presents the idea of life in the real state of exception in rather elliptic terms:

> Just as the biopolitical body of the West cannot be simply given back to its natural life in the *oikos*, so it cannot be overcome in a passage to a new body – a technical body or a wholly political or glorious body – in which a different economy of pleasures and vital functions would once and for all resolve the interlacement of *zoe* and *bios* that seems to define the political destiny of the West. This biopolitical body that is bare life must itself instead be transformed into the site for the constitution and installation of a form of life that is wholly exhausted in bare life and a *bios* that is only its own *zoe*. (Agamben 1998: 188)

Agamben's formulations in this fragment are easy to misunderstand. After all, doesn't a '*bios* that is only its own *zoe*' correspond precisely to the structure of the sovereign ban? It certainly does, since, as we have seen, the state of exception is the only site of political praxis left to us, neither pure *bios* nor pure *zoe* being any longer accessible. Yet while sovereignty operates by capturing and separating bare life from the positive forms of *bios* or, in what amounts to the same thing, crushing these forms down to the level of pure survival, Agamben makes the opposite move of articulating *zoe* and *bios* into a new figure, in which 'it is never possible to isolate something like naked life' (Agamben 2000: 9). Thus, as Catherine Mills (2005: 219) has argued, there are not two but *four* figures of life at work in Agamben's argument: besides *bios* and *zoe* that are no longer accessible to us, there is bare life that is obtained by the negation of *zoe* within *bios* and, finally, the articulation of *zoe* and *bios* into a new unity, which Agamben calls *form-of-life*, the hyphenation highlighting the *integrity* of this figure, in which life and its form are inseparable (Agamben 2000: 11; cf. Agamben 1999b: 208). In order to understand the logic of this articulation, we must return to the homology between bare life and the Voice in language or pure being in ontology.

> [In] the syntagm 'bare life', 'bare' corresponds to the Greek *haplos*, the term by which first philosophy defines pure Being. The isolation of the sphere of pure Being, which constitutes the fundamental activity of Western metaphysics, is not without analogies with the isolation of bare life in the realm of Western politics. Precisely these two empty and indeterminate concepts safeguard the keys to the historico-political destiny of the West. And it may be that only if we are able to decipher the political meaning of pure Being will we be able to master the bare life that

expresses our subjection to political power, just as it may be, inversely, that only if we understand the theoretical implications of bare life will we be able to solve the enigma of ontology. (Agamben 1998: 182)

On the basis of this homology, the political resolution of the problem of bare life follows strictly from the Heideggerian affirmation of existence as the sole content of the essence of the human (Heidegger 1962: 67). 'Today *bios* lies in *zoe* exactly as essence, in the Heideggerian definition of Dasein, lies in existence' (Agamben 1998: 188). If the essence of the human is unpresentable in terms of positive predicates ('what one is') but consists in the sheer facticity of its existence ('that one is'), then the form of *bios* proper to the human is indeed its own *zoe*, whose sheer facticity is no longer the negated foundation of *bios* but rather its entire content, there being no other form, essence, task or identity imposed on it. What Agamben calls form-of-life is 'a being that is its own bare existence, [a] life that, being its own form, remains inseparable from it' (ibid.: 188). The notion of form-of-life follows the logic of the *experimentum linguae* that brings to speech the very existence of language and of the coming community whose sole content is the fact of being-in-common. Just as in *Language and Death* Agamben breaks with the ineffability of the Voice and attempts to 'speak the unspeakable' by bringing the existence of language itself to language, so at the end of *Homo Sacer* he affirms the possibility of a form of life that 'brings bare life itself to life' (see Kishik 2012: 99–119).

In *The Kingdom and the Glory*, Agamben elaborates this notion of the form-of-life through an engagement with the theological idea of 'eternal life' (*zoe aionios*). While in Christian theology this idea ultimately took the form of the discourse on the resurrection of the kind we addressed in Chapter 2, Agamben highlights an earlier and more originary understanding of 'eternal life' in Pauline messianism, in which it does not pertain to a hypothetical future condition but rather designates a specific quality of life in the messianic time, characterised by the becoming-inoperative of every determinate identity or vocation, which now appear in the suspended form of the 'as not' (*hos me*) – the notion we shall return to in the following chapter.

Under the 'as not', life cannot coincide with itself and is divided into a life that we live and a life for which and in which we live. To live in the Messiah means precisely to revoke and render inoperative at each instant every aspect of the life that we live and to make the life for which we live, which Paul calls 'the life of Jesus', appear within it. (Agamben 2011: 248)

In this reading, eternal life has nothing to do with the afterlife but is rather a way of living *this* life that renders inoperative all its specific forms of *bios*, its functions, tasks and identities.

Agamben then proceeds from the theological to the philosophical context to elaborate this figure of eternal life in terms of the Spinozan idea of *acquiescentia* (self-contentment), 'the pleasure arising from man's contemplation of himself and his power of activity' (Spinoza cited in Agamben 2011: 250). In Agamben's interpretation it is precisely this contemplation of one's own power that articulates inoperativity and potentiality, opening one's existence to a free and profane use. To the glorious life of the sovereign stands opposed the eternal life of the *homo sacer* restored to its potentiality, a form of life wholly exhausted in the reappropriated bare life (see Chiesa and Ruda 2011).

> [The] life, which contemplates its (own) power to act, renders itself inoperative in all its operations, and lives only (its) livability. In this inoperativity the life that we live is only the life through which we live: only our power of acting and living. Here the *bios* coincides with the *zoe* without remainder. Properly human praxis is sabbatism that, by rendering the specific functions of the living inoperative, opens them to possibility. (Agamben 2011: 251)

Insofar as this 'sabbatical' life renders all positive forms of *bios* inoperative, it coincides with *zoe*, yet insofar as *zoe* is no longer negated as a foundation of *bios*, it does not take the degraded form of bare life. Rather than reduce political life to a pseudo-natural life through acts of dehumanisation, the 'eternal life' of contemplation affirms the potentiality of the human being and thus functions as a

> [metaphysical] operator of anthropogenesis, liberating the living man from his biological or social destiny, assigning him to that indefinable dimension that we are accustomed to call 'politics'. The political is neither a *bios* nor a *zoe*, but the dimension that the inoperativity of contemplation, by deactivating linguistic and corporeal, material and immaterial praxes, ceaselessly opens and assigns to the living. (Ibid.: 251)

What is eternal about this 'eternal life' is then evidently not its span, but rather the excess of potentiality over actuality that is freed when the actual positive forms of life are rendered inoperative in the mode of contemplation.

It is easy to see that, just as the appropriation of the event of language in speech, on which it is modelled, the politics of the form-of-life is made possible by the condition of nihilism, which renders void all positive contents of speech acts and forms of life. Just as the *experimentum linguae* is enabled by the nihilistic perception of the vanity and vacuity of all speech, the affirmation of the inoperative form-of-life in the real state of exception is fortified by the crisis or demise of all other political alternatives to the status quo, particularly in the post-Cold War era, which in the 1990s was optimistically labelled the 'end of history'. While today the diagnosis of the end of history is perceived as naive if not outright ludicrous, it is arguably less productive to endlessly refute it, pointing to every minor event as an apparent 'return' of history, than to rethink it, which is precisely what Agamben has done in his writings from the late 1980s onwards. In the following chapter we shall address Agamben's interpretation of modern nihilism as a post-historical condition and account for his messianic strategy of rendering the historical process inoperative.

Notes

1. This senselessness will become important to Agamben's theorisation of the Shoah in both *Homo Sacer* and *Remnants of Auschwitz*. Agamben rejects the use of the concept of the Holocaust to describe the extermination of European Jews, since it lends a sacrificial aura to the process whose horror is amplified by the total senselessness of the process: 'The Jews were exterminated not in a mad and giant holocaust but exactly as Hitler had announced, "as lice", which is to say, as bare life. The dimension in which the extermination took place is neither religion nor law, but biopolitics' (Agamben 1998: 114. See also Agamben 1999c: 28–31).
2. The twentieth century provides an abundance of examples of the totalitarian conversion of democracy, from the collapse of the Weimar Republic to the degeneration of the democracy of Soviets in post-revolutionary Russia into Stalinist autocracy. Yet Agamben's scandalous invocation of an 'intimate solidarity' between democracy and totalitarianism is not merely grounded in this historical evidence of the fragility of democratic institutions but goes considerably further (Agamben 1998: 10). What accounts for the intimate solidarity of the two regimes is the condition of nihilism that renders both forms of rule devoid of sense and accounts for their 'decadence'. The key inspiration here is Guy Debord's famous theory of the 'society of the spectacle' (1994), which has been important for Agamben's work since the 1970s. For Debord, both totalitarian and democratic regimes were forms of what he called the spectacle, in which authentic existence is replaced by representation and the commodity-form colonises social life as such. Socialist totalitarianism exemplified a 'concentrated' spectacle, in which the sphere of representation was controlled by the state apparatus, while liberal democracy exemplified a

'diffuse' spectacle, in which this control is disseminated throughout civil society. In his later *Comments on the Society of the Spectacle* Debord (2011) introduced the third figure of the 'integrated spectacle', a post-Cold War synthesis of democratic and totalitarian forms that combines enhanced state control with the proliferation of 'private' production of representations (see Agamben 2000: 73–89). This theory is important for understanding Agamben's pessimism about democracy at the very moment of its apparent triumph in the Cold War. What some commentators viewed as the 'end of history', whereby democracy became the 'only game in town', having triumphed over its adversaries, was for Agamben the premonition of democracy's own decay. We shall return to Agamben's diagnosis of the post-Cold War condition in Chapter 5.

Chapter 5

The Time of the End: Inoperative History

In this chapter we shall probe Agamben's affirmation of inoperativity in the domain of history. In the early 1990s Agamben joined other continental philosophers in the criticism of Francis Fukuyama's influential adaptation of the Hegelian-Kojèvian thesis on the *end of history* and developed an alternative notion of the deactivation of the historical process. Tracing Agamben's engagement with Hegel's and Kojève's thought, we shall reconstitute Agamben's version of the end of history in terms of the suspension of the Hegelian *Master–Slave dialectic*. Agamben's end of history has nothing to do with the fulfilment of the immanent logic of the historical process but rather consists in rendering this process inoperative in emancipatory social practices that *subtract* from the identities of both Master and Slave. We shall then elaborate this logic of inoperative historicity by engaging with Agamben's reading of Pauline *messianism*, focusing on his idea of messianic time as the eruption of the *kairos*, a moment of rupture within history that carries an emancipatory possibility. In the conclusion we shall contrast this 'profane messianism' with the katechontic logic of the political that restrains and delays the messianic suspension, perpetuating the reign of sovereign power.

The End of History Revisited

Agamben's *Homo Sacer* and other political works were written in the immediate post-Cold War period and their full appreciation is impossible without considering the context of their emergence and the political-theoretical standpoint they explicitly or implicitly targeted. One of the most influential theoretical responses to the end of the Cold War was the resurgence of the Hegelo-Kojèvian thesis on the end of history, forcefully propagated in Francis Fukuyama's seminal *The End of History and the Last Man* (1992). Even as today Fukuyama's reading of the demise of Soviet socialism as inaugurating the end of history has lost its erstwhile popularity, this should by no means be equated with a successful refutation of his argument.

On the contrary, the post-Cold War proliferation of triumphalist discourses on globalisation, 'transition to democracy', 'democratic peace', and so on is clearly conditioned by the presupposition of the exhaustion of the rivalry between opposed teleological projects and the global hegemony of Western liberal capitalism that was asserted by Fukuyama in the immediate aftermath of the demise of the Soviet Union.

In contrast to the predominant mood of derisive dismissal of Fukuyama's thesis among critical intellectuals, Agamben has engaged with the theme of the end of history seriously and repeatedly. As early as 1985, he argued that 'the one incomparable claim to nobility [that] our own era might legitimately make in regard to the past [was] *that of no longer wanting to be a historical epoch*' (Agamben 1995: 87; emphasis original). While Fukuyama's work is only alluded to but never directly addressed in his writings, Alexandre Kojève became a regular reference in Agamben's work since *Language and Death* and the discussion of his interpretation of the Hegelian dialectic became more direct and explicit starting from the 1992 article 'Notes on Politics' (2000: 109–120) that prefigures many of the theses of *Homo Sacer*. In this chapter we shall address Agamben's critique of Kojève's thesis in the wider context of his politics of inoperativity in order to reconstitute Agamben's alternative, non-dialectical version of the end of history.

Let us begin with Agamben's diagnosis of the era that Fukuyama described in terms of the victory of liberal democracy:

> The fall of the Soviet Communist Party and the unconcealed rule of the capitalist-democratic state on a planetary scale have cleared the field of the two main ideological obstacles hindering the resumption of a political philosophy worthy of our time: Stalinism on one side and progressivism and the constitutional state on the other. The 'great transformation' constituting the final stage of the state form is taking place before our very eyes: this is a transformation that is driving the kingdoms of the Earth (republics and monarchies, tyrannies and democracies, federations and national states) one after the other towards the state of the integrated spectacle (Guy Debord) and towards 'capitalist parliamentarism' (Alain Badiou). Contemporary politics is this devastating experiment that disarticulates and empties institutions and beliefs, ideologies and religions, identities and communities all throughout the planet, so as then to rehash and reinstate their nullified form. (Agamben 2000: 110)

For Agamben, the post-Cold War period is less a triumph of liberalism than a triumph of nihilism that transforms global politics into the 'society of the spectacle', in which the political and legal categories of the previous eras no longer have any meaning:

> terms such as sovereignty, right, nation, people, democracy and general will by now refer to a reality that no longer has anything to do with what these concepts used to designate – and those who continue to use these concepts uncritically literally do not know what they are talking about. (Ibid.: 110)

And yet in this nihilistic condition the 'old regime' of sovereign nation-states, democracy, international law, and so on is not succeeded by a new positive order but rather persists in a 'nullified form' and continues to be described by the concepts that no longer have any meaning (cf. Prozorov 2009b, Chapter 2).

It is this interpretation of the post-Cold War condition as the triumph of nihilism that draws Agamben's attention to the revival of the Hegelo-Kojèvian end of history thesis that he proposes to 'try and take seriously' (ibid.: 110). For Agamben, Fukuyama's liberal version of the end of history is one of the two dominant readings of the contemporary constellation in global politics, the other being the diverse field of globalisation theory. While the former theory views the liberal state as the endpoint of the historical dialectic, the latter approaches the alleged eclipse of the state by the globalising logic of capitalism as the proof of our present still being eminently historical and indeed constituting an 'epoch' of sorts. In contrast, Agamben insists that we should think 'the end of the state and the end of history *at one and the same time* [and] mobilize one against the other' (ibid.: 111; emphasis original).

> [T]he battlefield is divided today in the following way: on one side, there are those who think the end of history without the end of the state (that is, the post-Kojèvian or postmodern theorists of the fulfilment of the historical process of humanity in a homogeneous universal state); on the other side, there are those who think the end of the state without the end of history (that is, progressivists of all sorts). Neither position is equal to its task because to think the extinction of the state without the fulfilment of the historical telos is as impossible as to think a fulfilment of history in which the empty form of state sovereignty would continue to exist. (Ibid.: 110–11)

We easily recognise in the idea of a post-historical state that maintains its form but is devoid of all positive ideological or teleological content the logic of the state of exception that we have reconstituted in the previous chapter: 'What, after all, is a State that survives history, a State sovereignty that maintains itself beyond the accomplishment of its telos, if not a law that is force without signifying?' (Agamben 1998: 60). From this perspective, the post-Kojèvian thought of the post-historical state is equivalent to the affirmation of the 'fictive' state of exception, in which the latter remains tied to the pure form of law. In contrast, thinking the end of history and the end of the state together is equivalent to the affirmation of the real state of exception, a post-statist politics of the integral form-of-life in the community of whatever being. Just as Agamben's theory of the 'real state of exception' radicalised the logic of sovereignty through disseminating it throughout the social realm, his thought of the end of history points to something like a 'real' or 'proper' end of history that goes much further than Fukuyama's teleological liberalism. For Agamben, the end of history must necessarily presuppose a radical crisis of the state or any other form of constituted order:

> Simply because history designates the expropriation itself of human nature through a series of epochs and historical destinies, it does not follow that the fulfilment and the appropriation of the historical telos in question indicate that the historical process of humanity has now cohered in a definitive order (whose management can be handed over to a homogeneous universal state). (Agamben 2000: 111)

The search for a post-historical ethos of humanity becomes entirely heterogeneous to any statist project, but probes the possibilities of the human reappropriation of historicity, whereby time becomes available for free use in social praxis. '[T]his appropriation must open the field to a *nonstatal* and *nonjuridical* politics and human life – a politics and a life that are yet to be entirely thought' (ibid.: 112; emphasis original).

We are thus back to the main feature of Agamben's politics, the appropriation of inoperativity as the originary feature of the human condition that frees the potentialities of human existence from their confinement within the apparatuses of language, law and, as we shall see in this chapter, history itself. Yet what does it mean to render history inoperative? As we shall demonstrate below, Agamben's version of the end of history has little to do with the eschatological reading espoused by Kojève and Fukuyama, in which the end of history is understood as the *final stage* of the unfolding of the historical process that finds its fulfilment in the post-historical totality of the 'universal homogeneous state'. Instead, Agamben resumes Benjamin's project of mobilising the heritage of Judaeo-Christian messianism for a profane revolutionary act of *arresting* the development of history. In other words, history does not end by fulfilling its immanent logic but is rather *brought to an end* in the social practices that suspend its progress. In order to specify the character of these practices, we must first address the key modifications that Agamben introduces into Kojève's version of the end of history. Since it is specifically Kojève's reading of Hegel that Agamben engages with in his work, our discussion below does not address other readings of Hegel nor does it attempt to resolve the controversial question of Hegel's own stance on the end of history (see Grier 1996; Maurer 1996; Harris 1996). Our task is merely to reconstitute Agamben's conception of the end of history on the basis of his critique of Kojève's thesis.

The Workless Slave

In Kojève's reading of Hegel's *Phenomenology of Spirit* (1979 [1807]) history is understood in terms of 'negating action' that takes two forms: fight and work. The historical process is originally brought into motion by the primal human encounter that leads to the 'fight to the death for recognition'. In this fight, one of the participants risks his life and overcomes his antagonist, thereby becoming the Master and reducing the other to the role of the Slave. Yet while history is *initiated* by the violent confrontation and the fear of death that resigns the Slave to slavery, it is in fact work, i.e. the Slave's subsequent labour in the service of the Master, that forms the *substance* of the historical process as the realisation of the future by the negation of the present into the past. It is only through work, i.e. through negating action on the given reality, that humanity becomes 'truly' human, transcending the world of nature. Thus the history of human existence, or, better, human existence *as* history, is from the outset characterised by ineluctable negativity:

> Man is 'total' or 'synthetical', or, better, 'dialectical'; he exists 'for himself' or consciously and articulately, hence he is 'spiritual' or truly human, only to the extent that he implies the constituent-element of Negativity in his being, in his existence and in his 'appearances'. Taken in itself, Negativity is pure nothingness: it *is* not, it does not exist, it does not appear. Therefore, it can exist only as a real negation of Nature. Now, this existence of Negativity is, precisely, specifically human existence. (Kojève 1969: 221)

By his labour of negation the Slave transforms the natural world into the properly human, historical world: 'It is only by work that man is a supernatural being that is conscious of its reality; by working, he is "incarnated" Spirit, he is historical "World", he is "objectivized" History' (Kojève 1969: 23, 25). While the Master passively consumes the products of the Slave's work, the Slave represses his desire for the immediate consumption of the fruits of his activity and 'cultivates and sublimates his instincts', thus 'civilizing and educating' himself (ibid.: 24). Unlike the Master, who remains a static figure throughout the historical process that he initiates, the Slave's entire being is contained in the transformation of himself and its environment through negating action that ultimately leads to his liberation at the end of history:

> [In] transforming the World by this work, the Slave transforms himself too and thus creates the new objective conditions that permit him to take up once more the liberating Fight for recognition that he refused in the beginning for fear of death. Therefore, it is indeed the originally dependent, serving and slavish consciousness that in the end realizes and reveals the ideal of autonomous Self-Consciousness and is thus its 'truth'. (Kojève 1969: 29–30)

The entire dialectical process in the aftermath of the originary encounter is driven by the work of the Slave that actively negates the given reality and creates the human world that the Slave will inherit at the end of history, when his re-engagement in the struggle for recognition will enable him to defeat the Master and attain in the universal homogeneous state the freedom that he is deprived of throughout the historical process. Yet, what if we imagine, for a moment, a figure of the Slave who *suspends* his work without at the same time taking up the fight for recognition? Such a figure would evidently be distinct from the Master who has never worked at all and survives in the present only in order to maintain the forced character of the Slave's work. Yet this 'workless' Slave would also be distinct from the 'autonomous Self-Consciousness' of the Slave that has overcome itself through work and *mastered* history, producing the world in which he can become free. The Slave that has thus transcended his own condition does not work because he no longer *has to*, given the disappearance of the Master–Slave relationship. In contrast, a Slave that simply suspends his work is a figure that cannot be recuperated by the dialectical scheme, i.e. it is neither *identity* (by virtue of having worked before), nor *negativity* (by virtue of no

131

longer working in the present), nor *totality* (by virtue of suspending work prior to the fulfilment of the dialectical process).

Thus the workless slave does not correspond to any term in the dialectic of history and instead renders this entire dialectic inoperative. While for Kojève 'true Man can exist only where there is a Master *and* a Slave' (ibid.: 43; emphasis original), the workless slave exists in the zone of indistinction between the two figures. It is not that Slave and Master have been dialectically *overcome*, but rather that their interaction enters a *standstill*, in which there opens a space for human praxis that is neither fight nor work (Agamben 2004b: 83; cf. Benjamin 2002: 463, 865). While Kojève's reading conceives of the end of history in terms of its mastery by the reconciled humanity, the Slave's suspension of work suggests something like the end *of* the 'end of history', a *second end* that does not merely end history's perpetual evasion of human mastery but rather halts the drive for this mastery itself, whereby history is not completed but simply stopped in its tracks. In other words, the proper, definitive end of history consists in the annulment of the 'first', teleological end of history. Whereas the Kojèvian end of history is still graspable from a historical perspective as an end of history *within* history, the understanding of the end of history as the Slave's suspension of work dismantles the very terms in which this 'first end' could be intelligible. This 'second end' of history no longer presupposes anything like a 'universal homogeneous state' that would be the 'final term' of history (Kojève 1969: 9). Instead, this abrupt end carries no finality whatsoever, nor can it be presented in terms of the completion of some intelligible process. History truly comes to an end only when it is conceived as teleologically *endless*, devoid of any task in terms of which it could be fulfilled.

And yet if the 'jamming' of the dialectical machine of history is no longer governed by the desire for recognition that animated the historical process, what could possibly be its guiding principle, i.e. what does one abandon work *for*? As we have seen throughout this book, Agamben is singular among modern political thinkers to explicitly posit such a principle in terms of *happiness*, affirming the possibility of a comic overcoming of our confinement within the apparatuses of sovereignty and biopolitics for a 'happy life' of inoperative potentiality:

> The 'happy life' on which political philosophy should be founded cannot be either the naked life that sovereignty posits as a presupposition so as

to turn it into its own subject or the impenetrable extraneity of science and of modern biopolitics that everybody today tries in vain to sacralise. This 'happy life' should be, rather, an absolutely profane 'sufficient life' that has reached the perfection of its own power and of its own communicability – a life over which sovereignty and right no longer have any hold. (Agamben 2000: 114–15)

In Kojèvian terms, such a 'happy life' beyond any possibility of distinguishing between *bios* and *zoe* throws into question the very distinction between natural and historical worlds that grounds the dialectical process of negation. The Slave, who no longer seeks recognition and has suspended his work, cannot by definition be resigned solely to the natural world – in fact, he has irrevocably left it in his first encounter with the (future) Master, in which he did not risk his life and eventually entered the Master's service. Yet neither does he dwell in the historical world after abandoning his work, by the very definition of the historical process as contained entirely in the Slave's negation and transformation of his world through work. Indeed, this figure of the inoperative Slave is so problematic for Kojève's scheme that he hastily dismisses it as nothing but a relapse into the animal condition:

If *per impossibile* Man stopped negating the given and negating himself as given or innate – that is, stopped creating new things and creating himself as 'new man' – and were content to maintain himself in identity to himself and to preserve the place he already occupied in the Cosmos (or in other words, if he stopped living in relation to the future or to the 'project' and allowed himself to be dominated exclusively by the past or by 'memory'), he would cease to be truly human; he would be an animal, perhaps a 'knowing' and surely a very 'complicated' animal, very different from all other natural beings, but not essentially something other than they. (Kojève 1969: 220)

Thus for Kojève any suspension of work necessarily throws its subject to its merely natural, animal being, in which he would once again replay the encounter that launches the Master–Slave dialectic. In other words, if history stops 'along the way' (ibid.: 220, note 19), it must afterwards begin all over again from the very start rather than resume at the precise point of its stoppage. But this logically entails that with this 'stopping along the way' history has in fact *ended*, albeit not in the sense of a final accomplishment but rather in sense of the termination of its dialectical logic. We may therefore conclude that Kojève's scheme must admit the *non-dialectical* end of history as an ever-present possibility within history. What remains problematic in Kojève's account is his overly hurried reduction of the workless Slave that actualises this possibility to an animal, a reduction that diverts attention from the end of history to the necessity of its resumption. The suspension of work does not necessarily entail persisting in one's identity to oneself or preserving the place 'already occupied in the Cosmos'. On the contrary, this suspension by definition negates the Slave's self-identity *qua* Slave and hence has nothing to do with the affirmation of inert being against becoming. Rather than throw the human being back towards its animal existence, the suspension of work leads the former Slave to reclaim his present as the time of potentiality and hence freedom. As we have argued repeatedly in this book, the affirmation of inoperativity in Agamben's work has nothing to do with the valorisation of inertia or inaction but rather consists in the reappropriation of the potentiality of human existence captured and confined in various apparatuses that put human beings to work. As we shall demonstrate in the following section, Agamben's inoperative slave is therefore distinct not merely from Kojève's Master and Slave as historical subjects but also from Kojève's account of the post-historical subject.

The Snob and the Messiah

In Chapter 2 we saw that Agamben borrowed his concept of inoperativity from none other than Kojève himself. In his review of Raymond Queneau's novels (1952), Kojève termed their characters 'lazy rascals' (*voyous désoeuvrés)* and compared them to the Hegelian figure of the 'wise man' at the end of history. Yet rather more famous is another figure of the post-historical subject presented by Kojève, i.e. the *snob*. In Kojève's early argument in the 1930s, the end of history logically leads to the 'disappearance of Man', who was, after all, defined precisely by his participation in the historical process of negating action. Yet this disappearance only entails the radical cessation of Action ('the disappearance of wars and bloody revolutions') (Kojève 1969: 158–9), leaving the natural world and the natural or animal life of the human intact. As 'man no longer changes himself essentially' (ibid.: 159), philosophy will follow the historical process into oblivion, having reached its completion in Hegel's *Phenomenology of Spirit*. Nonetheless, Kojève argues that 'all the rest can be preserved indefinitely: art, love, play, etc., etc.' (ibid.: 159). Once the struggle for recognition is completed under the aegis of the 'universal homogeneous state' and there are no longer

Masters or Slaves, all that remains is the newly animalised humanity engaging in art, love and play that are devoid of all human meaning and reduced to something like purely natural pleasures.

However, in the 1962 note to the second edition of his *Introduction to the Reading of Hegel* Kojève abandons the idea of the post-historical animalisation of mankind. He describes the experience of his visit to Japan that led him to rethink the status of the post-historical man in terms of a caricaturistic figure of the *snob*, who is 'anything but animal' (Kojève 1969: 161). In the absence of properly historical 'Religion, Morals and Politics', the Japanese civilisation nonetheless created '[disciplines], negating the "natural" or "animal" given, which in effect surpassed those that arose from historical action' (ibid.: 161). Referring to the Noh Theatre, tea ceremonies and ikebana, Kojève claims that this snobbish disposition leads to a life 'according to totally formalized values – that is, values, completely empty of all "human" content in the "historical sense"' (ibid.: 162). The snob may therefore retain or borrow historical values, using them in the ritualised, purely formal manner that deprives them of all their meaning. Since 'no animal can be a snob' (ibid.: 162), post-historical beings will remain human, although this humanity will no longer consist in the transformative work of negation that *produced* new content, but rather in the formalised rituals that the snob tirelessly *reproduces* with no developmental or progressive effects whatsoever. Kojève ventures that the interaction between Japan and the Western world will eventually end in 'the Japanization of the Westerners (including the Russians)' (ibid.: 162).

Kojève's description of snobbery corresponds almost to the letter to Agamben's formula of 'being in force without significance': snobbish rituals maintain the pure form of historical action with no positive transformative effects, so that the avowedly 'historical' machine keeps running on empty, negating the natural (be it the animal voice, the *factum pluralitatis* or *zoe*) without producing positive, historico-cultural forms of life. In the condition of nihilism, modern societies only pretend to engage in historical action but in fact merely go through the motions of its formal reproduction. Post-historical snobbery is thus an apparatus that, similarly to the glorious body, the religious hymn or the sovereign state of exception, confines inoperativity in a separate sphere, putting it to work of its own glorification. The snob works tirelessly at exhibiting its own worklessness.

Agamben's politics of inoperativity may then be rigorously defined as the attempt to bring the Kojèvian end of history itself to an end, to *suspend the suspension* that is already at work in the condition of nihilism. In this approach inoperativity is understood as neither sheer laziness, attributable to a caricaturised 'wise man', nor a snobbish action devoid of significance, but rather as a more radical yet also more originary condition of 'whatever being' of pure potentiality, lacking an identity or a vocation yet not for this reason reducible to nature or animality. Agamben's post-historical subject does not become inoperative as a result of having fulfilled all of its tasks and actualised all of its potential, but rather reclaims its inoperativity from the apparatuses of sovereignty, law and governance that have all appropriated it as their own *modus operandi*. The dialectic of history that has been running on empty in the condition of nihilism is terminated without thereby being in any way fulfilled.

In its emphasis on bringing the dialectic to a standstill, Agamben's vision of the end of history resonates with Benjamin's messianism, whose logic Agamben has developed in a series of studies from the 1980s onwards (see 2007a: 89–106; 1999b: 48–61, 243–71). For Agamben, Benjamin is singular among modern philosophers in supplementing the traditional metaphysical search for the foundation or origin with the perspective of fulfilment of redemption, which alone permits us to break out of the apparatus of history, whose negating action has long lost all meaning:

> [In] our tradition, a metaphysical concept, which takes as its prime focus a moment of foundation and origin, coexists with a messianic concept, which focuses on a moment of fulfilment. What is essentially messianic and historic is the idea that fulfilment is possible by retrieving and revoking foundation, by coming to terms with it. If we drop the messianic theme and only focus on the moment of foundation and origin – or even the absence thereof (which amounts to the same thing) – we are left with empty, zero degree, signification and history as its infinite deferment. (Agamben 2005b: 104)

While the discussion of the full extent of Benjamin's influence on Agamben's reconstruction of messianism in profane and profanatory terms is beyond the scope of this chapter, we may briefly illuminate its significance by considering Benjamin's argument on the relation between the messianic and the profane in his 'Theologico-Political Fragment'. In Benjamin's famous expression, 'from the standpoint of history [the Messianic Kingdom] is not the goal but the end' (Benjamin 1978: 312). This means that, to the extent that the end of history can be considered an accomplishment, it is not an accomplishment *of* history but rather of something extraneous to it. Unlike Kojève, both Benjamin and Agamben consider the advent of messianic time in terms of a simple termination of the historical process rather than the fulfilment of its internal logic: 'nothing historical can relate itself on its own account to anything Messianic' (ibid; see also Agamben 1999b: 144–5). Nonetheless, while Benjamin's and Agamben's notion of the messianic is thoroughly heterogeneous to history, it is not transcendent in relation to the historical world, but is rather irreparably profane, governed by the worldly ideal of happiness, which Benjamin famously conceived of as the 'rhythm of Messianic nature': 'the order of the profane should be erected on the idea of happiness' (Benjamin 1978: 312). Insofar as it is entirely unattainable through work (Agamben 2007b: 19–21), happiness is a profane condition that is unrelated to anything historical and for this reason corresponds in its effects to those of the advent of the Messianic Kingdom: 'Just as a force can, through acting, increase another that is acting in an opposite direction, so the order of the profane assists, through being profane, the coming of the Messianic Kingdom' (Benjamin 1978: 312).

The parallel between the advent of the messianic kingdom and the profane 'rhythm' of happiness makes possible the reappropriation of the emancipatory potential of messianism in the absence of any theological content. If messianic time has no necessary connection with the actual arrival of the Messiah but shares its 'rhythm' in bringing about a profane, 'earthly restitution' (Benjamin 1978: 312), then messianism no longer refers to an experience of perpetual expectation but rather offers a paradigm of bringing history to an end in the here and now, at any historical moment whatsoever (Agamben 2005b: 99–103). In order to understand this possibility we must introduce two concepts of time that are central to Agamben's reinterpretation of messianism, *chronos* (linear homogeneous time) and *kairos* (the time of rupture or decision). As early as the 1978 book *Infancy and History* (2007a), Agamben attempted to challenge the continuous concept of time, which fused the Antique circular notion of time with the Christian linear notion. Instead, Agamben proposes the idea of kairological time, which marks the human appropriation of its temporal existence and thus frees the human being from its subjection to history. In this manner, the experience of temporality is no longer conceived in terms of servitude and work but rather as an experience of pleasure, akin to the Spinozan *acquiescentia* that we analysed in the previous chapter as a mode of 'eternal life'. Insofar as eternity in this figure refers not to the never-ending span of life (or its 'sempiternity') but rather to its location *outside* history, we may understand kairological time in terms of the eruption of the eternal within the historical process:

> Contrary to what Hegel stated, it is only as the source and site of happiness that history can have a meaning for man. In this sense, Adam's seven hours in Paradise are the primary core of all authentic historical experience. For history is not, as the dominant ideology would have it, man's servitude to continuous linear time, but man's liberation from it: the time of history and the *kairos* in which man, by his own initiative, grasps favourable opportunity and chooses his own freedom in the moment. Just as the full, discontinuous, finite and complete time of pleasure must be set against the empty, continuous and infinite time of vulgar historicism, so the chronological time of pseudo-history must be opposed by the kairological time of authentic history. (Agamben 2007a: 115)

How is this messianic *kairos* of 'authentic history' related to the more familiar (if ultimately alienating) experience of chronological time that guides the Hegelo-Kojèvian historical process? In *The Time that Remains* (2005b), Agamben cites the following definition from the *Corpus Hippocraticum*: '*chronos* is that in which there is *kairos*, and *kairos* is that in which there is little *chronos*' (Agamben 2005b: 69). The continuous temporality of *chronos* contains moments of *kairos* within itself, while the latter is defined by the contraction and abridgement of *chronos*, the time where there is little time left for anything. Contrary to frequent misunderstandings, the messianic *kairos* is not the equivalent of a chronological 'end of time', the *eschaton*. As an 'image devoid of time' (ibid.: 70), the *eschaton* may never be grasped but can only be perpetually deferred as the endpoint of transition. '[E]very transition tends to be prolonged into infinity and renders unreachable the end that it supposedly produces' (ibid.: 70). In contrast, kairological temporality rather consists in the attempt to grasp, in the here and now, what transition only promises in the unforeseeable future.

Agamben presents the difference between messianism and eschatology in terms of the distinction between the 'end of time', which the apocalyptic prophet that resembles the Hegelian figure of the Philosopher (see Kojève 1969: 157–67) observes and describes, and the 'time of the end' that is experienced in the messianic suspension of the apparatus of history.

> What interests the apostle is not the last day, it is not the instant in which time ends, but the time that contracts itself and begins to end, or if you prefer, the time that remains between time and its end. (Agamben 2005b: 62)

Messianic time is neither *chronos* nor its end (*eschaton*) but rather the time that *remains* between the two, 'the time that time takes to come to an end' (ibid.: 67). The kairological mode of temporality is constituted by the secondary division that divides the division between *chronos* and *eschaton*, being neither the former nor the latter but implicated in both.

Thus, kairological time is not external to the linear and continuous *chronos* but rather refers to a specific mode of grasping and reclaiming this temporality, rendering its ordinary progression inoperative and putting it in relation to the *eschaton* that it both promises and defers. Thus, any historical moment whatsoever may become the moment of *kairos,* in which the chronological movement of history is deactivated. Yet, to the extent that it negates the historical process itself, how does this suspension differ from the negating action of the Slave, either the working slave of the historical process or the self-emancipating slave of the end of history? What is this mode of praxis that does not seek liberation within history but rather strives to attain a happy 'eternal life' outside it? In order to understand this difference we must address the two forms of negation that define respectively Kojève's and Agamben's approaches to the end of history.

Destruction and Subtraction

In a key footnote to his 'Note of Eternity, Time and the Concept' Kojève defines historical action as characterised by 'the primacy of the future' (1969: 136, note 25). Historical action negates the existing reality, transforming it into the past, and in this manner actualises its vision of the future *in* and *as* the new present.

> [We] say that a moment is 'historical' when an action that is performed in it is performed in terms of the idea that the agent has of the future (that is, in terms of a *Project*): one decides on a *future* war, and so on; therefore, one acts in terms of the *future*. But if the moment is to be truly 'historical' there must be change; in other words, the decision must be *negative* with respect to the given: in deciding for the future war, one decides *against* the prevailing peace. And, through the decision for the future war, the peace is transformed into the past. (Ibid.: 136, note 24; emphasis original)

Every historical action must be oriented towards the fulfilment of some future-oriented project through the negation of the present reality into the past. In contrast, the messianic suspension of history in the inoperative praxis of the workless slave evidently frees human action from the very horizon of the project to which existence is subjected. Thus, the second end of history is only thinkable as the negation of the project itself rather than its fulfilment. Yet since we still seem to be stuck with negation, does not Agamben's inoperativity remain eminently historical despite its best efforts to halt the historical process? Does not the workless slave still negate given reality, even if it is only the reality of his own negation?

It is here that we ought to introduce two distinct modes of negation. In Kojève's argument, negating action must necessarily take the form of the *destruction* of the existing world: '[The] idea can be transformed into truth only by negating action, which will destroy the World that does not correspond to the idea and will create by this very destruction the World in conformity with the ideal' (ibid.: 98). Throughout the historical process, this destruction is undertaken in the service of the Master who appropriates the new present created by this destruction as the object of his consumption and enjoyment. At the end of this process, the Slave will refuse his enslavement, taking up the struggle for the revolutionary destruction of the world of the Master, overcoming his initial fear of death and becoming a 'free Worker who fights and risks his life' (ibid.: 57). The formula 'free worker' occurs very rarely in Kojève's text (see also ibid.: 230, note 25) and is evidently paradoxical in terms of his theory. If the Slave overcomes his fear of death and confronts the Master, his freedom is indeed realised in the destructive struggle, but in what sense can he then remain a 'worker' and, moreover, what is the meaning of this work, given Kojève's insistence that it is only forced, slavish work that matters in the historical process? This paradoxical concept is deployed as a transition point between the working Slave who is not yet free and the emancipated ex-Slave who no longer works. Yet the transition in question is ultimately contained in the move from one mode of destructive negation to another, from the negation of the world *for* the Master to the negation of the world *of* the Master. At the very moment the 'worker' frees himself from the forced character of his destruction of the real, he immediately becomes a fighter on a quest to destroy the world that he has himself produced in the service of the Master.

Moreover, in the context of Kojève's reading of the Master–Slave dialectic destruction is not merely a metaphor but must be taken quite literally (see ibid.: 29). While on the ontological level Hegel's dialectic is famously fulfilled through the synthesis of identity and negativity that constitutes totality, on the phenomenological level of the *existential* dialectic, we find no parallel synthetic operation:

> In truth, only the Slave 'overcomes' his 'nature' and finally becomes Citizen. The Master does not change: he dies rather than cease to be Master. The final fight, which transforms the Slave into Citizen, overcomes Mastery in a *nondialectical* fashion: the Master is simply killed and he dies as Master. (Ibid.: 225, note 22; emphasis original)

By murdering the Master, the Slave *alone* achieves the synthesis of Mastery and Slavery, since his re-engagement in the struggle for recognition entails that he is no longer a Slave, and the murder of the Master (as opposed to his enslavement) entails that there is no longer anyone left to become the Master *of* (ibid.: 231). The murder of the Master is the final act in the drama of destruction coextensive with human history, the last project of realising the future by negating the present into the past. Even the negation of slavery that ushers in the end of history takes the form that defined the Slave's activity to begin with.

To what extent does Agamben's inoperative praxis succeed in negating the historical world of Mastery and Slavery without assuming the same form of the destruction of the real? Our discussion of Agamben's wariness of constituent power in Chapter 4 demonstrates his attunement to the problem: even if it affirms and enacts popular sovereignty, revolutionary destruction ends up reproducing the very logic of the historical process, in which the subject was enslaved in the first place. It is therefore not surprising that for all the fury of the destruction it unleashed, the politics of popular sovereignty often subjected the populace to a sovereign power at least as intense and exactly as exceptionalist as the one it overthrew. Just as in the context of sovereignty the idea of constituent power is abandoned by Agamben for a more originary potentiality with no relation to the actuality of law, so in the domain of history the process of negating action is itself negated in the singular manner that avoids the replication of its destructive logic. In order to grasp the specificity of inoperativity as a mode of negation we may make use of Badiou's distinction between destruction and subtraction. In *Being and Event* (2005a: 407–8), Badiou introduces this distinction in the context of his theory of the truth procedure in order to emphasise the irreducibility of novelty to the destruction of the existent:

> [E]mpirically, novelty is accompanied by destruction. But it must be clear that this accompaniment is not linked to intrinsic novelty. Destruction is the ancient effect of the new supplementation amidst the ancient. Killing somebody is always a matter of the (ancient) state of things; it cannot be a prerequisite for novelty. (Ibid.: 408)

In contrast to destruction, the *subtractive* procedure, presented by Badiou as the true source of novelty and thus the 'affirmative' element in every negation, consists in the production of something that is indiscernible within the negated situation, that cannot be rendered positive in its terms and thus avoids any engagement or incorporation in this situation instead of destroying it (Badiou 2005a: 371). Agamben draws on and develops this logic of subtraction in his theory of the coming community (1993a: 75, 85–7): the inoperative community of whatever singularities subtracts itself from the myriad of positive identities that divide its members and thus establishes itself as something new that is literally inaccessible to the apparatuses governing the situation and remains impervious to their grasp. While destruction does nothing but perpetuate the dialectical process of negating action, subtraction suppresses the movement of the dialectic by virtue of its avoidance of any engagement with what it negates.

In his *Highest Poverty* Agamben finds a paradigm of subtractive negation in the practices of Franciscan monasticism, which has been a key reference for many of Agamben's concepts, from profanation to the form-of-life. While numerous monastic movements of the thirteenth century challenged the authority of the Church, positing themselves as the 'true Church' and thus inevitably entering into conflict with the existing hierarchy, the singularity of the Franciscan movement consisted in its avoidance of such an open conflict through the cultivation of a radical distance from the institution of the Church as well as other authorities. The 'form of life' cultivated by the Franciscans did not consist in the application of any existing rules or laws to life, nor in the establishment of new rules or laws that could serve as alternatives to the existing church office and liturgy, but was rather 'completely extraneous to both civil and canon law', having its entire content in the life of Christ alone (Agamben 2013: 122). 'Life according to the form of the holy Gospel is situated on a level that is so distinct from that of the life according to the form of the holy Roman Church that it cannot enter into conflict with it' (ibid.: 122). Rather than locate this form of life on the level of positive institutions as a new and 'true' rule, law or liturgy, which logically leads to a frontal antagonism with the established authorities that can only be resolved through the destructive negation of the opponent, the Franciscan movement subtracted itself from the institutional apparatuses without any polemic against them in order to invent a form of life that is strictly inaccessible to them and may therefore evade their capture.

While Kojève's fighting 'free worker' evidently exemplifies the logic of destruction, which Badiou explicitly links to Hegel's account of revolutionary Terror (2007: 53–4), the slave that simply suspends his work, without simultaneously opting for the destruction of the Master and his world, is a paradigm of the logic of subtraction. By subtracting himself from the very relationship that sets the dialectic into motion, this figure that is neither Slave nor Master, a non-Slave that does not thereby become Master or a non-Master that does not thereby become Slave, embodies the kind of novelty that could never be recuperated by the dialectic and for this very reason renders the latter inoperative. Subtraction is thus a mode of negation that consists entirely in its own withdrawal from the Master–Slave relation: in contrast to Kojève's pathos of destruction, the Master is here negated solely by virtue of the inoperativity of the Slave.

As Not

Having defined subtraction in logical terms as a non-destructive mode of negation, let us now address it as an ethos, a way of life of the post-historical subject. What does it mean to subtract oneself from the historical process in one's lifeworlds that are still historical, even if, as Agamben insists, their historical content is increasingly null and void? In his reinterpretation of Pauline epistles Agamben isolates a formula that defines subtraction as a mode of subjectivation proper to messianic time. Paul uses the expression 'as not' (*hos me*) in the First Letter to the Corinthians to describe the ways of being and acting in the 'contracted' time of the end:

> But this I say, brethren, time contracted itself, the rest is, that even those having wives may be as not having, and those weeping as not weeping, and those rejoicing as not rejoicing, and those buying as not possessing, and those using the world as not using it up. For passing away is the figure of this world. But I wish you to be without care. (I Cor. 7: 29–32, cited in Agamben 2005b: 23)

The formula 'as not' should be rigorously distinguished from the rather more familiar concept of 'as if', which, from Kant onwards, was widely used in philosophy to posit fictitious conditions as 'regulative ideas', guiding action in the present without themselves being realisable in it (Agamben 2005b: 36–7. See also Taubes 2004: 53–4, 74–6). In contemporary political philosophy, this logic is operative in the Derridean version of messianism. Derrida's famous idea of 'democracy to come' presupposes, precisely by virtue of its clear distinction from any 'future democracy' (see Derrida 2005: 90–3), that it is never actually going to arrive (i.e. it will remain 'to come' at any point in the future) but must rather motivate contemporary praxis *as if* it were already here. This is why Agamben has repeatedly criticised Derridean messianism as 'thwarted' or 'paralyzed', producing perpetual deferral and incapable of attaining fulfilment (see Agamben 1991: 39; 2005a: 64; 2005b: 103; 1999b: 171). In contrast to Derrida's refusal of the very problematic of the 'ends' (of man, history or politics) and his insistence of the inaccessibility of the *eschaton*, which makes the perspective of messianic redemption wholly fictitious, Agamben asserts the possibility of redemption in the here and now, any moment in time being a potential *kairos* for the subtraction from the historical dialectic.

In contrast to the fictitious vantage point of the 'as if', the Pauline 'as not' does not leave the subject any vantage point from which to imagine a hypothetical redemption, but rather 'dislocates and, above all, nullifies the entire subject' (Agamben 2005b: 41). The significance of the formula is thus contained in the tension it introduces into the object or practice to which it is applied (i.e. weeping, rejoicing, possessing, using, and so on), which is undermined from within by the revocation of its content without necessarily altering its form. The workless slave does not simply abandon all his activities in the world but rather works *as not* working, diverting his actions from the task of negation in the service of the Master. As we have argued repeatedly with regard to the notion of inoperativity, it is not a matter of abandoning all activity, opting for *not* weeping, *not* possessing, etc., but rather a matter of neutralising the force and function of the activity in question from within, opening it up to a different use. Thus, Agamben's messianic subject certainly continues to inhabit the world with its apparatuses of government but subtracts itself from its intraworldly identities and roles that are constituted by these apparatuses. It is truly *in* the world but not (fully) *of* the world. Such a subtraction requires neither the exodus from the world into fantasy and fiction nor the violent destruction of the world. Recalling Agamben's mini-malist approach to messianism as a 'tiny displacement' that leaves things 'almost intact' (Agamben 1993a: 53), we may conclude that this displacement consists precisely in the subtraction of the subject from its prescribed place in the world that makes it possible to 'reside in the world without becoming a term in it' (Coetzee 1985: 228).

As we can see, Agamben's messianic subject exhibits all the familiar features of the post-statist community of whatever being, grounded in the sheer *factum pluralitatis* that we have addressed in Chapters 3 and 4: subtraction from positive identity, suspension of particularistic forms of life, life without relation to law, and so on. Indeed, it is an important methodological feature of Agamben's work that despite the dazzling variety of thematic contexts that he addresses (such as poetry, pornography, monasticism, law, language) we encounter the same concepts in different paradigmatic guises, so that a myriad of terms, both traditional ones and neologisms, refer to the same underlying ontological constellation of inoperativity, potentiality and whatever being. Thus, in the context of Pauline messianism inoperativity is presented through the paradigm of the Pauline concept of *katargesis*, the fulfilment of law through its deac-tivation (Agamben 2005b: 98–9), and the *experimentum linguae* is discussed in terms of Paul's 'word of faith' not exhausted in signified contents but rather contained in the 'pure and common potentiality of saying, open to a free and gratuitous use of time and the world' (ibid.: 135–6). The messianic end of history thus appears to be yet another name for the comic politics of taking leave of the appara-tuses that govern our existence. Rather than indicate anything like a resurgence of the 'theological' element in Agamben's work, his version of messianism is entirely directed towards the profanation of all apparatuses, including the theological one, and return of what they captured and confined to free use, be it language, life or time.

Removing the Katechon

From this perspective, it is important to specify what tradition of political thought Agamben is actually opposing with his profanatory messianism. It is evidently not an avowedly theological or theocratic politics, which in the condition of nihilism may only be affirmed at best in bad faith and at worst as a farcical parody that does not even pretend to believe in itself. Yet neither is it a purely 'secular' politics – as we have seen in Chapter 2, for Agamben secularisation merely transfers a force from one domain to another without deactivating it. What Agamben targets is rather a politics that, to wit, 'theologises' nothing but *itself*, a politics that valorises not any hypothetical end or goal of political action, but the essence of the political itself, irrespectively of whether it is understood in terms of the friend–enemy distinction, agonistic contestation, acting in common or rational argumentation. Just like Agamben's version of messianism, this tradition may be traced back to the Pauline epistles, specifically the notion of the katechon in Paul's (disputed) Second Letter to the Thessalonians (see Hell 2009; Prozorov 2012). In this letter, Paul responds to the audience's agitation concerning the imminence of the Second Coming addressed in the First Letter, explaining the present delay of the return of Christ and elaborating the process by which it will eventually take place:

> [Let] no one deceive you in any way. Because it will not be unless the apostasy shall have come first, and the man of lawlessness, the son of destruction is revealed. He opposes and exalts himself above every so-called god and object of worship. As a result, he seats himself in the sanctuary of God and declares himself to be God. You know what it is that is now holding him back, so that he will be revealed when the time comes. For the mystery of anomy is already at work, but only until the person now holding him back (*ho katechon*) is removed. Then the lawless one (*anomos*) will be revealed, whom the Lord will abolish with the breath of his mouth, rendering him inoperative by the manifestation of his presence (*parousia*). (2 Thessalonians 2, 6–8, cited in Agamben 2005b: 109)

Since the notion of the katechon does not occur anywhere else in the Scripture, the interpretation of this passage remains ambiguous, particularly with respect to what or who the katechon is and what its relation is to the Antichrist (the 'lawless one'), whose revelation and elimination would pave the way for the divine *parousia*. In Schmitt's reading, the function of the katechon has historically been fulfilled by sovereign power, starting from the Roman Empire. The katechon is the worldly force that delays the advent of the Antichrist, which in turn would eventually lead to the messianic redemption (Schmitt 2003: 59–60). It is as this delaying or restraining force, as opposed to a direct agent of the Good, that sovereign power receives its valorisation. For Schmitt, the concept of the katechon made it possible to link the eschatological promise of Christianity and the concrete experience of history, explaining the delay of *parousia* and giving meaning to historical and political action, which the imminence of the Second Coming would understandably devalue:

I do not believe that any historical concept other than katechon would have been possible for the original Christian faith. The belief that a restrainer holds back the end of the world provides the only bridge between the notion of an eschatological paralysis of all human events and a tremendous historical monolith like that of the Christian empire of the German kings. (Schmitt 2003: 60)

For Schmitt the idea of the katechon made it possible simultaneously to endow Christianity with political form and incorporate pre-Christian forms of political authority into the eschatological context of Christianity, deactivating the 'paralysing' force of that context. It is evident that the paralysis in question pertains precisely to the messianic experience of the suspension of chronological history in the kairological moment of the 'time of the end'. The idea of katechon is thus profoundly incompatible with any messianism and may rather be grasped as an intricate mode of its negation, which prolongs history indefinitely in the face of its ending, keeping the historical dialectic in process and the Slaves at work. Indeed, the entire duration of history is nothing but the delay that the katechon is able to produce by restraining the messianic, and the entire existence of constituted power, from empires to nation-states, Christian or otherwise, is contained in the katechontic gesture of 'holding back'. It is thus clear why Schmitt, the apologist of the political, did not simply valorise the katechon, but in a certain sense *worshipped* it: 'I believe in the katechon; for me he is the sole possibility for a Christian to understand history and find it meaningful' (Schmitt cited in Meier 1998: 162).

In Agamben's argument, this *belief* in the katechon characterises every theory of the State, 'which thinks of it as a power destined to block or delay catastrophe' (2005b: 110). In this secularised (yet not profaned!) sense the katechon refers to any constituted authority whose function is to restrain social anomie (violence, anarchy or chaos), while simultaneously withholding a radical redemption from it. In contrast to this tradition, Agamben's interpretation of the Pauline text asserts that rather than grounding something like a Christian 'doctrine of State power' (ibid.: 109), it harbours no positive valuation of the katechon whatsoever. Indeed, in the above-cited fragment, the katechon is something that is to be 'removed' or 'taken out of the way' in order to reveal the 'mystery of anomie' that is 'already at work': '[T]he katechon is the force – the Roman Empire as well as every constituted authority – that clashes with and hides *katargesis*, the state of tendential lawlessness that characterizes the messianic, and in this sense delays unveiling the "mystery of law-lessness"' (ibid.: 111). The valorisation of the katechon thus begs a simple question: 'if we longed for *parousia*, should we not be impa-tient with the interference of the katechon?' (Rasch 2007: 106). This, as Agamben shows, is precisely Paul's attitude, yet clearly not the approach taken by the philosophers of the political, for whom the katechon has assumed an autonomous value:

> [What] if, after two thousand years and untold promises, we have lost our faith in the *parousia* and grown weary of waiting for the arrival of divine violence? Then would not delaying the Antichrist be what we should hope for? The katechon, as a figure for the political, rejects the promise of the *parousia* and protects the community from the dangerous illusions of both ultimate perfection and absolute evil. (Rasch 2007: 107)

In Rasch's view, what the defenders of the katechon fear is not so much the Antichrist but the Messiah himself, who, moreover, might well appear to them indistinct from the Antichrist: both are 'figures who promise us perfection, figures who offer us redemption and bestow upon us the guilt of failing perfection or rejecting their offer' (ibid.: 107). There is a certain irony in the 'Christian doctrine of state power' ultimately coming down to the apostasy of any recognisable Christianity in the nihilistic vision of an exhausted humanity that can no longer distinguish between the Antichrist and the Messiah. However, Agamben's reading of Paul leads us to a different case of indistinction. If the katechon conceals that all power is 'absolute outlaw' and thereby defers the reappropriation of this anomie by the messianic community, then it would not be too much to suggest that the katechon actually *is* the Antichrist that perpetuates its reign by concealing the fact of its long having arrived. Thus, Agamben argues that

> [it] is possible to conceive of *katechon* and *anomos* [Antichrist] not as two separate figures, but as one single power before and after the final unveiling. Profane power is the semblance that covers up the substantial lawlessness of messianic time. In solving the 'mystery', semblance is cast out and power assumes the figure of the *anomos*, of that which is the absolute outlaw. (2005b: 111)

The katechon may thus be understood as an insidious device, by which 'substantially illegitimate' anomic power perpetuates its reign, converting the seekers of redemption into the guardians of its perpet-ual inaccessibility and thereby ensuring the survival of greater evil in the guise of the lesser one. As Rasch sums up Agamben's argument, 'embracing the political is equivalent to building concentration camps while awaiting the Antichrist' (Rasch 2007: 106).

It is precisely this survival of evil in the guise of a victory over it, whereby the Antichrist as katechon inserts itself between us and the messianic redemption, that constitutes what Paul calls the 'mystery' of anomie. This mystery, whose survival over the centuries Agamben has traced in his detailed genealogies of sovereignty and government, finds its ultimate 'resolution' in the reappropriation of anomie by the messianic community in the real state of exception, which reclaims its inoperativity by subtracting itself from the historical dialectic. Yet, as we have seen, this resolution is furthest away from a Kojèvian synthesis, fulfilment or accomplishment: when the katechon is removed and its delaying function rendered inoperative, history simply ends without either the grand execution of the Master or the still grander emancipation of the Slave. In full accordance with the comic logic of the 'slight adjustment', the end of history in its messianic sense does not lead to either paradisiacal bliss or the agonies of perdition. As Agamben argued in *The Coming Community*, 'the life that begins on earth after the last day is simply human life' (1993a: 7). On the basis of the preceding three chapters we can certainly appreciate how this life would be 'simple', insofar as it is no longer fractured by the negativity of the Voice, bare life or history as negating action but rather exists as its own form, living its own potentiality in the absence of identity or tasks. Yet, there remains a question: insofar as this life has overcome all these fractures that have defined human existence as we know it, to what extent can it still be called *human*? This is the question we address in the following chapter that traces the unfolding of Agamben's politics of inoperativity in the fourth and widest domain, that of humanity as such.

Chapter 6

Outside of Being: Inoperative Humanity

This chapter probes Agamben's affirmation of inoperativity in the domain of humanity. Many representatives of continental philosophy have recently engaged with the *anthropocentric* foundations of the Western political tradition, targeting exclusion and domination involved in it. In his work of the 2000s Agamben developed an original solution to the problem of anthropocentrism that does not attempt to include non-human or non-living beings within the domain of human politics but rather disrupts the very distinction between humans and non-humans. Agamben demonstrates how this distinction is always contingent and arises from the operation of the apparatus that he terms *anthropological machine*. In this chapter we shall discuss Agamben's attempt to render this machine inoperative in his work *The Open: Man and Animal* (2004b), focusing in particular on Agamben's critique of Heidegger's attempt to distinguish humanity from animality on the basis of the exclusively human faculty of the *disclosure of the world*. Reversing Heidegger's line of reasoning, Agamben rather approaches this faculty as an indicator of an extreme affinity between humanity and animality, paving the way for the deactivation of the machine in the figure of *saved life* beyond all separations and divisions between humanity and animality. We shall address this figure of post-anthropocentric 'life outside of being' as the most radical and thoroughgoing version of the comic affirmation of inoperativity in Agamben's work.

Problematising the Human

Our discussion of Agamben's politics in the preceding pages has tended to emphasise continuity in Agamben's thought, demonstrating the persistence of the same themes in his work from his earliest writings on aesthetics, language and ontology to his most recent studies of government and religion. Rather than indicate a discontinuous 'turn' towards politics in the post-Cold War period, the *Homo Sacer* series and subsequent works must be understood as taking explicit stock of Agamben's politics as it has been theorised implicitly or elliptically in the previous decades.

Nonetheless, there is also an important discontinuity in Agamben's work that we encounter in the fourth and final domain that we shall consider in our analysis of his politics of inoperativity. This discontinuity pertains to the question of anthropocentrism, the centrality (primacy, privilege or uniqueness) of the human being in both onto-logical and political terms (and, as we have seen, for Agamben the two are always connected, if not identical). This site is crucial for understanding Agamben's political thought, since it is here that the various strands of his work, analysed in the preceding three chapters, ultimately converge: what is at stake in the *experimentum linguae* and the experience of infancy, in the deactivation of the logic of sovereignty and the constitution of the form-of-life, in the suspen-sion of historical action and the messianic reappropriation of time is ultimately a reconsideration of what it means to be human: a being endowed with language, a political animal, a self-negating subject of the historical process. This reconsideration is all the more important, since it connects with the problematisation of anthropocentrism and humanism in various currents of contemporary critical thought, such as speculative realism and object-oriented philosophy, new ver-sions of materialism, trans- and post-humanist theories (Meillassoux 2008; Harman 2011; Brassier 2007; Bennett 2010; Latour 2004; Bryant 2011; Barad 2007; Pettman 2012), which were previously very distant from the main concerns of Agamben's philosophy.

> [The] main focus of nearly all of Agamben's published writings thus far has been avowedly anthropocentric. Despite his unflinching and far-reaching criticisms of metaphysical humanism, it is clear that he has never shown a sustained interest in exploring the anthropocentric dimen-sions and consequences of his metaphysical project. Especially those texts published prior to and including *The Coming Community* can be read as contribution to and deepening of the anthropocentrism underlying the metaphysical tradition. (Calarco, 2007: 164)

In Calarco's argument, this anthropocentrism began to be problema-tised, if not overcome, in the more political works of the *Homo Sacer* series and this problematisation reaches its peak in *The Open: Man and Animal*, a brief text that is nonetheless one of the most impor-tant in Agamben's entire *oeuvre*. This discontinuity must nonetheless not be overstated. It would be a mistake to produce an image of an 'anthropocentric' early Agamben and a later advocate of inoperative humanity: rendering humanism inoperative was on the agenda at least since *Infancy and History*. The difference is rather between two *interpretations* of this inoperativity: while in the earlier work it functions as yet another marker of *difference* between humans and animals, in the later work it serves as a pathway towards the *erasure* of that difference. It is precisely in its attempt to render inoperative the separation of humanity and animality that Agamben's critique of anthropocentrism belongs to the comic logic that we have reconstituted in this book.

Let us begin by recapitulating the theme of human existence in Agamben's texts discussed in the previous chapters. In all the three domains that we have covered so far human existence was constituted as profoundly different from that of animals. Aside from the exceptional case of the axolotl, it is only the human being that is originally 'infant', lacking language, and must enter into it in a dual move of subjectivation (as a speaking being) and desubjectivation (as a living being). It is only human speech that rests on the negative foundation of the removed voice, which introduces scission into the experience of language, which can never be as 'natural' as the 'chirping of the cricket' or the 'braying of an ass'. It is this idiosyncratic condition of 'having language' (as opposed to 'being language' in the case of animals) that simultaneously resigns human existence to negativity and makes possible human freedom as the experience of both potentiality *to* and potentiality *not to*. While animal potentiality is contained in the finite set of possibilities inscribed in the genetic code, so that animals *can* do certain things and *cannot* do others, human beings are capable of their own impotentiality, i.e. they can *not* do or be and are hence never tied to any genetic inheritance, specific environment or particular vocation. Since Agamben's vision of political community is based on the strict homology between *factum loquendi* and *factum pluralitatis* and the essence of this community is wholly contained in the inoperative exposure of potentiality, it apparently follows that this community can only be a human one, the animal resigned to endlessly wander in the actuality of its being-language, at one with its chirping and braying.

By the same token, the discussion of the sovereign state of exception and bare life as its product is clearly restricted to human beings, for whom alone the distinction between *zoe* and *bios* would make any sense in the first place. Although in *Homo Sacer* Agamben illustrates the idea of the ban with the figure of the werewolf, which occupies the threshold *between* the human and the animal

(1998: 104–11), the idea of bare life is otherwise addressed squarely *within* human existence as the negation of *zoe* within *bios* (akin to the 'removal' of *phone* within *logos*). This is all the more true for *Remnants of Auschwitz*, where the animal enters the discussion only figuratively, be it as the 'lice' to which Hitler compared the Jews or the 'stray dogs' to which the guards compared the *Muselmann* in the camps. The negation of *zoe* in the production of bare life is analysed as the movement of de-humanisation, which is capable of the infinite destruction of the human without ever really reaching the animal, which must have already been negated for us to become human in the first place and to which the negation of the human cannot any longer return us (Agamben 1999c: 132–4).

Finally, Agamben's approach to the end of history followed Kojève's *a priori* restriction of the historical dimension to human existence. While Hegel's stance on the issue was at least ambivalent (Kojève 1969: 216–18), Kojève's interpretation is entirely unequivocal: there is no such thing as the dialectic of nature and only human beings are capable of the negating action that constitutes history. For this reason, the question of the *end* of history is also only meaningful for human beings, animals forever resigned to traversing empty and homogeneous time without any modification in their being. Agamben's own reinterpretation of the end of history from the perspective of inoperativity is therefore by definition focused on the liberation of human existence from history as a singularly human curse.

Thus, in all three domains of Agamben's work there is an evident anthropocentric bias that is hardly overcome by his critique of conventional humanism – all the critical operations on humanism are performed *within* the human and do not bring one closer to the overcoming of the *separation* of man and animal. Nonetheless, such a reading would be overly hasty, since the move away from anthropocentrism is also observable at least implicitly in all the three domains. Agamben's idea of 'calling into question the prestige that language has enjoyed in our culture, as a tool of incomparable potency, efficacy and beauty' in the *Sacrament of Language* (Agamben 2009a: 71) clearly targets the sublimation of the human being as *zoon logon echon*. The *experimentum linguae* that Agamben proposes actually brings human language closer to the 'chirping of the cricket': by suspending the signifying function and communicating nothing but its own communicability language becomes almost indistinguishable from the natural voice prior to its negation.

In turn, the deconstruction of the sovereign ban and the affirmation of the real state of exception remove the prestige that could be accorded to the human as *zoon politikon*: if all that political life meant in the state of exception was exposure to death, it could not possibly be used to distinguish humans from animals, let alone elevate the former above the latter. If the proud subject of human rights is ultimately the one that can be compared to lice or dogs, then politics does not transcend nature but may well form the quickest path of the return to its least pleasant aspects.

Finally, Agamben's idea of the messianic end of history that suspends, without completing or fulfilling, the historical process of negating action renders vain Kojève's efforts to distinguish the end of history from a mere relapse into the non-historical animality:

> After the end of History Man no longer negates, properly speaking. However, Man does not become an animal since he continues to speak (negation passes into the dialectical *thought* of the Wise Man). But post-historical Man, omniscient, all-powerful and satisfied Man (the Wise Man) is not a Man in the strict sense of the world either: he is a 'god' (a mortal god, admittedly). (Kojève 1969: 220, note 19)

While Kojève resorts to every possible sleight of hand to maintain the difference of the post-historical being from an animal (transposing 'real' negation into 'verbal' or 'intellectual' activity he otherwise derides, maintaining negation in the ritualised form of snobbery, converting the workless Wise Man into a 'mortal god'), it is evident that the inoperativity of the post-historical being renders its difference from the animal unobservable and informulable, and 'the face of the wise man who, on the threshold of time, contemplates this end with satisfaction, necessarily fades into an animal snout' (Agamben 2004b: 7).

Indeed, this is the thesis with which Agamben begins *The Open*, which explicitly takes up these themes in the most thoroughgoing investigation of the impact of the idea of inoperativity on the notion of humanity. Written as a series of vignettes on various aspects of the man–animal division, *The Open* nonetheless follows a clear logic that is already familiar to us: the identification of the apparatus of government that Agamben terms the 'anthropological machine', the deactivation of its logic through a critical engagement with Heidegger's approach to humanity and animality, and, finally, the deactivation of the machine through the articulation of a form of life, in which the very separation between the two is overcome. In the remainder of this chapter we shall consider these three stages of the argument in turn.

The Anthropological Machine

In Agamben's argument, it is only at the end of history that the problem of the division between man and animal assumes its full ontological importance. If the end of history entails the disappearance of the human 'properly so called', then the entire apparatus that separated humanity and animality for the entire duration of history is thrown into disarray:

> If animal life and human life could be superimposed perfectly, then neither man nor animal – and, perhaps, not even the divine – would any longer be thinkable. For this reason, the arrival at posthistory necessarily entails the reactualization of the prehistoric threshold, at which that border has been defined. Paradise calls Eden back into question. (Agamben 2004b: 21)

The perspective of the end of history permits us to problematise the historical apparatus that ceaselessly separated man and animal, which Agamben terms the *anthropological machine*.

As is the case with every apparatus (language, law, history, and so on), this machine operates through the capture, confinement and ordering of beings. The key principle of its operation is the division between animality and humanity that it draws *within* both humans and animals. Even a cursory familiarity with the history of this apparatus demonstrates that this division does not have any secure ontological foundation but, similarly to the sovereign decision on the exception, is radically contingent. For example, in his analysis of Carl Linnaeus's attempts to formulate the difference between men and anthropoid apes Agamben highlights the historical fluidity of boundaries between the human and the animal: since in the eighteenth century the possession of language, which later became the key distinguishing principle, was thought to also characterise animals, the only 'specific difference' that Linnaeus could assign to human beings was not a positive feature but rather an old philosophical imperative: *nosce te ipsum* (know thyself!): 'Man has no specific identity other than the ability to recognize himself. Man is the animal that must recognize itself as human to be human' (ibid.: 26). Yet this is no longer a stable ontological difference but rather an intricate epistemic device:

> [a] machine for producing the recognition of the human, constructed of a series of mirrors in which man, looking at himself, sees his own image

always already deformed in the features of an ape. *Homo* is a constitutively 'anthropomorphous' animal who must recognize himself in a
non-man in order to be human. (Ibid.: 26–7)

A human being is thus an animal that *resembles* a human being
and has learned to *recognise* this resemblance. It does not have any
essence other than the capacity to set itself apart from the animal
from which it otherwise does not essentially differ: 'Homo is constitutively nonhuman, he can receive all natures and all faces' (ibid.:
30).

Agamben proceeds from this undecidability of the human to
identify two historical versions of the anthropological machine, the
modern and the ancient one. The overall structure of the machine is
strictly identical to that of the sovereign state of exception analysed
in Chapter 4:

> Insofar as the production of man through the opposition man/animal,
> human/inhuman, is at stake here, the machine necessarily functions by
> means of an exclusion (which is also always a capturing) and an inclusion
> (which is also always already an exclusion). Indeed, precisely because
> the human is already presupposed every time, the machine actually pro-
> duces a state of exception, a zone of indeterminacy in which the outside
> is nothing but the exclusion of an inside and the inside is in turn only the
> inclusion of an outside. (Ibid.: 37)

The modern version of the machine operates by the animalisation of the human being, by drawing the dividing line within the
human itself and thus isolating the non-human within the human.
Agamben's example here is the 'ape-man' or *homo alalus*, a figure
of nineteenth-century biology that marked the passage from the
anthropoid apes ('man-apes') to humans proper. This being was
no longer an ape in its strictly anatomical characteristics, but not
yet human due to its not possessing language. Nonetheless, as subsequent evidence showed, this figure was clearly fictitious, 'only a
shadow cast by language, a presupposition of speaking man' (ibid.:
36): all that the idea of the 'ape-man' does is perform the animalisation of man by subtracting the potentiality for language from his
existence. The ape-man is thus not the 'pre-human' being, from
which 'man proper' originates, but rather a 'post-human' being
produced by a subtractive and reductive gesture that corresponds
exactly to the production of bare life in the sovereign exception.
Evidently, this version of the machine can easily be shown to operate
beyond biological science and directly intervene in the narrowly

political domain, as the dehumanisation of Jews in the Nazi camps but also other, less extreme forms of discrimination and exclusion testify. Since the criterion that separates humans from animals has no ontological foundation, it is always possible to try to isolate and separate an animal within the human.

The version of the machine that Agamben terms 'ancient' (but which one can certainly observe in modern times as well) proceeds in the diametrically opposed way, not by excluding the inside in the movement of animalisation but by including the outside in the mode of the 'humanisation' of an animal, producing the animal in human form, be it the 'man-ape', *homo ferus*, the *enfant sauvage*, the werewolf or, metaphorically and closer to immediately political concerns, the slave, the barbarian or simply the foreigner. While animalised humans were understood as animal though still in some sense human, humanised animals were taken to belong to humanity despite being in some sense animal. Yet, irrespectively of the direction the division took in the machine, its end result is the production of a life that is neither animal nor human but precisely *bare*, lacking any positive determination and existing solely as the object of inclusive exclusion:

> Like every space of exception this zone [of indistinction between man and animal] is, in truth, perfectly empty, and the truly human being who should occur there is only the place of a ceaselessly updated decision, in which the caesurae and their rearticulation are always dislocated and displaced anew. What would thus be obtained, however, is neither an animal life nor a human life, but only a life that is separated and excluded from itself – only a *bare life*. (Ibid.: 38)

Just as the state of exception suspends the law, rendering it informulable and unobservable, the ceaseless caesurae of the anthropological machine necessarily fail to stabilise the human–animal distinction and instead separate ever more forms of life from themselves by drawing this distinction *within* living beings. Once again, we encounter the idea of bare life not as a synonym of natural, physical or animal life but rather as its negation: while there exist living beings, animal and human, bare life exists nowhere but in the machine that seeks to both separate and articulate the two and ends up negating both. The idea of the anthropological machine makes it clear why any 'post-anthropocentric' politics that simply attempts to *include* animals within the sphere of 'human politics', for example through their endowment with rights, freedom and equality with humans, remains insufficient if not counter-productive. If humanity itself is produced through an isolation of bare life within it, the inclusion of other living beings within this category only serves to feed the machine by providing it with ever more 'ape-men' or 'man-apes' to capture and dominate.

For this reason, the solution to the violence of this apparatus cannot consist in its reform or replacement but only in rendering it inoperative: 'It is not so much a matter of asking which of the two machines is better or more effective – or rather less lethal and bloody – as it is of understanding how they work so that we might, eventually, be able to stop them' (ibid.: 38). The next step that Agamben takes towards this understanding consists in a critical re-engagement with Heidegger, who, more than any other philosopher in the twentieth century, insisted on the radical difference between humanity and animality. In the following section we shall address Agamben's deconstructive reading of Heidegger's 1929–30 lectures entitled *The Fundamental Concepts of Metaphysics*.

Boredom

Even a cursory familiarity with the philosophy of Heidegger reveals the centrality of the themes of humanity and animality to his investigation of the question of being (see Garrido 2012: 36–62). In *Being and Time* Heidegger famously rejected the traditional metaphysical definitions of the human being as *animal rationale*, which add the possession of language or reason to 'simply living being' (1962: 71–7). In these conceptions life is interpreted in a 'privative' mode as something that remains when everything proper to the human being is subtracted, as 'what must be the case if there can be anything like mere-aliveness' (ibid.: 75). Rather than define *Dasein* in terms of an ontologically indeterminate 'life as such', to which something else is then added, Heidegger seeks to uncover a more fundamental structure of *Dasein*'s being in the world that is simultaneously presupposed and concealed in the more 'specific' interpretations of human and animal life in the disciplines of biology, anthropology, and psychology. While in *Being and Time* the question of animal or biological life is quickly dismissed as secondary and epiphenomenal to the question of being, in the 1929–30 lectures Heidegger engages with biology in much greater detail. In these lectures animal life becomes the main focus of a properly ontological investigation, albeit as a paradoxical mode of being that lacks access to being. Since it is this mode of being that Agamben will take up in his critique of Heidegger, let us reconstitute Heidegger's line of reasoning in more detail.

Heidegger begins with the threefold thesis: 'the stone is world-less (*weltlos*); the animal is poor in world (*weltarm*); man is world-forming (*weltbildend*)' (Heidegger 1995: 176–7). The stone (or any other non-living being) has no access to the world at all, hence there is no question of them being 'deprived' or 'lacking' of the world that human beings can, on the contrary, access and form. Things are much more complicated in the intermediate category of animals: they are not completely devoid of access to the world but their mode of access is itself characterised by lack, privation and, ultimately, inaccessibility. Relying on the contemporary zoological studies of Jakob von Uexkull, Heidegger analyses the animal's relation to its environment in terms of captivation (*Benommenheit*), whereby the animal always remains closed in the circle of its 'disinhibitors', i.e. the elements of the environment that interest the animal and on which its receptive organs are focused. In Heidegger's argument, insofar as the animal is completely absorbed in its disinhibitors, it cannot truly act in relation to them *as* beings but only 'behave' with regard to them as if 'taken' by them (ibid.: 242). What is withheld from the animal is the very possibility of apprehending something as such, *as* a being. The animal's poverty-in-world thus pertains to its impotentiality for the disclosure of beings:

> Beings are not revealed to the behavior of the animal in its captivation, they are not disclosed and for that reason are not closed off from it either. Captivation stands outside that possibility. We cannot say: beings are closed off from the animal. This would be the case only if there were some possibility of openness at all, however slight that might be. But the captivation of the animal places the animal essentially outside of the possibility that beings could be either disclosed to it or closed off from it. The animal as such does not stand within a potentiality for revelation of beings. (Ibid.: 248)

Thus the animal only 'has' the world in the mode of not having it (cf. Garrido 2012: 56–7). In terms of Agamben's concept of potentiality, the animal simultaneously lacks the potentiality for the disclosure and the non-disclosure of beings: beings as beings are neither revealed to it nor concealed from it but simply remain inaccessible. And yet, the animal certainly *relates* to beings that form its disinhibiting ring, even if it does not relate to them as beings. Heidegger terms this relation 'opening' and contrasts it rigorously to the disconceal-ment or disclosure proper to the human being: yes, the disinhibitor is open (*offen*) for the animal but not disclosed to it as such (*offenbar*, literally 'openable') (Heidegger 1995: 253).

> For the animal, beings are open but not accessible; that is to say, they are open in an inaccessibility and an opacity. This openness without dis-concealment distinguishes the animal's poverty in world from the world-forming, which characterizes man. The animal is not simply without world, for insofar as it is open in captivity, it must, unlike the stone, which is worldless – do without world, lack it; it can, that is, be defined in its being by a poverty and a lack. (Agamben 2004b: 55)

The opening that Heidegger grants the animal is thus entirely dis-tinct from the poetic understanding of the kind offered in Rilke's eighth *Duino Elegy*, in which it is the animal rather than the human that dwells in and sees the open 'with all its eyes' (ibid.: 57–8). For Heidegger, any such anthropomorphisation of the animal is inadmis-sible and groundless. The animal is only open to what is inaccessible and opaque to it: look 'with all its eyes' it might, but it will never see anything in the open. Nonetheless, on some occasions in the lectures Heidegger converts this 'poverty in world' into a kind of plenitude or wealth that is in turn withheld from humans, who, while remaining *living* beings, are somehow deprived of access to 'life' as such: 'life is a domain that possesses a wealth of being-open, of which the human world may know nothing at all' (Heidegger 1995: 255). Human beings are capable of the understanding of their *being* but not of their *life*.

Yet if this is so, if the modes of animal and human being are so heterogeneous, then to what extent is it possible to claim that human beings even share the same world with 'world-poor' animals? From a Heideggerian perspective, no being-with-animals appears to be pos-sible since being *with* logically presupposes being *in* the same world, which is not the case for humans and animals. While we can easily transpose ourselves into the place of another human being and defi-nitely cannot transpose ourselves into the place of the stone (because it does not *have* such a place, not having a world to begin with), with respect to the animal things are more complicated. Heidegger claims that while it is possible for a human being to 'transpose oneself' into the place of the animal, it is impossible to, in a strict sense, 'go along with it', if 'going-along-with means directly learning how it is with this being, discovering what it is like to be this being' (ibid.: 202).

Discussing the example of domestic animals, he demonstrates how problematic it is to speak of 'living with' animals:

> We keep domestic pets in the house with us, they 'live' with us. But we do not live with them if living means: being in an animal kind of way. Yet we are with them nonetheless. But this being-with is not an existing-with because a dog does not exist but merely lives. Through this being with animals we enable them to move within our world. [The] dog feeds with us – and yet, we do not really 'feed'. It eats with us – and yet, it does not really 'eat'. Nevertheless, it is with us. A going along with ... a transposedness, and yet not. (Ibid.: 210)

This 'and yet not' appears to be the most concise definition of the world-poverty of the animal: having world and yet not having it, open to its exterior yet not to beings within it, displaying a sphere of transposability yet refusing any going along with. In this interpretation, the human–animal relation is not, in a strict sense, a relation at all, which makes all talk of being-with or community with animals meaningless and misleading. Anthropocentrism appears to have been vindicated. Nonetheless, Heidegger refrains from positing a complete divergence between the human world and animal environment and finds a way to connect them with a reference to the passage in Paul's Letter to the Romans (8: 19) about the worldly creatures' groaning for redemption. The animal can yearn for redemption precisely because its very opening to the opacity creates an 'essential disruption' within it (Heidegger 1995: 273), a disruption that, while not equivalent to the ecstatic existence of *Dasein*, nonetheless creates a possibility of conceiving of a connection or even a passage between the two modes of being.

In his reading of Heidegger, Agamben traces such a passage through a comparison of animal captivation with the attunement of 'profound boredom', first discussed by Heidegger at the beginning of the course as the fundamental mood, in which the world and its beings are disclosed. In his phenomenology of boredom Heidegger moves from the most familiar form of boredom as being-bored-*by*-something (a determinate object or situation) through the more general being-bored-*with*-something that arises from within *Dasein* and has no determinate object to the most 'profound' boredom, which is precisely the attunement through which the world is disclosed (ibid.: 82–8, 113–25, 136–43). This profound form of boredom is characterised by the intensification of the two 'structural moments' that define boredom as such: *being left empty* and *being held in limbo*.

The first moment refers to *Dasein*'s 'being delivered to beings' telling refusal of themselves as a whole' (ibid.: 137), whereby it finds itself in a state of indifference that envelops all beings, including *Dasein* itself. In this state beings around us do not disappear but rather manifest themselves as such precisely in their indifference. The things we do in order to pass the time when bored, the diversions with which we try to entertain or amuse ourselves, fail to engage us, leaving us suspended in the withdrawal of beings. No possibility of action or use is available to us in the midst of beings that 'refuse themselves' and have 'nothing to offer' to us. 'In becoming bored by something we are precisely still held fast by that which is boring, we do not yet let it go, or we are compelled by it, bound to it for whatever reason' (ibid.: 92). It is easy to observe an uncanny proximity of *Dasein* in its fundamental mood to the captivation of the animal: 'In becoming bored, Dasein is delivered over to something that refuses itself, exactly as the animal, in its captivation, is exposed in something unrevealed' (Agamben 2004b: 65). Both animal and man are 'open to a closedness' (ibid.: 65).

The second moment, being held in limbo, is closely related to this opening. The beings that refuse themselves are nothing other than possibilities of *Dasein*'s existence that are left unexploited (Heidegger 1995: 141). What refuses itself to *Dasein* are the things it could have done, experienced or used, which now stand before it as wholly inaccessible and yet present. 'Beings in their totality have become indifferent. Yet, there [also] occurs the dawning of the possibilities that Dasein could have, but which lie inactive precisely in this "it is boring for one", and, as unutilized, leave us in the lurch' (ibid.: 141). Nonetheless, this withdrawal of concrete or specific possibilities impels *Dasein* towards a more extreme and originary possibility that characterises its very mode of being. In other words, the suspension of particular possibilities reveals what makes these possibilities possible in the first place and thus makes *Dasein* itself possible as the being whose essence is contained in its potentiality for being.

> Those beings refusing themselves in their totality do not make an announcement concerning arbitrary possibilities of myself, they do not report on them, rather insofar as announcement in refusal is a *calling*, it is that which makes authentically possible the Dasein in me. This calling of possibilities as such, which goes together with the refusal, is not some indeterminate pointing to arbitrary, changing possibilities of Dasein, but an utterly unequivocal pointing to *whatever it is* that makes possible,

bears and guides all essential possibilities of Dasein. (Ibid.: 143; emphasis original)

This description of the disclosure of the originary possibility clearly resonates with Agamben's dual structure of potentiality. *Dasein*, which for Heidegger exists in the mode of possibility, is made possible by the suspension and deactivation of concrete factical possibilities as a result of beings refusing themselves: potentiality is always also, and primarily, a potentiality *not to*. Thus, *Dasein* is simultaneously entranced by the emptiness of the beings' total indifference and impelled towards what Heidegger calls the 'moment of vision' (ibid.: 151–2; cf. Heidegger 1962: 371–80), a resolute grasp of the authentic possibility of existence, which is itself nothing but existence in the mode of possibility.

We may now clearly see both the similarities and the differences between animal captivation and human boredom. While both animal and man can be left empty by beings that refuse themselves, no animal can ever be held in limbo. 'What the animal is unable to do is suspend and deactivate its relationship with the ring of its specific disinhibitors. The animal environment is constituted in such a way that something like a pure possibility can never become manifest within it' (Agamben 2004b: 68). It is this difference which leads Agamben to a striking conclusion that remains only implicit in Heidegger since it runs contrary to the privilege his thought grants to *Dasein*. If the passage from animal to man (anthropogenesis) proceeds through the limbo as the structural moment of boredom, then this passage

> does not open onto a further, wider and brighter space, achieved beyond the limits of the animal environment and unrelated to it; on the contrary, it is opened only by means of a suspension and a deactivation of the animal relation with the disinhibitor. (Ibid.: 68).

It is only when this relation is suspended that the animal captivation can be grasped as such – a possibility that, as we recall, is not available to the animal itself: 'the open and the free-of-being do not name something radically other with respect to the neither-open-nor-closed of the animal environment: they are the appearing of an undisconcealed as such' (Ibid.: 69). If the animal was open to a closedness that it could never access, the human being is able to do precisely that; it is able to grasp the inaccessible *as* inaccessible. Yet this obviously does not amount to much or, in fact, to anything at all. The 'privative' understanding of animal life as a subtraction from human being is thus reversed: it is rather the human being-in-the-world, standing out in the clearing of being, that is derived from the suspension of the animal captivation: '[The] jewel set at the centre of the human world and its *Lichtung* (clearing) is nothing but animal captivation. Whoever looks in the open sees only a closing, only a not-seeing' (Ibid.: 69).

This line of reasoning permits us to understand Heidegger's intricate arguments on the coexistence of being and nothing. In the lecture 'What is Metaphysics?', delivered during the same year as *The Fundamental Concepts of Metaphysics*, *Dasein* is explicitly defined as 'being held out into the nothing' (Heidegger 1977: 108) and this nothing is posited as the paradoxical 'ground' in which all beings come to appear: *Ex nihilo omne ens qua ens fit* [from the nothing all beings as beings come to be] (ibid.: 108). The lectures on the essence of animality permit us to understand where this negativity of being comes from:

> From the beginning, being is traversed by the nothing: the *Lichtung* is also originarily *Nichtung*, because the world has become open for man only through the interruption and nihilation of the living being's relationship with its disinhibitor. Being appears in the 'clear night of the nothing' only because man, in the experience of profound boredom, has risked himself in the suspension of his relationship with his environment as a living being. (Agamben 2004b: 70)

Anthropogenesis is thus a negative operation that does not 'enrich' animal captivation but impoverishes it even further by making opacity, closedness, the undisconcealed manifest as such: 'Dasein is simply an animal that has learned to become bored. This awakening of the living being to its own being-captivated, this anxious and resolute opening to a not-open, is the human' (ibid.: 70).[1] This understanding of *Dasein* clearly breaks with the tradition of twentieth-century philosophical anthropology, which valorised the 'open' character of the human condition, its independence from its environment, its lack of a determinate identity or task, and so on. While, as we have seen, influences of that approach could still be found in Agamben's early works on infancy, in *The Open* his approach is much more sober and austere: yes, the human can access the open that the animal is simply exposed to, yet all that can be accessed in this 'clearing of being' is the manifestation of the inaccessible in all its nullity. Man is an animal that knows life *as* being, which is to say, as *nothing*.

On the basis of this reading Agamben is able to reinterpret Heidegger's more famous argument in the 'Origin of the Work of

Art' (1977: 143–206) about the perpetual strife of 'world' and 'earth' in terms of the struggle *within* the human being of humanity (the world, openness, disconcealment) and animality (earth, closedness, opacity). Yet, more importantly, he is also able to advance beyond it, since, unlike Heidegger, Agamben has no illusions about the productive character of this strife, whereby the mastery and overcoming of animality would produce positive forms of life (*bios*), endowed with a historical destiny. In Agamben's diagnosis of modern nihilism that we have addressed at length, all that historical projects of nations and states have produced and keep producing is the state of exception, in which the law is in force without significance and the historical machine of negating action is running on empty. In a word, like all other apparatuses at the end of history, the anthropological machine is 'idling' (Agamben 2004b: 80). The human mastery and overcoming of its own animality only leads to the degrading reduction of humanity itself to bare life, be it in the extreme form of concentration camps or in the admittedly more benign 'positive' biopolitics of the management of life as such:

> Do we not see around and among us men and peoples who no longer have any essence or identity, who are delivered over to their inessentiality and their inactivity, and who grope everywhere, and at the cost of gross falsifications, for an inheritance and a task, *an inheritance as task*? Even the pure and simple relinquishment of all historical tasks (reduced to simple functions of internal or international policing) in the name of the triumph of the economy, often today takes on an emphasis in which natural life itself and its well-being seem to appear as humanity's last historical task. (Ibid.: 76)

Yet what does it mean for humanity to assume the management of its own animality, its own biological life? From a Heideggerian perspective, such a humanity abandons its constitutive feature of keeping itself open to the opacity of animality and instead seeks to *secure* (by opening, if necessary!) this not-open at all cost. In Agamben's concise phrase, such a humanity makes being itself 'its specific disinhibitor' (ibid.: 77) and becomes a paradoxical animal that is captivated by its own captivation. This is precisely the animalised, or, in a more refined argument, snobbish humanity that emerges at the Kojèvian end of history, which is the triumph of nihilism. 'The total humanization of the animal coincides with a total animalization of man' (ibid.: 77).

The Saved Night

Just as the snobbish end of history could be opposed by its messianic version, the biopolitical 'animalisation' whereby man dominates its own animality by means of technology is not the only possibility available to us. The alternative is presented by Agamben in the following manner: 'Man, the shepherd of being, appropriates his own concealedness, his own animality, which neither remains hidden nor is made an object of mastery, but is thought as such, as pure abandonment' (ibid.: 80). While this idea of appropriation has evident Heideggerian overtones, at this stage in the argument Agamben actually abandons Heidegger's text and, as he frequently did on other occasions, turns to Benjamin, whom he once called 'an antidote that allowed me to survive Heidegger' (Agamben cited in De la Durantaye 2009: 53). The final pages of *The Open*, offering nothing less than the manifesto of anti- or post-biopolitics, are among the most esoteric in Agamben's *oeuvre*. In the remainder of this chapter we shall explicate Agamben's argument by demonstrating its dependence on and radicalisation of the already familiar affirmation of inoperativity as both the goal and method of his comic politics.

Agamben's point of departure in his elaboration of the alternative to the biopolitical domination of animality is Benjamin's figure of the 'saved night'. While, similarly to Heidegger, Benjamin approaches nature or animal life in terms of the concealed and the opaque ('night') in contrast to the revelatory character of humanity and history, for him the role of such historical endeavours as works of art and ideas is not to disclose this concealed figure but rather to *maintain* it in its undisconcealed status, to leave it 'in the night' and thereby to 'save' it (Agamben 2004b: 81–2). The Pauline idea of nature's yearning for redemption is thus rethought: the salvation that natural creatures groan for consists precisely in remaining 'in the night', i.e. remaining unsaved and unsavable by human disclosure and mastery:

> The 'saved night' is the name of this nature that has been given back to itself. The salvation that is at issue here does not concern something that has been lost and must be found again, something that has been forgotten and must be remembered; it concerns, rather, the lost and the forgotten as such – that is, something unsavable. (Ibid.: 82)

This idea of the unsavable or 'irreparable' has been central to Agamben's theorisation of whatever being and form-of-life and offers a good illustration of the comic mood of his thought. It is clear that if we define comedy in terms of a happy ending after tragic tribulations, the theme of salvation should be central to any comic disposition. And yet, in full accordance with the minimalist or austere character of this disposition, discussed in Chapter 1, Agamben's salvation introduces no new positive content, nor does it restore positivity to the tradition that nihilism has already rendered vacuous. We can never go back on nihilism but it does not follow from this that the horizon of salvation is itself to be annulled. For Agamben, salvation does not consist in reclaiming what was lost or making the profane sacred but rather in the 'irreparable loss of the lost, the definitive profanity of the profane' (Agamben 1993a: 102). What is worthy of salvation for Agamben is never any particular form of life, specific language or a historical project but only the inoperative potentiality of 'whatever being', constitutive of and confined within them. Insofar as the essence of whatever being is its own inoperative existence and the form of this life is its own potential formlessness, it is devoid of any discernible features in terms of which it would strive for salvation. The salvation of a whatever being could therefore not possibly consist in abandoning one set of identity predicates for another. What is saved is saved along with all of its predicates, as 'consigned without remedy to [one's] way of being' or *irreparable* (ibid.: 90). To be saved as unsavable or irreparable is to be saved *from* the salvation promised by the myriad of historical apparatuses that capture and dominate one's animality in order to perfect one's humanity, to be let be in one's being-thus, in the night of one's originary inoperativity (Agamben 2005b: 39–41; 2007b: 35. See De la Durantaye 2009: 197–9).

In terms of the logic of the anthropological machine this imperative entails bringing to a standstill the ceaseless project of articulating humanity and animality either through animalisation or humanisation. The 'stoppage' of the machine entails that it is no longer possible either to master animality in a historical project of human (self-)realisation or to master humanity by, as it were, returning the human to the nature from which it originates. Since the machine operates by the identification of one term through the exclusion of the other, its jamming entails the inoperativity of both of them and the emergence of something else in the space between them:

[Neither] must man master nature nor nature man. Nor must both be surpassed in a third term that would represent their dialectical synthesis.

What is decisive here is only the 'between', the interval or the play between the two terms, their immediate constellation in a non-coincidence. In the reciprocal suspension of the two terms, something, for which we perhaps have no name and which is neither animal nor man, settles in between nature and humanity and holds itself in the mastered relation, in the saved night. (Agamben 2004b: 83)

Following Benjamin's esoteric allusion to sexual fulfilment as the 'hieroglyph' of this saved being, Agamben elaborates the idea of the unsavable in an analysis of Titian's painting *Nymph and Shepherd*, which depicts the two lovers in a somewhat melancholic scene of 'exhausted sensuality'. In Agamben's interpretation, the melancholy in question has little to do with the lovers' realisation of having sinned and their looming expulsion from Eden but rather pertains to the transformation that the consummation of the erotic encounter effects in the lovers:

In their fulfilment the lovers learn something of each other that they should not have known – they have lost their mystery – and yet have not become any less impenetrable. But in this mutual disenchantment from their secret, they enter a new and more blessed life, one that is neither animal nor human. It is not nature that is reached in their fulfilment but rather a higher stage beyond both nature and knowledge, beyond concealment and disconcealment. These lovers have initiated each other into their own lack of mystery as their most intimate secret. Bare or clothed, they are no longer either concealed or unconcealed – but rather *inapparent*. In their fulfilment, the lovers who have lost their mystery contemplate a human nature rendered perfectly inoperative – the inactivity and *désoeuvrement* of the human and the animal as the supreme and unsavable figure of life. (Ibid.: 87)

In their encounter the lovers have been initiated into each other's 'mystery', i.e. the disclosure of the animality of the other.[2] Yet this mystery has no positive content aside from its own mystification: what is revealed in this disclosure is the impenetrability of nature, its opacity to any knowledge. Thus, the lovers only come to *know* each other in the sense of knowing that there is nothing to be known about each other. Their mystery is thus not really 'solved' but simply 'severed' (ibid.: 83–4). Insofar as humanity was defined by the task to solve this mystery by mastering animal nature, as a result of this severance it ends up rendered inoperative. But, insofar as the mystery itself was revealed as the lack of mystery, it can no longer transfix one in the mode akin to animal captivation, hence animality ends up inoperative as well. Yet these inoperative lovers remain alive and presumably well. The key to understanding this form of life beyond both animality and humanity is Agamben's figure of the knowledge the lovers gain about each other, the knowledge that knows nothing but its own ignorance:

> [This life] surely 'does not see the open' in the sense that it does not appropriate it as an instrument of mastery and knowledge but neither does it remain simply closed in its own captivation. The *agnoia*, the non-knowledge which has descended upon it, does not entail the loss of every relation to its own concealment. Rather, this life remains serenely in relation with its own proper nature as a zone of nonknowledge. (Ibid.: 90–1)

In order to specify the character of this nonknowledge or a-knowledge (*ignoscenza*) we must return to Heidegger's characterisation of the human and animal relation to being. We recall that only *Dasein* is endowed with the potentiality for the disclosure of beings and worlds by standing in the open (the clearing of being, the Nothing). It is only to *Dasein* that beings become manifest in their being, while the animal can never disclose its disinhibitor as such, as a being. The ethical principle of Heideggerian ontology is thus 'letting be': 'man makes himself free for the possible and in delivering himself over to it, lets the world and beings be as such' (ibid.: 91). Yet if what lies at the heart of world disclosure is the suspension of animal captivation, letting be inevitably means *letting the animal be*. *Where*, however, is this animal let be once *Dasein* discloses the 'mystery' of its captivation? As we have seen, the 'world-poor' animal does not know being, remaining outside it 'in an exteriority more external than any open and inside in an intimacy more internal than any closedness' (ibid.: 91). Evidently the only possibility to let the animal be is then to let it be *outside of being* (ibid.: 91).

Being with Animals

Let us attempt to interpret this arcane expression that arguably marks the culmination of Agamben's confrontation with the Western ontopolitical tradition. What does it mean to be outside of being? Evidently it does not refer to *non-being* in the sense of nothingness or death. The claims about being 'outside of being' pertain not to being itself but rather to the *understanding* or knowledge of being, which for Heidegger was the defining attribute of *Dasein*. The animal that lives outside of being certainly *is*, yet it dwells in the zone that is neither the open which is opened to and by the human that knows and understands being, nor the closed where the animal dwells in an informulable yearning for seeing the open:

> The zone of nonknowledge that is at issue here is beyond both knowing and not knowing, beyond both disconcealing and concealing, beyond both being and the nothing. But what is thus left to be outside of being is not thereby negated or taken away; it is not, for this reason, inexistent. It is an existing, real thing that has gone beyond the difference between being and beings. (Ibid.: 90–1)

If letting the animal be means leaving it as 'unsavable' in the zone outside of being, what about the human: can a human being who lets the animal be also dwell, unconcerned with being, in this zone? In his cautious admission of the possibility of transposition into the animal sphere (if not going-along-with), Heidegger clearly recognised the possibility for the human being to enter this zone. Agamben's explication of anthropogenesis in terms of the openness to the animal opacity demonstrates why this possibility is in fact ever-present. In fact, if humanity is obtained only by the *suspension* of animal captivation, the human *never really leaves* the zone outside of being but only changes its perspective on it. Once the anthropological machine is stopped and the animal is let be, the zone outside of being is opened as the formerly unthinkable site of the coexistence of humanity and animality that involves neither humanisation nor animalisation. Contrary to Heidegger, it is indeed possible to *be with* the animal, just as long as this takes place outside of being. This is evidently not a matter of the disappearance of humanity: just as animals or stones, the human being that has moved outside its understanding of being still *is* and has not been consumed by non-being. If being is not life, then life is not being and it is possible to live outside of being, which is precisely what the animal does in its captivation. Of course, this life can no longer distinguish (as only *Dasein* can) between worldlessness, poverty in world and world formation, yet it still remains *there*, in the world that it no longer opens or is captivated by:

> In being with the animal – in worldlessness – Dasein finds itself having the experience of not being able to understand, of not being able to be-with or to coinhabit. It is the experience of being with what is *unconcerned with being* and therefore of what stands *out of the world*. Life (animality) becomes, in this particular sense, the *other of being*. Life shows itself as what exceeds the horizon of ontology. (Garrido 2012: 60; emphasis original. Cf. Bull 2012: 112–15)

The ethos of letting be outside of being thus makes possible a community of truly whatever being that is no longer restricted to human beings but extends to animals and, although Agamben himself does not go that far, even inorganic entities:

> On Heidegger's account, it is a priori impossible to go along with or to follow stones. In that they are worldless, they do not offer a sphere of transposition. But precisely for that reason, stones may bear witness to the most original possibility of being-with. To be 'with' a stone – to touch its impenetrability, to sense its opacity, to experience its absolute inaccessibility – is 'to be with' something in absolute worldlessness – beyond being, beyond existence, beyond life. Is it not a radical way to think the originarity of being-with? (Garrido 2012: 59)[3]

It is important to appreciate the radicality of Agamben's position: the idea of a being 'outside of being' goes far beyond not only his own earlier concept of 'whatever being', which, insofar as it was modelled on the experience of language, was always restricted to humanity, but also the various attempts in twentieth-century continental philosophy to conceive of a non-identitarian and impersonal mode of being. In his *Third Person* Roberto Esposito provides a brief genealogy of the philosophy of the impersonal that proceeds from Simone Weil's valorisation of the impersonal aspects of the human, through Benveniste's account of the singularity of the third-person pronoun and impersonal expressions, Kojève's argument for the impersonality of the post-historical state, Levinas's Other, Blanchot's Neuter and Foucault's 'infamous men', finding its culmination in Deleuze's notion of 'becoming-animal' (Deleuze and Guattari 1994: 242–59; Esposito 2012: 104–49). Since it was precisely the 'animalisation' of the human in states of exception and concentration camps that was the main 'problem' with what Esposito calls the 'dispositif of the person' (Esposito 2012: 56–63), the notion of becoming-animal appears to be a surprising solution to this problem. And yet for Esposito it is precisely the radical affirmation of that very animality that this dispositif was intended to master and control that may successfully deactivate it:

> The vindication of animality as our own most intimate nature breaks with a fundamental interdiction that has always ruled over us. Becoming-animal, for Deleuze, does not signify sinking into the darkest pit of the human being; nor is it a metaphor or a literary phantasm. On the contrary, it is our most tangible reality, as long as what we mean by real is the process of mutation that our nature has always undergone. What we

are talking about is not humankind's *alter*, or the *alter* in humankind, but rather humankind brought back to its natural alteration. What matters in the becoming-animal, even before its relationship with the animal, is especially the becoming of a life that only individuates itself by breaking the chains and prohibitions, the barriers and the boundaries that the human has etched within it. (Esposito 2012: 150)

Even though Esposito does not mention Agamben in this genealogy, we may suggest that his figure of a being outside of being is the true culmination of the genealogy of the impersonal, going beyond Deleuze's becoming-animal precisely in rendering inoperative the very possibility of differentiating between humanity and animality. While there are evident resonances between Agamben's approach and Deleuze and Guattari's complex and intricate theory of becoming-animal, there is also a key difference between them. The Deleuzian animal is defined by transgression of barriers, openness to the outside, metamorphosis and mutation – the features that are furthest away from the Heideggerian captivation and rather bring to mind the attributes of the *human* in both Hegel (self-transcendence through negation) and Heidegger (ecstatic character of existence). To become animal for Deleuze is to transgress one's confinement within a specific environment, form of life or identity, subvert one's vocation, task or function – in short, *negate* that which the philosophical-anthropological tradition subsumed under the category of animality as world-poverty. There is quite simply something very 'human' about the Deleuzian animal, which suggests that rather than halt the anthropological machine this approach only reverses its direction, making what was once the index of humanisation the sign of animality and the other way round.

In contrast to this continuing valorisation of self-transcendence and exposure to the open, in Agambenian terms to 'become animal' would be to become captivated by what refuses itself. Rather than move outside of being, such a being would rather be *stuck with being that refuses all access*. To become an animal in this sense would be to assume poverty in the world and, unlike the animal, to do so voluntarily, by, as it were, renouncing the opening of the world and recoiling into the closed sphere of captivation. What Agamben proposes instead could be termed 'unbecoming' both animal and man, ceasing the very process of becoming this or that but rather dwelling in the zone where humanity and animality are not separable and hence no difference between them (be it cast in Heideggerian or Deleuzian terms) is possible to mark. Rather than affirm yet another version of becoming something else, Agamben focuses on the possibilities of *being-with* on the basis of nothing but *being-thus*, a being together of man and animal in which one does not become the other but both are let be outside of being.

In his *Anti-Nietzsche*, Malcolm Bull (2012: 98–102) addresses this possibility of such a non-exclusive community in terms of 'sub-humanism', an ironic reversal of Nietzsche's famous reference to the superhuman. This community is made possible by renouncing the potentiality for mastering the animal within or outside oneself and rather occupying the *sub*-human position of the animal with a crucial difference of no longer being captivated by its disinhibitors. The sub-human is no longer the proud Heideggerian 'shepherd of being', yet neither is it a sheep. It is an animal that is no longer poor in world or a human being who no longer sees the open and cannot even be bothered to try. Neither *captivated* (taken, mastered) nor itself *captivating* (mastering, capturing), neither passive nor active – like Kafka's Bucephalus, the children of limbo or Bartleby, this is a being that just *is* without being anything, a whatever life that does not articulate its own concept, a life that lives and speaks without negating itself in the apparatuses of language, law and history. Evidently, this life outside of being resonates with Agamben's most famous concept of 'bare life', yet the meaning of 'bareness' is completely transformed here. This life is not *bared* or *stripped* in the sense of being separated from its form but rather is exposed in a nudity that is nothing but the pure appearance of the inapparent, the complete exposure of the opaque, the revelation of the absence of secrets:

> The only thing that the beautiful face can say, exhibiting its nudity with a smile, is 'You wanted to see my secret? Then look right at it if you can. Look at this absolute, unforgivable absence of secrets!' The matheme of nudity is, in this sense, simply this: *haecce*! There is nothing other than this. Yet, it is precisely the disenchantment of beauty in the experience of nudity, this sublime, but also miserable exhibition of appearance beyond all mystery and all meaning, that can somehow defuse the theological apparatus and allow us to see beyond the prestige of grace and the chimeras of corrupt nature, a simple, inapparent human body. This simple dwelling of appearance in the absence of secrets is its special trembling – it is the nudity that signifies nothing and, precisely for this reason, manages to penetrate us. (Agamben 2010: 91)

Thus, at the endpoint of Agamben's investigations into post-humanism we re-encounter bare life, this time in the sense of a life that makes its nudity its own form and hence renounces any positive form imposed on it by the law and other apparatuses of sovereign power; a life that exposes itself in the absence of any signified content or meaning; a life that no longer struggles to dominate, mobilise and negate its own nature in a historical project but dwells in time at one with its natural opacity; a life no longer marked by the apparatuses of language, law, history and humanity.

In the conclusion to his 'Theory of Signatures' Agamben contemplated the possibility of a discourse that could go beyond the study of signatures, the acts of the passage of the semiotic into the semantic, towards the dimension that logically precedes them yet can only be accessed by rendering them inoperative: 'Whether a philosophical inquiry is possible that reaches beyond signatures toward the Non-marked that, according to Paracelsus, coincides with the paradisiacal state and final perfection is, as they say, another story, for others to write' (Agamben 2009b: 80). This reticence is arguably an instance of false modesty on Agamben's part: actually, he has been writing that 'another story' *all along*, since his early works on infancy. If, according to Paracelsus, signatures that exist everywhere in nature are, for human beings, markers of original sin, of 'falling into nature, which leaves nothing unmarked' (ibid.: 33), then Agamben's comic politics, which leaves the tragic logic of sin and guilt behind is precisely a pathway towards the non-marked, not in the sense of the transcendence of the nature irredeemably marked by signatures, but in the sense of the *erasure* of the signatures themselves, whereby *phone* and *logos*, *zoe* and *bios*, Master and Slave, man and animal become indistinct.

The idea of an unmarked life, appearing as inapparent, is the culmination of the many strands of Agamben's thought we have addressed in the preceding chapters. The notion of inoperativity that has been our guiding thread through Agamben's philosophy may evidently be grasped in terms of the deactivation of all signatures that assign a being to this or that identity or function in various apparatuses of government. It is also easy to observe the aspiration towards the unmarked in the four domains of Agamben's work that we have covered. Firstly, the *experimentum linguae* that speaks the pure being of language beyond all signification literally strips language of all signifying marks, restoring it as pure communicability that precedes and exceeds the actual communicative function. Secondly, the post-sovereign 'form-of-life' wholly exhausted in bare life, a *bios* that is only its own *zoe*, is similarly a life unmarked, either negatively or positively, by the signatures of 'good life' produced by the apparatuses of government and hence no longer threatened by the sovereign potentiality of stripping life of all these signatures in the state of exception. Thirdly, the post-historical condition is produced through the erasure of the marks defining the historical struggle for recognition: the 'workless slave' as the post-historical subject is neither Master nor Slave but an inoperative figure subtracted from the process of negating action. Finally, the figure of a 'saved' and yet unsavable life, in which one cannot distinguish between humanity and animality, points to a being that has travelled furthest towards the unmarked towards the outside of being as such, forgoing its understanding of being in favour of the possibility of going-along and being-with all other beings in the mode of whatever being.

Of course, *contra* Paracelsus, this unmarked life outside of being has nothing to do with 'final perfection', if only because inoperativity ensures that there is no longer anything final or perfect in the sense of completion or accomplishment. The unmarked Eden cannot be found on any map not because it is transcendent, an 'other place' beyond the present world, but precisely because it is wholly disseminated in the immanence of the latter. The unmarked is *things as they are* in their whatever being, irreparable and profane, inoperative and potential. On second thought, maybe this *is* final perfection, since in a strict logical sense there is nothing that can come *after* it. There is only this, thus, whatever, nothing else.

Notes

1. A somewhat similar interpretation of Heidegger's lectures was offered by Derrida, whose attempt to destabilise the difference between humans and animals proceeds by questioning the human capacity for the disclosure of beings *as* beings, as such, without particular perspective, interest or design. For Derrida, 'there is no pure and simple "as such"' (2008: 160), which means that humans are not blessed with what the animal is supposedly deprived of.

2. The reference to lovers is not fortuitous here, since in his earlier work Agamben already defined love in terms of 'intimacy with the stranger', in which the loved one remains 'inapparent': 'To live in intimacy with a stranger, not in order to draw him closer, or to make him known, but rather to keep him strange, remote: unapparent, so unapparent that his name contains him entirely. And, even in discomfort, to be nothing else, day after day, that ever open place, the unwaning light, in which that one being, that thing remains forever exposed and sealed off' (Agamben 1995: 61). In Agamben's reading, the experience of love has nothing to

do with the ecstatic fusion of singularities into a fantasmatic unity, but rather consists in sharing the disjunction whereby these singularities are exposed in their mutual opacity, open to and touching each other without ever grasping each other as objects of knowledge.

3. See Nancy 1994: 158–66 for the discussion of the possibility of attributing freedom to non-human and non-living beings that follows a similar line of reasoning. See Prozorov 2013a, Chapter 3 for a detailed discussion of the derivation of freedom, equality and community from the sheer being of beings, so that these notions no longer have humanity as their exclusive or even privileged referent.

Conclusion
An Optimist Against All Odds

We have now completed our inquiry into Agamben's affirmative politics of inoperativity. In conclusion, let us address the possible problems with this vision of politics that have been identified by Agamben's numerous critics and discuss the possibility of their resolution within his theoretical scheme. Throughout the book we have already encountered various criticisms of Agamben's political thought from alternative normative standpoints and his response to them. It is possible to group these criticisms into two categories. On the one hand, Agamben's politics has been criticised from the perspective of *constituted power*, i.e. the institutions of the state, law, public sphere, communicative action, and so on, as not sufficiently appreciative of the capacity of these institutions to deal with the problems of sovereignty and biopolitics that he highlights (see Connolly 2007; Fitzpatrick 2005; Mills 2008; Rasch 2007). On the other hand, Agamben has been criticised from the perspective of *constituent power*, be it in the form of Negri's multitude (2000), Rancière's people (1999), Badiou's militant subject (2005b), and so on, as not sufficiently appreciative of the capacity of the political subject to depose and dismantle the structures of sovereign biopolitics and replace them with an alternative form of sovereignty, order, state, etc. (see Laclau 2007; Chiesa and Ruda 2011; Toscano 2011).

These extrinsic forms of criticism are as plausible as they are ineffective, insofar as Agamben's theory of sovereignty demonstrates both the indispensability of the state of exception to the 'normal' functioning of the state, law and other constituted structures of authority, and the complicity of constituent power in the state of exception as the manifestation of the sovereign potentiality not to be. Thus, Agamben always already anticipates and ventures to respond to and disarm the objections of his critics. While it would be naive to expect this disarming to be entirely convincing and successful, as long as one subscribes to the basic logic of Agamben's thought, his opposition to both the 'reformist' path of improving positive institutions and the 'revolutionary' path of overthrowing them in a voluntarist act of popular sovereignty appears entirely plausible.

Of course, the problem is precisely that this basic logic, which we have analysed in terms of inoperativity, is so difficult to subscribe to. The idea of a comic redemption through a generalised inoperativity is so counter-intuitive that Agamben almost seems to be purposefully audacious. After all, our idea of politics is conventionally phrased in the activist terms of the positive transformation of social reality, and a politics of disengagement, deactivation, subtraction and suspension can only be accepted as a temporary and partial solution, always to be followed by the next productive, constructive and affirmative step (cf. Hardt and Negri 2000: 204). Hence the disappointment of all those critics who, while sympathetic to Agamben's work as a critical diagnosis of the situation and even the idea of inoperativity as a means of undermining the dominant apparatuses, end up frustrated when their impatient question 'What then?' is answered by a curt 'nothing' (or at best an elliptical and enigmatic allusion to happy life).

And yet this is the price to be paid for a politics that takes leave of what has arguably been the defining feature of sociopolitical life, if not for Agamben's proverbial 'forty millennia', then for at least the last two centuries, i.e. the mobilisation of human existence by political authority, be it revolutionary or counter-revolutionary, liberal or socialist. In full accordance with this tradition, Agamben's critics, particularly on the Left, repeatedly emphasise the insufficiency of merely negative 'resistance' and the need to theorise the 'morning after' of the construction of a new post-revolutionary positive order. In their account, Agamben's privilege granted to inoperativity and deactivation makes him less radical, shunning the 'dirty work' of post-revolutionary construction (cf. Žižek 2003: 27–8; 2012: 128). Yet what if a 'less radical' stance is precisely the one that remains committed to the conventional distinctions between constituent and constituted power, between revolutionary turmoil and a stable order, destruction and construction, whereby every revolution must be followed by the sobering work of the 'morning after'? What if there is no morning after? Or, a bit less ominously, what if the morning after is precisely the *novissimas dies* of 'simply human life' that Agamben proclaims as the effect of the messianic suspension of all apparatuses?

While the elliptical character of Agamben's response to the

questions of what happens after the apparatuses have been rendered inoperative is understandably frustrating, any possible elaboration of inoperative politics in terms of the construction of a positive order would contradict the fundamental logic of Agamben's thought. Just as one cannot consistently uphold *both* the generic universality of whatever being and sexual or ethnic difference (a self-evident point that nonetheless continues to inspire fervent criticism), so it is impossible to combine the affirmation of inoperativity with a new historical project of emancipation. Yet is there *really* a lack of such projects? While the projects seem to be in great abundance, it is emancipation that somehow seems to be in short supply. Perhaps this is so because its cause is not really served by *projects*, i.e. new sets of tasks that submit human existence to negating action in the present in the name of the bright future. Thus, while it is easy to understand the reluctance of many critics to embrace the fundamental attunement of Agamben's political thought, it is important to appreciate both its principled divergence from the dominant tradition of activist-voluntarist politics and its consistency and fidelity to this divergence.

Since extrinsic criticism grounded in an alternative normative perspective always risks relapsing into an interminable polemic on first principles, it would be more productive to focus on an *immanent* mode of criticism that focuses on the internal contradictions and inconsistencies in an author's work that undermine it from within. A good starting point for such a critique of Agamben's politics would be the apparent incompatibility between its grand ambitions (nothing less than the deactivation of the apparatuses of language, law, history and humanity) and its valorisation of inoperativity in opposition to all historical action, emancipatory projects, and so on. Bluntly put, do not the ambitions of Agamben's politics demand far more *work* than the idea of inoperativity can sustain? While we may well entertain the 'eternal Sabbath' as the *ideal* of comic politics, how can it possibly also be its *method*? And if it cannot, then doesn't inoperative politics become yet another exercise in utopianism, promising us comedy while we remain stuck in tragedy? It is thus possible to simultaneously share the ambitions of Agamben's politics and remain deeply sceptical or pessimistic about the possibilities of its realisation.

Nonetheless, Agamben himself has explicitly rejected any attribution of a 'personal or psychological pessimism' to his work and, on one occasion, proclaimed that his critical interlocutor was 'more pessimistic than he was' (Agamben 2004a: 124; see Prozorov 2010).

Agamben's optimism regarding the possibility of the actualisation of his political vision rests on three principles that we shall consider in this conclusion. Firstly, Agamben is optimistic because the intensification of the global state of exception under modern nihilism entails that we have *nothing to lose* from a radical disruption of the existing apparatuses of government, which have degraded into a combination of the 'killing machine' of sovereignty and the meaningless 'spectacle' of ad hoc government without ontological foundation. The contemporary condition that Agamben, following Schmitt, likens to a 'global civil war' (2005a: 3) is not a result of a malfunctioning ineffectiveness or betrayal of any of the classical political paradigms but rather a holistic crisis of Western politics, which reveals the nullity of its foundational distinctions that was there all along but was formerly concealed by the relatively ordered character of political life. In this holistic crisis there is literally nothing in our tradition that we can rely on as a foundation for political transformation, hence there is nothing to lose from a complete 'halting of the machine'.

Agamben rejects as illusory any attempt to find the locus of radical transformation in either the state and the legal system or the immanence of social praxis, but, rather than draw from this disillusionment the pessimistic conclusion about the impossibility of an alternative politics, finds in it the possibility of radical change, which is no longer constrained by any institutional structures of the contemporary order, but jams the entire biopolitical apparatus in both its sovereign and governmental aspects. Simply put, all that the contemporary apparatuses of government offer us is the choice between sovereign violence in the state of exception and the nihilistic management of life itself, the choice between Death and Nothing, which is really not much of a choice at all. Yet it is precisely the falsity of this alternative that liberates us from *having to* choose between different versions of nihilism and enables us to probe the possibilities of forms of life outside all governmental apparatuses.

Secondly, insofar as the nihilistic drive of the biopolitical machine does all the work of emptying out positive forms of life, identities and vocations, we literally *do not have much to do* to attain an inoperative life of whatever being. In full accordance with the 'Hölderlin principle', radical transformation is actually made possible by nothing other than the unfolding of biopolitical nihilism itself to its extreme point of vacuity, whereby the apparatuses of government no longer produce anything positive but are, at best, running on empty or, at worst, functioning as killing machines. Agamben's metaphor for this condition is *bankruptcy*: 'One of the few things that can be declared with certainty is that all the peoples of Europe (and, perhaps, all the peoples of the Earth) have gone bankrupt' (2000: 142). It is precisely this diagnosis that makes intelligible his politics of profanation: it is nihilism itself that reveals the fundamental inoperativity of the human being, the experience of language prior to all signification, the sovereign potentiality of the human being, and so on, and it is only a matter of *reclaiming* these ontological attributes from their expropriation by historically contingent apparatuses that isolate them into a separate sphere of glory and make their free use impossible.

We must therefore rigorously distinguish Agamben's approach from utopianism. As Foucault has argued, utopias derive their attraction from their discursive structure of a *fabula*, which makes it possible to describe in great detail a better way of life, precisely because it is manifestly impossible (Foucault 1970: xvii). While utopian thought easily provides us with elaborate visions of a better future, it cannot really lead us there, since its site is by definition a non-place. In contrast, Agamben's works tell us rather little about life in an inoperative community of whatever being, but they are remarkably concrete about the practices that are constitutive of this community, precisely because these practices require nothing that would be extrinsic to the contemporary condition of biopolitical nihilism. Thus, Agamben's coming politics is manifestly *anti-utopian* and draws all its resources from the condition of contemporary nihilism; it attempts not to introduce anything new or 'positive' into the condition of nihilism but rather to *use* this condition itself in order to reclaim human existence from its biopolitical confinement.

Thirdly, Agamben's political thought is optimistic because the inoperative form-of-life that it affirms is no longer posited as a historical task, something to be attained in reformist or revolutionary praxis, but merely requires the *subtraction* of the subjects from the existing apparatuses, whereby they reappropriate their own potentiality for 'whatever being'. Agamben's politics is not a matter of a painstaking process of the composition of a social movement or coalition of parties, of raising awareness and mobilising the civil society, of articulating and aggregating particular interests into a (counter)hegemonic bloc, and so on. All of the above would contradict Agamben's affirmation of inoperativity as not merely a distant ideal but an actual method of politics. Politics need not take the form of (yet another) historical project but rather consists in one's subtraction from the apparatuses that govern us and the identities that they prescribe, rendering them inoperative and in this manner reclaiming our own inoperativity. Thus, the passage from the worst to the best, from tragedy to comedy, literally takes a single step.

Yet why would this step be taken by the subjects of contemporary societies? Why not prefer to go on dwelling in the inauthentic realm of the degraded sociality of late-modern nihilism? Even if we agree that the sole choice that the existing apparatuses offer is between Death and Nothing, *why not choose Nothing*, especially since it is clearly preferable to death, despite being metaphysically or metaphorically close to it? Surely the subtractive step outside the apparatuses cannot be a matter of historical (or post-historical) necessity, since what is at stake is precisely the overcoming of every claim to necessity in the affirmation of radical freedom understood in terms of potentiality (not to). Neither, however, is it possible to conceive of the move towards the inoperative community of whatever being as a matter of free *will*, since Agamben refuses to frame this transformation in terms of a project, a decision, or even, as we shall see below, as an *act* as such.

This problem is somewhat concealed by the focus of Agamben's commentators on his most controversial claim about the concentration camp as the paradigmatic *nomos* of modernity. If this identification is accepted, then the problem of will does not really arise, as it would be obscene to pose the question of why anyone would want to leave the concentration camp. Yet, as we have argued, the camp is only an extreme and hyperbolic example of the far more general logic that is otherwise manifested in relatively more benign cases of, for example, community policing, counter-terrorist policies, the management of migration, and so on. Once we abandon the focus on the camp, it is by no means guaranteed that the subjects of the contemporary biopolitical societies would want to abandon the existing apparatuses of law, order and security for a 'real state of exception' devoid of all protections granted by these apparatuses.

The same applies *a fortiori* to the socioeconomic apparatuses of the capitalist 'society of the spectacle', whose profanation Agamben advocates in order to liberate the pure means, the facticity of being-thus, confined in them. While the desire for liberation can be safely presupposed in the case of the camp, what about shopping malls and reality shows, self-help books and package tours, bingo halls and porn websites? Since what is at stake in profanation is a non-canonical or unconventional use of the practices that the apparatuses have captured and diverted for their purposes, Agamben must account precisely for this *turn* towards experimentation and free use. Even if the vacuity of contemporary apparatuses is increasingly evident to everyone, is it not *too* optimistic to expect late-modern societies to opt en masse for the unconventional and experimental modes of use as opposed to sticking to the tried and true, nullified as it is? To recall Heidegger's discussion of the 'They' (*das Man*) in *Being and Time*, this inauthentic mode of being-in-the-world attains its hold over *Dasein* not so much by oppression but rather by 'accommodating' it, making its everydayness more comfortable precisely insofar as it conforms to the average understandings, however vacuous or absurd. If, as Heidegger suggests, 'fallenness' is 'tempting' and 'tranquilizing', then how is this temptation to be overcome? (Heidegger 1962: 164–8, 224)

Contrary to first impressions, the problem with Agamben's comic politics is not its excessive radicalism but its relative modesty in the wider social context. Agamben proposes what appears to be a self-consciously *minoritarian*, if not outright 'bohemian', form of life that can hardly be expected to be replicated across the whole of society, simply because the *attraction* of profanatory experiments and playful subversions of the existing apparatuses is far from self-evident. Why would anyone who is not *already* outside the apparatuses in question (for example, critical intellectuals, avant-garde artists) want to exit them in order to engage in these practices, especially insofar as Agamben refuses to frame this move in terms of a revolutionary project of emancipation, which would involve articulating some form of normative justification for these practices?

Of course, the problem of how a theoretical design of transformation is to be translated into political practice is not unique to Agamben, yet in his work it becomes more acute due to his refusal of any construction of politics in terms of a project and the affirmation of inoperativity as both a means and an end of the coming politics. What Agamben's work lacks is an equivalent of Badiou's valorisation of militant political action in terms of its 'fidelity' to the event and its participation in the production of the 'truth' of the situation (see Badiou 2005b). While Badiou's politics is also presented in terms of a subtractive break with the existing state of affairs, this break is explicitly cast as an ethico-political injunction, a call to disciplined militant action that is framed precisely in terms of an emancipatory and egalitarian project that Agamben seeks to dispense with. Badiou is explicitly concerned with championing militant activism, not least by philosophically linking it with the production of truth. In contrast, since for Agamben the truth of being is exhausted in the facticity of whatever being, access to it no longer requires a long-term political project in which militancy, asceticism and discipline could be valorised in a Badiouan manner, but only a single act of subtraction, which nonetheless remains very difficult to account for (see Agamben 1991: 84–106; 1999b: 116–37).

It is of course possible to dismiss this question altogether in the manner best exemplified by Foucault's approach to the function of his work. Rather than posit normative criteria that would tell people why they must act in this or that manner, Foucault claimed to be content with simply demonstrating *how* one could resist, *if one wanted*, without imposing this mode of praxis as normatively privileged (Foucault 1990b: 9).

> It is absolutely true that when I write a book I refuse to take a prophetic stance; that is, the one of saying to people: here is what you must do, and also: this is good and this is not. I say to them, roughly speaking, it seems to me that things have gone this way; but I describe those things in such a way that the possible paths of attack are delineated. Yet, even with this approach I do not force or compel anyone to attack. So then, it becomes a completely personal question, if I choose, if I want, to take certain courses of action with reference to prisons, psychiatric asylums, this or that issue. (Foucault 1996: 261)

This is certainly a valid option, though it is arguably less appropriate for Agamben's works, which are marked by a strong messianic pathos completely alien to Foucault and which promise a global transformation that Foucault refused even to discuss. Moreover, it is important that Foucault referred to his practical disposition in terms of 'pessimistic activism' rather than optimism (cf. Foucault 1988: 156), an activism alongside others who are *already* resisting the apparatuses of power from a minoritarian position. While Agamben could also claim that his idea of an inoperative form-of-life is a 'toolkit', intended for 'users' rather than an 'audience' (Foucault 1980: 145), this limitation of the vision of transformation to those already interested or involved in it would certainly result in a thorough desublimation of the messianic pathos that made his political philosophy so attractive. In contrast to Foucault's somewhat contrived indifference as to whether his toolkits are indeed applied, Agamben grants an unequivocal ethical privilege to inoperativity and potentiality and even goes so far as to pronounce their negation 'evil':

[The] only ethical experience (which, as such, cannot be a task or a subjective decision) is the experience of being (one's own) potentiality, of being (one's own) possibility – exposing, that is, in every form one's own amorphousness and in every act one's own inactuality. The only evil consists instead in the decision to remain in a deficit of existence, to appropriate the power to not-be as a substance and a foundation beyond existence or to regard potentiality itself, which is the most proper mode of human existence, as a fault that must always be repressed. (Agamben 1993a: 44)

In *The Coming Community* Agamben recognises the paradox of formulating as a matter of injunction, demand or duty precisely the freedom from any essence, identity or vocation:

> there is in effect something that humans *are and have to be*, but this something is not an essence or properly a thing: it is the simple fact of one's own existence as possibility or potentiality. But precisely because of this things become complicated. (Agamben 1993a: 43; emphasis added)

The originary inoperativity and potentiality of the human condition do not mean that human beings are 'simply consigned to nothingness and therefore can freely decide whether to be or not to be, to adopt or not to adopt this or that destiny (nihilism and decisionism coincide at this point)' (ibid.: 43). Since inoperativity does not simply mean remaining stuck in nihilism and potentiality does not simply mean deciding on a way of life in a sovereign manner, they cannot be simply enjoyed within the apparatuses of sovereign power and nihilistic management but must be reappropriated in political praxis, even if this praxis takes a minimal form of subtraction. Yet as soon as we speak of this praxis as something that 'must' or 'has to' be, we risk converting and perverting inoperativity into a new historical project in whose actualisation potentiality is exhausted. In short, while the subtraction from the apparatuses is definitely not merely a possible action among others but rather is affirmed with a strong ethical *exigency* (cf. Agamben 2005b: 39), this exigency cannot serve as a foundation for political activism, an emancipatory project or any act of will, so as not to contradict the very inoperativity and potentiality that it affirms. One's subtraction from the apparatuses is ethical and one's dwelling within them is evil, yet the apparently self-evident passage from the evil to the ethical ends up extremely problematic, perpetually at the risk of relapsing back into the evil it ventures to leave behind. It is as if the activist or voluntarist concept of politics were an insidious device that trapped us within the 'deficit of existence' precisely by offering us an easy yet ultimately illusory way out of them.

The problem may be illustrated by revisiting the figure of Bartleby, who, as we recall, was 'capable without wanting', his 'preference not to' being distinct from any alternative preference. Despite all efforts to present Bartleby as the embodiment of absolute contingency, beyond both will and necessity, Agamben cannot avoid bringing the themes of will and decision back to account for the question of how Bartleby became what he is, how he entered the state of absolute contingency: Bartleby '*decided* to stop copying', he '*must* stop copying, *must* give up his work' (Agamben 1999b: 268; emphasis added). This is neither a careless slip nor the abandonment of an earlier stance – logically, Bartleby must have decided to become inoperative, must have originally preferred to prefer not to. And yet this decision cannot simply be an act of will that actualises one potentiality and negates others, since this would be a relapse into the logic of historical action that Agamben seeks to deactivate. It must rather be something like a meta-decision in favour of potentiality *as such*, in favour of actualising the potentiality *for* potentiality, setting aside the potentiality for potentiality not to be. To the extent that such a 'passive decision' can be accounted for at all, it is as a matter of conversion or *metanoia*, a radical perspectival shift that unfolds in an almost magical manner, as something that happens to or befalls us rather than something that we choose or produce.

In the context of Agamben's work magic would not be an accidental metaphor, since the comic mood of his thought is inextricably linked to it.

> Whatever we can achieve through merit and effort cannot make us truly happy. Only magic can do that. At that point, when we have wrenched it away from fate, happiness coincides entirely with our knowing ourselves to be capable of magic. (Agamben 2007b: 19)

While historical apparatuses promise us chimerical happiness in the future in return for our subjection and work in the present, genuine happiness is only possible when these apparatuses are rendered inoperative and the irreducibly potential character of our existence is restored.

If the only way to achieve happiness is not to aspire to reach it, then the decision in favour of potentiality and inoperativity is only conceivable as itself inoperative and potential, something that *can not be.* It is neither something that was *meant to happen* in accordance with the immanent logic of history nor something that was *made to happen* through a voluntarist domination of history that breaks it into two. It is simply something that *happens* – or not, in a strictly contingent manner. Yet to what extent can one remain an optimist when affirming this radical contingency? At first glance, any contingency worthy of the name is entirely indifferent to either optimism or pessimism since it warrants nothing but the possibility of things being otherwise without any specification of the likelihood of this possibility.[1] The nihilistic degradation of the global biopolitical apparatuses does indeed open the possibility of the reappropriation of our potentiality in an inoperative community of whatever being but this very possibility must presuppose its own potentiality not-to-be. It is therefore just as possible that we remain within the deficient mode of existence that we misrecognise for our authentic ethos, remain stuck in the worst, just one step away from the best. It is perfectly possible that *nothing will happen* – it is not for nothing that the time we live in is called the age of nihilism.

Agamben clearly recognises these possibilities but adds to them a crucial caveat: 'This – *but not only this* – is possible' (Agamben 1999b: 126; emphasis original). It is precisely the supplementary 'but not only this' that permits Agamben to retain his optimism in the face of absolute contingency. Even if it all amounts to nothing, if the subjects caught up in the apparatuses of biopolitical nihilism end up not wanting what they are capable of, if they shrug and say 'whatever' in response to Agamben's vision of whatever being, this only means that 'not only this is possible', that the possibility of a happy life *remains* a possibility, that whatever is can *not* be. This is the ultimate limit of Agamben's optimism, beyond which his thought cannot venture, having dispensed with both will and necessity and finding its ground in absolute contingency alone. Devoid of all assurances of teleology and the hopes invested in voluntarism, Agamben's thought is nonetheless characterised by a strong belief in the power of the possible, in potentiality as the power to render inoperative all the apparatuses that govern our existence and expropriate our potentialities. This belief, which can only be strengthened with each successive failure, resonates with Wallace Stevens' moving words in *Notes on the Supreme Fiction*, 'It is possible, possible, possible, it must be possible. It must be that in time the real will from its crude compoundings come' (Stevens 1990: 404). It remains up to each of us whether and how to act on this belief.

Note

1. As Quentin Meillassoux (2008: 82–111) has demonstrated, the absolute contingency of things (e.g. of the laws of physics) can coexist without any contradiction with their utmost stability over millennia. The abandonment of Leibniz's principle of sufficient reason only asserts that everything is contingent and can be otherwise without specifying the likelihood of such transformation.

Bibliography

Agamben, G. (1991), *Language and Death: The Place of Negativity*, Minneapolis, MN: University of Minnesota Press.

Agamben, G. (1993a), *The Coming Community*, Minneapolis, MN: University of Minnesota Press.

Agamben, G. (1993b), *Stanzas: Word and Phantasm in Western Culture*, New York: SUNY Press.

Agamben, G. (1995), *The Idea of Prose*, New York: SUNY Press.

Agamben, G. (1998), *Homo Sacer: Sovereign Power and Bare Life*, Stanford, CA: Stanford University Press.

Agamben, G. (1999a), *End of the Poem: Studies in Poetics*, Stanford, CA: Stanford University Press.

Agamben, G. (1999b), *Potentialities: Selected Essays in Philosophy*, Stanford, CA: Stanford University Press.

Agamben, G. (1999c), *Remnants of Auschwitz: The Witness and the Archive*, New York: Zone Books.

Agamben, G. (2000), *Means without End: Notes on Politics*, Minneapolis, MN: University of Minnesota Press.

Agamben, G. (2004a), 'I Am Sure that You Are More Pessimistic than I Am: An Interview with Giorgio Agamben', *Rethinking Marxism*, 16: 2, 115–24.

Agamben, G. (2004b), *The Open: Man and Animal*, Stanford, CA: Stanford University Press.

Agamben, G. (2005a), *State of Exception*, Chicago, IL: The University of Chicago Press.

Agamben, G. (2005b), *The Time that Remains: A Commentary on the Letter to the Romans*, Stanford, CA: Stanford University Press.

Agamben, G. (2006), 'Falling Beauty', in *Cy Twombly: Sculptures*, Munich: Pinakothek.

Agamben, G. (2007a), *Infancy and History: On the Destruction of Experience*, London: Verso.

Agamben, G. (2007b), *Profanations*, New York: Zone Books.

Agamben, G. (2007c), 'The Work of Man', in M. Calarco and S. DeCaroli (eds), *On Agamben: Sovereignty and Life*, Stanford, CA: Stanford University Press.

Agamben, G. (2009a), *The Sacrament of Language: An Archaeology of the Oath*, Stanford, CA: Stanford University Press.

Agamben, G. (2009b), *The Signature of All Things: On Method*, New York: Zone Books.

Agamben, G. (2009c), *What is an Apparatus? And Other Essays*, Stanford, CA: Stanford University Press.

Agamben, G. (2010), *Nudities*, Stanford, CA: Stanford University Press.

Agamben, G. (2011), *The Kingdom and the Glory: For a Theological Genealogy of Economy and Government*, Stanford, CA: Stanford University Press.

Agamben, G. (2013), *The Highest Poverty: Monastic Rules and Form-of-Life*, Stanford, CA: Stanford University Press.

Arendt, H. (1973), *The Origins of Totalitarianism*, New York: Harcourt.

Badiou, A. (2001a), *Ethics: An Essay on the Understanding of Evil*, London: Verso.

Badiou, A. (2001b), *Saint Paul: The Foundation of Universalism*, Stanford, CA: Stanford University Press.

Badiou, A. (2005a), *Being and Event*, London: Continuum.

Badiou, A. (2005b), *Metapolitics*, London: Verso.

Badiou, A. (2005c), 'Universal Truths and the Question of Religion', *Journal of Philosophy and Scripture*, 3: 1, 38–42.

Badiou, A. (2007), *The Century*, London: Polity.

Badiou, A. (2008), *The Meaning of Sarkozy*, London: Verso.

Badiou, A. (2009), *Logics of Worlds*, London: Continuum.

Badiou, A. (2010), *The Communist Hypothesis*, London: Verso.

Barad, K. (2007), *Meeting the Universe Halfway: Quantum Physics and the Entanglement of Matter and Meaning*, Durham, NC: Duke University Press.

Bataille, G. (2001), *Eroticism*, Harmondsworth: Penguin.

Benjamin, W. (1968), *Illuminations*, New York: Schocken Books.

Benjamin, W. (1978), *Reflections*, New York: Schocken Books.

Benjamin, W. (2002), *The Arcades Project*, Cambridge, MA: Harvard University Press.

Bennett, J. (2010), *Vibrant Matter: A Political Ecology of Things*, Durham, NC: Duke University Press.

Bernstein, J. M. (2004), 'Bare Life, Bearing Witness: Auschwitz and the Pornography of Horror', *Parallax*, 10: 1, 2–16.

Blanchot, M. (1988), *The Unavowable Community*, New York: Station Hill.

Bosteels, B. (2011), *The Actuality of Communism*, London: Verso.

Brassier, R. (2007), *Nihil Unbound: Enlightenment and Extinction*, Basingstoke: Palgrave.

Brodsky, J. (1987), *Nobel Prize for Literature 1987 Banquet Speech*, available online at: www.nobelprize.org/nobel_prizes/literature/laureates/1987/brodsky-lecture.html?print=1 (accessed 1 March 2013).

Bryant, L. (2011), *Democracy of Objects*, Ann Arbor, MI: Open Humanities Press.

Bull, M. (2012), *Anti-Nietzsche*, London: Verso.

Calarco, M. (2007), 'Jamming the Anthropological Machine', in M. Calarco and S. DeCaroli (eds), *Giorgio Agamben: Sovereignty and Life*, Stanford, CA: Stanford University Press.

Calarco, M. (2008), *Zoographies: The Question of the Animal from Heidegger to Derrida*, New York: Columbia University Press.

Chiesa, L. (2009), 'Giorgio Agamben's Franciscan Ontology', *Cosmos and History*, 5: 1, available online at http://cosmosandhistory.org/index.php/journal/article/view/130/239 (last accessed 20 April 2013).

Chiesa, L. and Ruda, F. (2011), 'The Event of Language as Force of Life: Agamben's Linguistic Vitalism', *Angelaki*, 16: 3, 163–80.

Clemens, J. (2008), 'The Role of the Shifter and the Problem of Reference in Giorgio Agamben', in J. Clemens, N. Heron and A. Murray (eds), *The Work of Giorgio Agamben: Law, Literature, Life*, Edinburgh: Edinburgh University Press.

Clemens, J. (2010), 'The Abandonment of Sex: Giorgio Agamben, Psychoanalysis and Melancholia', *Theory and Event*, 13: 1, available online at http://muse.jhu.edu/journals/theory_and_event/summary/v013/13.1.clemens.html (last accessed 20 April 2013).

Coetzee, J. M. (1985), *The Life and Times of Michael K*, Harmondsworth: Penguin.

Critchley, S. (2012), *The Faith of the Faithless: Experiments in Political Theology*, London: Verso.

Debord, G. (1994), *The Society of the Spectacle*, New York: Zone Books.

Debord, G. (2011), *Comments on the Society of the Spectacle*, London: Verso.

Deines, T. (2006), 'Bartleby the Scrivener, Immanence and the Resistance of Community', *Culture Machine*, 8, available online at http://culturemachine.tees.ac.uk (last accessed 31 May 2012).

De la Durantaye, L. (2009), *Giorgio Agamben: A Critical Introduction*, Stanford, CA: Stanford University Press.

Deleuze, G. (1988), *Foucault*, London: The Athlone Press.

Deleuze, G. (1992), 'What is a *Dispositif?*', in T. J. Armstrong (ed.), *Michel Foucault: Philosopher*, New York: Harvester Wheatsheaf.

Deleuze, G. (1997), 'Bartleby, or the Formula', in *Essays Critical and Clinical*, Minneapolis, MN: University of Minnesota Press.

Deleuze, G. and Guattari, F. (1988), *A Thousand Plateaus*, London: The Athlone Press.

Deranty, J.-P. (2008), 'Witnessing the Inhuman: Agamben or Merleau-Ponty', in A. Ross (ed.), *The Agamben Effect*. South Atlantic Quarterly Special Issue, 107: 1, 165–86.

Derrida, J. (1992), 'Force of Law: The "Mystical Foundations of Authority"', in D. Cornell, M. Rosenfeld and D. G. Carlson (eds), *Deconstruction and the Possibility of Justice*, London: Routledge.

Derrida, J. (1995), *The Gift of Death*, Chicago, IL: The University of Chicago Press.

Derrida, J. (2005), *Rogues: Two Essays on Reason*, Stanford, CA: Stanford University Press.

Derrida, J. (2008), *The Animal that Therefore I Am*, New York: Fordham University Press.

Derrida, J. (2009), *The Sovereign and the Beast, vol. 1: The Seminars of Jacques Derrida*, Chicago, IL: The University of Chicago Press.

Dickinson, C. (2011), *Agamben and Theology*, London: Continuum.

Dubreuil, L. (2008), 'Leaving Politics? Bios, Zoe, Life', *Diacritics*, 36: 2, 83–98.

Esposito, R. (2012), *Third Person*, London: Polity.

Esposito, R. (2013), *Living Thought: The Origins and Actuality of Italian Philosophy*, Stanford, CA: Stanford University Press.

Foucault, M. (1970), *The Order of Things: An Archaeology of the Human Sciences*, London: Tavistock.

Foucault, M. (1977), *Discipline and Punish: The Birth of the Prison*, New York: Knopf.

Foucault, M. (1980), 'Power and Strategies', in *Power/Knowledge: Selected Interviews and Other Writings: 1972–1977*, New York: Knopf.

Foucault, M. (1988), 'Practicing Criticism', in L. Kritzman (ed.), *Michel Foucault: Politics, Philosophy, Culture. Interviews and Other Writings 1977–1984*, London: Routledge.

Foucault, M. (1990a), *History of Sexuality. Volume One: An Introduction*, Harmondsworth: Penguin.

Foucault, M. (1990b), *History of Sexuality. Volume Two: The Use of Pleasure*, New York: Random House.

Foucault, M. (1996), 'Friendship as a Way of Life', in S. Lotringer (ed.), *Foucault Live: Interviews, 1961–1984*, New York: Semiotext(e).

Foucault, M. (2003), *'Society Must be Defended': Lectures at the Collège de France 1975–1976*, London: Picador.

Foucault, M. (2007), *Security, Territory, Population: Lectures at the Collège de France 1977–1978*, Basingstoke: Palgrave.

Foucault, M. (2008), *The Birth of Biopolitics: Lectures at the Collège de France 1978–1979*, Basingstoke: Palgrave.

Franchi, S. (2004), 'Passive Politics', *Contretemps*, 5, 30–41.

Fukuyama, F. (1992), *The End of History and the Last Man*, New York: Free Press.

Garrido, J.-M. (2012), *On Time, Being and Hunger: Challenging the Traditional Way of Thinking Life*, New York: Fordham University Press.

Grier, P. T. (1996), 'The End of History and the Return of History', in J. Stewart (ed.), *The Hegel Myths and Legends*, Chicago, IL: The Northwestern University Press.

Hallward, P. (2003), *Badiou: A Subject to Truth*, Minneapolis, MN: University of Minnesota Press.

Hardt, M. and Negri, A. (2000), *Empire*, Cambridge, MA: Harvard University Press.

Hardt, M. and Negri, A. (2004), *Multitude: War and Democracy in the Age of Empire*, New York: Penguin.

Harman, G. (2002), *Tool-Being: Heidegger and the Metaphysics of Objects*, Chicago, IL: Open Court.

Harman, G. (2011), *The Quadruple Object*, Alresford: Zero Books.

Harris, H. S. (1996), 'The End of History in Hegel', in J. Stewart (ed.), *The Hegel Myths and Legends*, Chicago, IL: The Northwestern University Press.

Hegarty, P. (2005), 'Supposing the Impossibility of Silence and of Sound, of Voice: Bataille, Agamben and the Holocaust', in A. Norris (ed.), *Politics, Metaphysics and Death: Essays on Giorgio Agamben's* Homo Sacer, Durham, NC: Duke University Press.

Hegel, G. W. F. [1807] (1979), *The Phenomenology of Spirit*, Oxford: Oxford University Press.

Heidegger, M. (1961), *Introduction to Metaphysics*, New York: Anchor Books.

Heidegger, M. (1962), *Being and Time*, New York: HarperCollins.

Heidegger, M. (1977), *Basic Writings*, New York: HarperCollins.

Heidegger, M. (1995), *The Fundamental Concepts of Metaphysics: World, Finitude, Solitude*, Bloomington, IN: Indiana University Press.

Heidegger, M. (1998), *Pathmarks*, Cambridge: Cambridge University Press.

Hell, J. (2009), 'Katechon: Carl Schmitt's Imperial Theology and the Ruins of the Future', *The Germanic Review*, 84: 4, 283–326.

Hobbes, T. [1651] (1985), *Leviathan*, Harmondsworth: Penguin.

Kafka, F. (2002), *Metamorphosis and Other Writings*, London: Continuum.

Kant, I. [1781] (2008), *Critique of Pure Reason*, Harmondsworth: Penguin.

Kalyvas, A. (2005), 'The Sovereign Weaver: Beyond the Camp', in A. Norris (ed.), *Politics, Metaphysics and Death: Essays on Giorgio Agamben's* Homo Sacer, Durham, NC: Duke University Press.

Kearney, R. (2009), 'Paul's Notion of the *Dynamis*: Between the Possible and the Impossible', in J. D. Caputo and L. M. Alcoff (eds), *St Paul among the Philosophers*, Bloomington, IN: Indiana University Press.

Kishik, D. (2012), *The Power of Life: Agamben and the Coming Politics*, Stanford, CA: Stanford University Press.

Kojève, A. (1952), 'Les Romans de la Sagesse', *Critique*, 60, 387–97.

Kojève, A. (1969), *Introduction to the Reading of Hegel: Lectures on the* Phenomenology of Spirit, Ithaca, NY: Cornell University Press.

Kuhn, T. (1970a), 'Reflections on my Critics', in I. Lakatos and A. Musgrave (eds), *Criticism and the Growth of Knowledge*, Cambridge: Cambridge University Press.

Kuhn, T. (1970b), *The Structure of Scientific Revolutions*, 2nd edn, Chicago, IL: The University of Chicago Press.

LaCapra, D. (2007), 'Approaching Limit Events: Siting Agamben', in M. Calarco and S. DeCaroli (eds), *Giorgio Agamben: Sovereignty and Life*, Stanford, CA: Stanford University Press.

Laclau, E. (2007), 'Bare Life or Social Indeterminacy', in M. Calarco and S. DeCaroli (eds), *On Agamben: Sovereignty and Life*, Stanford, CA: Stanford University Press.

Latour, B. (2004), *Politics of Nature: How to Bring the Sciences into Democracy*, Cambridge, MA: Harvard University Press.

Lewis, T. (2013), 'Education as Free Use: Giorgio Agamben on Studious Play, Toys and the Inoperative Playhouse', *Studies in the Philosophy and Education*, 30 (forthcoming).

Marchart, O. (2007), 'Zwischen Moses und Messias: Zur Politischen Differenz bei Agamben', in J. Böckelmann and F. Meier (eds), *Die Gouvernementale Maschine. Zur Politischen Philosophie Giorgio Agambens*, Münster: Unrast.

Martell, J. (2011), *Divine Violence: Walter Benjamin and the Eschatology of Sovereignty*, London: Routledge.

Masterman, M. (1970), 'The Nature of a Paradigm', in I. Lakatos and A. Musgrave (eds), *Criticism and the Growth of Knowledge*, Cambridge: Cambridge University Press.

Maurer, R. K. (1996), 'Hegel and the End of History', in Jon Stewart (ed.), *The Hegel Myths and Legends*, Chicago, IL: The Northwestern University Press.

McCormick, J. (1997), *Carl Schmitt's Critique of Liberalism: Against Politics as Technology*, Cambridge: Cambridge University Press.

Meier, H. (1998), *The Lesson of Carl Schmitt: Four Chapters on the Distinction between Political Theology and Political Philosophy*, Chicago, IL: The University of Chicago Press.

Meillassoux, Q. (2008), *After Finitude: An Essay on the Necessity of Contingency*, London: Continuum.

Mesnard, P. (2004), 'The Political Philosophy of Giorgio Agamben: A Critical Evaluation', *Totalitarian Movements and Political Religions*, 5: 1, 139–57.

Mills, C. (2005), 'Linguistic Survival and Ethicality: Biopolitics, Subjectivation and Testimony in *Remnants of Auschwitz*', in A. Norris (ed.), *Politics, Metaphysics and Death: Essays on Giorgio Agamben's Homo Sacer*, Durham, NC: Duke University Press.

Mills, C. (2008), *The Philosophy of Agamben*, Stocksfield: Acumen.

Murray, A. (2010), *Giorgio Agamben*, London: Routledge.

Nancy, J.-L. (1991), *The Inoperative Community*, Minneapolis, MN: University of Minnesota Press.

Nancy, J.-L. (1993), *The Birth to Presence*, Stanford, CA: Stanford University Press.

Nancy, J.-L. (1994), *The Experience of Freedom*, Stanford, CA: Stanford University Press.

Nedoh, B. (2011), 'Kafka's Land Surveyor K: Agamben's Anti-Muselmann', *Angelaki*, 16: 3, 149–61.

Negri, A. (2012), 'The Sacred Dilemma of Inoperosity: On Giorgio Agamben's *Opus Dei*', available online at http://www.uninomade.org/negri-on-agamben-opus-dei (last accessed 30 March 2013). Originally published in Italian in *Il Manifesto*, 24 February 2012.

Norris, A. (ed.) (2005), *Politics, Metaphysics and Death: Essays on Giorgio Agamben's* Homo Sacer, Durham, NC: Duke University Press.

Ojakangas, M. (2005), 'Impossible Dialogue on Biopower: Agamben and Foucault', *Foucault Studies*, 2, 5–28.

Ojakangas, M. (2006), *A Philosophy of Concrete Life: Carl Schmitt and the Political Thought of Late Modernity*, Oxford: Peter Lang.

Ojakangas, M. (2012), 'Michel Foucault and the Enigmatic Origins of Bio-politics and Governmentality', *History of the Human Sciences*, 25: 1, 1–14.

Passavant, P. A. (2007), 'The Contradictory State of Giorgio Agamben', *Political Theory*, 35: 2, 147–74.

Patton, P. (2007), 'Agamben and Foucault on Biopower and Biopolitics', in M. Calarco and S. DeCaroli (eds), *On Agamben: Sovereignty and Life*, Stanford, CA: Stanford University Press.

Pettman, D. (2012), *Human Error: Species-Being and Media Machines*, Minneapolis, MN: University of Minnesota Press.

Power, N. (2010), 'Potentiality or Capacity: Agamben's Missing Subjects', *Theory and Event*, 13: 1, available online at http://muse.jhu.edu/journals/theory_and_event/v013/13.1.power.html (last accessed 30 April 2013).

Prozorov, S. (2007), *Foucault, Freedom and Sovereignty*, Aldershot: Ashgate.

Prozorov, S. (2009a), 'The Appropriation of Abandonment: Giorgio Agamben on the State of Nature and the Political', *Continental Philosophy Review*, 42: 3, 327–53.

Prozorov, S. (2009b), *The Ethics of Postcommunism: History and Social Praxis in Russia*, Basingstoke: Palgrave.

Prozorov, S. (2009c), 'Generic Universalism in World Politics: Beyond International Anarchy and the World State', *International Theory*, 1: 2, 215–47.

Prozorov, S. (2009d), 'Giorgio Agamben and the End of History: Inoperative Praxis and the Interruption of the Dialectic', *European Journal of Social Theory*, 12: 4, 523–42.

Prozorov, S. (2010), 'Why Giorgio Agamben is an Optimist', *Philosophy and Social Criticism*, 36: 3, 1053–73.

Prozorov, S. (2011), 'Pornography and Profanation in the Political Philosophy of Giorgio Agamben', *Theory, Culture and Society*, 28: 4, 71–95.

Prozorov, S. (2012), 'The Katechon in the Age of Biopolitical Nihilism', *Continental Philosophy Review*, 45: 4, 483–503.

Prozorov, S. (2013a), *Ontology and World Politics: Void Universalism I*, London: Routledge.

Prozorov, S. (2013b), 'What is the "World" in World Politics?: Heidegger, Badiou and Void Universalism', *Contemporary Political Theory*, 12: 2, 102–22.

Rancière , J. (1999), *Disagreement: Politics and Philosophy*, Minneapolis, MN: University of Minnesota Press.

Rasch, W. (2007), 'From Sovereign Ban to Banning Sovereignty', in M. Calarco and S. DeCaroli (eds), *Giorgio Agamben: Sovereignty and Life*, Stanford, CA: Stanford University Press.

Santner, E. (2006), *On Creaturely Life: Rilke, Benjamin, Sebald*, Chicago, IL: The University of Chicago Press.

Scheuerman, W. (1999), *Carl Schmitt: The End of Law*, Boulder, CO: Roman and Littlefield.

Schmitt, C. (1976), *The Concept of the Political*, New Brunswick, NJ: Rutgers University Press.

Schmitt, C. (1985a), *Political Theology: Four Chapters on the Concept of Sovereignty*, Cambridge, MA: The MIT Press.

Schmitt, C. (1985b), *The Crisis of Parliamentary Democracy*, Cambridge, MA: The MIT Press.

Schmitt, C. (2003), *The Nomos of the Earth in the International Public Law of the Jus Publicum Europaeum*, New York: Telos Press.

Sharpe, M. (2009), 'Only Agamben Can Save Us? Against the Messianic Tone Recently Adopted in Critical Theory', *The Bible and Critical Theory*, 5: 3, 11–19.

Slomp, G. (2009), *Carl Schmitt and the Politics of Hostility, Violence and Terror*, Basingstoke: Palgrave.

Snoek, A. (2012), *Agamben's Joyful Kafka: Finding Freedom Beyond Subordination*, London: Continuum.

Stevens, W. (1990), *The Collected Poems of Wallace Stevens*, New York: Vintage.

Sumic, J. (2011), 'Giorgio Agamben's Godless Saints: Saving What Was Not', *Angelaki*, 16: 3, 137–47.

Taubes, J. (2004), *The Political Theology of Paul*, Stanford, CA: Stanford University Press.

Thoburn, N. (2003), *Deleuze, Marx and Politics*, London: Routledge.

Thurschwell, A. (2005), 'Cutting the Branches for Akiba: Agamben's Critique of Derrida', in A. Norris (ed.), *Politics, Metaphysics and*

Death: Essays on Giorgio Agamben's Homo Sacer, Durham, NC: Duke University Press.

Toscano, A. (2011), 'Divine Management: Critical Remarks on Giorgio Agamben's *The Kingdom and the Glory*', *Angelaki*, 16: 3, 126–35.

Vatter, M. (2008), 'In Odradek's World: Bare Life and Historical Materialism in Agamben and Benjamin', *Diacritics*, 38: 3, 45–70.

Wall, T. C. (1999), *Radical Passivity: Levinas, Blanchot, Agamben*, New York: SUNY Press.

Weber, S. (2008), *Benjamin's-abilities*, Cambridge, MA: Harvard University Press.

Weil, S. (1952), *Gravity and Grace*, New York: Putnam.

Whyte, J. (2009), 'I Would Prefer Not To: Giorgio Agamben, Bartleby and the Potentiality of the Law', *Law and Critique*, 20, 309–24.

Wolfe, C. (2009), *What is Posthumanism?* Minneapolis, MN: University of Minnesota Press.

Žižek, S. (2003), *Organs without Bodies: Deleuze and Consequences*, London: Routledge.

Žižek, S. (2006), *The Parallax View*, Cambridge, MA: The MIT Press.

Žižek, S. (2008), *In Defense of Lost Causes*, London: Verso.

Žižek, S. (2009), *Violence*, London: Profile Books.

Žižek, S. (2012), *Less than Nothing: Hegel and the Shadow of Dialectical Materialism*, London: Verso.

Index

animal
  animality/humanity distinction, 8, 34,
    136, 150, 154–5, 158, 164–7, 170–2
  becoming-animal, 171–2
  humanisation of, 165
anthropocentrism, 8, 71, 150–3, 157, 161
anthropogenesis, 69, 99, 123, 163–4, 170
anthropological machine, 8, 22, 154,
  156–7, 165, 170
apparatus
  definition of, 10, 17–19, 23, 32
  in Foucault, 17–18
Arendt, Hannah, 83, 108–9
Aristotle, 4, 30, 34–5, 71, 94, 96–7
Axolotl, 2, 73, 152

Badiou, Alain, 54–6, 59, 82–4, 127, 141–3,
  177, 183–4
bankruptcy, of peoples, 181
bare life
  analogy with the concept of being, 93,
    97–9
  and natural life, 95–7
  concept of, 7, 12, 54, 95, 105–11, 153–8,
    165
  reappropriation of, 121–3, 173–4
  Bartleby (novella), 49–58, 87, 109, 118,
    173, 186
Bataille, Georges, 34, 58
being-thus, 77, 89, 119, 67, 173
Benjamin, Walter, 7, 21–2, 25, 43–5, 81,
  90, 93, 115–16, 119–20, 130, 136–7,
  166–8
Benveniste, Émile, 42, 65, 171
biopolitics
  Agamben's concept of, 93–6
  and nihilism, 121, 132, 165–6, 179–81,
    187
  and sovereignty, 98–103, 108–11,
    114–15
  Derrida on, 96–7
  Foucault's concept of, 93
bios, 94–8, 114–15, 120–4, 152
Blanchot, Maurice, 33, 51, 171
body, 16, 30, 38–41, 98, 108, 111, 118,
  121, 173

boredom, 11, 161–5
Brodsky, Joseph, 20, 22
Bucephalus (Kafka's character), 20–3, 47,
  173
Bull, Malcolm, 170, 173

camp, the, 13, 19, 115, 153, 165, 171
  as a paradigm of modern politics, 87,
    109–12, 182
capitalism, 82, 127, 128
  as a religion, 44–6
  and the society of the spectacle, 48,
    124–5
captivation
  and animal poverty in the world, 159–60
  human suspension of, 162–5
chronos, 137–9
Clemens, Justin, 4, 58
Coetzee, John M., 145
comedy
  in aesthetic theory, 12–13
  in Dante, 13–15
  in Kafka, 16–21
communicability, 60, 67, 81, 120, 133 153,
  174
community, 50, 53, 60, 88–90, 115, 119,
  129, 142, 145, 148, 182, 185
  and the experience of language, 74–9,
    152
  and universality, 79–85
  with animals, 161–2, 169–3
constituent power, 58, 116–18, 141, 176
constituted power, 116–18, 147
contingency, 19, 105, 186–8

Debord, Guy, 48, 124–5
decreation, 52, 59, 120
De la Durantaye, Leland, 33, 59, 111
Deleuze, Gilles, 50–1, 55, 171–2
Derrida, Jacques, 64, 96–7, 144, 175
disinhibitor, 159–60, 163–5, 169, 173

empty throne, 46–8, 119
end of history
  Agamben's interpretation of, 135–9,
    145–9